A MYRIAD OF TONGUES

A
MYRIAD
OF
TONGUES

*How Languages Reveal Differences
in How We Think*

CALEB EVERETT

Harvard University Press

CAMBRIDGE, MASSACHUSETTS
LONDON, ENGLAND
2023

Library of Congress Cataloging-in-Publication Data
Names: Everett, Caleb, author.
Title: A myriad of tongues : how languages reveal differences in how we think /
    Caleb Everett.
Description: Cambridge, Massachusetts ; London, England : Harvard University
    Press, 2023. | Includes bibliographical references and index.
Identifiers: LCCN 2022059014 | ISBN 9780674976580 (cloth)
Subjects: LCSH: Anthropological linguistics. | Language and Languages—Variation.
Classification: LCC P35 .E898 2023 | DDC 306.44—dc23/eng/20230213
LC record available at https://lccn.loc.gov/2022059014

Interior illustrations: Getty Images / Garry Killian.

For Shan and Kris

CONTENTS

A MYRIAD OF TONGUES

Introduction

THE FRIGID GUSTS are many degrees below freezing and, judging from the grimaces passing by, unpleasant even by the standards of Manhattanites. I take refuge in a closet-sized coffee shop at the base of the inclement canyon that is 8th Avenue. The city seems taken aback by the brutal January snowstorm as snow piles up alongside the crawling traffic of the morning commute. With sensation returning to my cheeks and a cappuccino in hand, I find that the view through the shop window becomes enchanting. This enchantment is soon interrupted by the scene on the corner of 8th and 42nd, where things do not seem ideal for a silver Prius that became mired in the snow as it attempted a right turn. The front tires are spinning in place as vehicles accumulate in the intersection, their horns blaring despite the clear helplessness of the hybrid's driver. A full minute seems to pass before the car's tires achieve traction, having spun through several layers of snow to reach the asphalt. The hatchback sleds off, headed uptown amid the current of impatient commuters.

A question occurs to me: Was it really snow that the car was stuck in? That word choice does not seem quite right. "Crushed snow" seems more appropriate, as "snow" by itself seems inaccurate or at least inadequate. "Packed snow"? It was not sleet, because it came down as flakes, not as ice pellets. I feel linguistically challenged as I grasp for a better descriptor. It clearly was a kind of snow, but each available term feels semantically imprecise. The car's wheels were stuck in "snowy ice," or "icy snow," or "snowy slush." All the terms that come to mind have a somewhat cobbled-together and unconventional feel, and most are a compound, with "snow" being modified by or modifying some other term.

Then a geographic coincidence occurs to me. I am sitting just a few miles away from the former workplace of Franz Boas, who planted the some-languages-have-many-words-for-snow tree of thought and is considered by many the founder of American anthropology. Boas was a professor at Columbia University and the first scholar to suggest that English's terminology for snow is relatively impoverished when he observed in 1911 that the language of the Inuit has at least four distinct and basic terms that are all translatable with the English word "snow" and associated descriptors. There is *qana,* or "falling snow"; *piqsirpoq,* or "drifting snow"; *qimuqsuq,* "snow that is already in a drift"; and *aput,* "snow that is on the ground." In a cycle of exponential exaggeration, Boas's observation eventually yielded the notion, in the zeitgeist if not among scholars, that Eskimos have dozens or even hundreds of words for snow. Such claims have been repeated in places like the *New York Times.* As noted in a decades-old humorous essay by the linguist Geoff

Pullum, many of the claims surrounding the words-for-snow trope were comically inaccurate. Such inaccuracy does not imply, however, that languages do not vary in unexpected and profound ways with respect to how they describe certain physical phenomena. The extent of such variation was perhaps overlooked in some quarters precisely because of exaggerated claims like those surrounding Eskimo snow, claims that could easily be debunked. As we will see in this book, some analogous dismissals of linguistic diversity have surfaced repeatedly in the study of the world's languages. Setting aside that larger point, what is clear is that there has been plenty of subsequent debate about, and interpretation of, the exaggerated notion that some languages have boundless terms for snow. Much of this debate missed a key, simple point that Boas's example drives home: languages tend to reflect the environments in which they evolve. Populations in Greenland are likely to refer to different kinds of "snow" because they confront different kinds of snow so often and, relatedly, because they must coordinate their behavior and actions around it. In contrast, a group of indigenes in Australia may be wholly unfamiliar with snow and need no basic words to refer to it, much less varieties of it. The words-for-snow trope is, at its core, just a simple illustration of the fact that languages are influenced by their speakers' specific social needs and environments. The world's languages are incredibly diverse in part due to the varied physical and social environments in which humans live. In this book I will survey some key findings obtained from work on linguistic and cultural diversity, discussing new insights into how people communicate and think. This work aims to highlight particularly vibrant strands of the research produced by psychologists, linguists, anthropologists, and others that is reshaping our understanding of human speech and associated thought and behavior.[1]

The world's linguistic diversity is extreme and, in my experience, underestimated by most people. Consider this: When I teach an introductory course on anthropological linguistics at my university, in the first lecture of the semester I often ask the students to name as many languages as they can. The group of fifty students will struggle to name more than several dozen languages. They typically include Latin or Klingon or some other language of dubious qualifications. Individual students may struggle to name twenty languages. (This is not meant as a criticism, since most intelligent and well-read people struggle with this task—I leave it to you to try it if you are so inclined.) Yet there are, by most counts, over seven thousand languages in existence today. Furthermore, most of the languages that come to the minds of my students have European origins and are closely related. Setting aside a few commonly named languages like Mandarin and Arabic, the most frequently cited ones—German, Spanish, French, Italian, and even Latin—are representatives of only one of the roughly 350 language families in the world. These easily labeled languages trace their ancestry back to one language, Proto-Indo-European, which was spoken near the Black Sea roughly six thousand years ago. In short, most college students' awareness of linguistic diversity is formed by their extensive exposure to a small fraction of the languages that exist in the world today. And this fraction represents only one of the thousands of ancestral tongues that were likely spoken when Proto-Indo-European began its rise to prominence millennia ago.[2]

This bias extends beyond undergraduates. Languages of European ancestry have for centuries received inordinate attention from scholars in the West. This common fixation has clear and understandable historical roots, but since it helped to shape many theories of language, many cognitive scientists rightfully see it as problematic. Even during the twentieth century, when scholars were already aware that a very large number of languages existed around the globe, linguistic theories were informed in large measure by our understanding of European languages like English, languages that most of these theorists spoke natively. In some circles this theoretical bias remains even today. It has contributed to an unfortunate tendency to think of languages as being broadly similar, since many Indo-European languages are in fact similar to each other due both to their relatedness and to the frequent interactions between their speakers. This narrow focus helped foster the once-prominent view that languages exhibit only superficial variation that obfuscates profound similarities or even a "universal grammar." The universalist perspective is becoming less influential in the language sciences, judging from the research that is most impactful these days, and I suspect the reason why is simple. Once linguists really expanded the scope of their inquiries to look closely at the world's languages, they found that those languages were much more diverse than many theories presumed. If biologists primarily studied a few related species in one ecosystem, only occasionally studying species elsewhere, they would likely underestimate the world's range of biodiversity. Thankfully, there has been a radical shift that is still underway in the study of language, alongside a parallel shift in the study of human thought and behavior. These shifts have resulted in a clear focus not on the hypothetical universal features evident in all languages, but on the critical ways in which languages diverge—and what that divergence can tell us about humans more broadly. For instance, a new study authored by a team of well-known scholars, widely shared on social media in late 2022, surveyed the many ways in which overreliance on English has limited our understanding not just of languages but of human thought. The authors of that study note that a recognition of the extensive linguistic and cognitive diversity of *Homo sapiens* is essential to a deeper understanding of our species. This diversity is at the heart of the story this book will tell, though subtle and pervasive tendencies in the world's languages are part of the story too.[3]

In a paper just over a decade old, entitled "The Myth of Language Universals," linguists Nick Evans and Stephen Levinson offered a litany of ways in which linguistic diversity contravenes the notion that the world's languages have meaningful universals. Many linguists who have spent extensive time doing fieldwork on diverse languages in remote locales (myself included) agreed with the central claims of the article, which was published in the journal *Behavioral and Brain Sciences*. The lack of linguistic universals is in some ways surprising given that all human populations have the same basic anatomy associated with thinking and speaking, all of which evolved prior to our African exodus. It is also somewhat surprising because language serves similar functions across populations. Still, while these functional pressures do yield many similarities of form across languages, the pressures are insufficient to yield any true linguistic universals. In fact, Evans and Levinson suggested that the principal question linguists should try to answer is why languages are so diverse. They noted that ours is the only known species whose communication system varies so much across population groups. The countless studies that have focused on languages from diverse families and regions present unequivocal evidence of this profound variation, which includes everything from the kinds of tenses languages use (see Chapter 1), to the basic word orders they use (see Chapter 8), to, yes, the kinds of words for snow they use (see Chapter 5). No single book could catalog all this variation, but by reading this one you will get a better sense of the extent of the linguistic and associated cognitive diversity that exists across the globe.[4]

Linguists are still coming to grips with how incredibly distinct the world's languages are. Meanwhile, psychologists and others are better appreciating the diversity of thought and behavior across human populations. In another famous paper published in *Behavioral and Brain Sciences* a little over a decade ago, psychologists Joseph Henrich, Steven

Heine, and Ara Norenzayan made a critical point about our understanding of human cognition: nearly all of it is based on studies of people from Western, educated, industrialized, rich, and democratic (WEIRD) societies. These societies are weird indeed when contrasted to the bulk of human societies that exist or ever have existed. Henrich and colleagues suggested that "members of WEIRD societies, including young children, are among the least representative populations one could find for generalizing about humans." This is true for a variety of reasons, including the dramatic effects that industrialization and literacy have had on the social and material environments in which many of us WEIRD people were raised.[5]

The fact that WEIRD populations are a weak proxy for all humanity is also due to the effects that intensive schooling has had on the kinds of symbolic and mathematical thought with which we are routinely engaged from a young age. In my previous book, *Numbers and the Making of Us*, I discussed research suggesting that humans' numerical practices vary more substantially across cultures than many people realize. That book was based partially on my own work with indigenous populations who use number systems very distinct from those with which most of us are familiar. I suggested in the book that most human populations that have existed over the course of our species' history, and certainly those that developed prior to our ancestors' emigrations from Africa about one hundred thousand years ago, were not affected by repeated exposure to mathematical symbols and words. Our understanding of human psychology regarding things like numerical thought is informed largely by one strain of human populations, a strain that is hardly representative of our species in either a contemporary or historical sense. After all, most major universities and research centers have relatively easy access to WEIRD populations, primarily college students. This is perhaps one reason why the cross-cultural diversity of human cognition, like the diversity of languages, has been underestimated. As cognitive scientists have begun to seriously take up the call for studying human cognition via representative samples of populations with diverse histories, ecologies, and subsistence types, the extent of human cognitive heterogeneity has become more visible. That visibility continues to grow today, just like awareness of linguistic diversity. Yet the awareness of profound linguistic and cognitive diversity has not been disseminated sufficiently into the public consciousness, nor even into the consciousness of many scholars outside the fields of linguistics and cognitive science more broadly. This book highlights major insights that studies of many diverse languages worldwide, not just those of WEIRD people, have offered to cognitive science, linguistics, and other key fields of research on humanity.[6]

I should probably mention here that I spent much of my childhood in the jungles of Amazonia. It was that childhood experience that ultimately led me into the fields of anthropology and linguistics, fascinated as I am by the range of human linguistic and cognitive diversity. This pursuit has led me down research paths that rely on a variety of methods. Some of those paths have led me back to indigenous peoples in Amazonia, and that regional focus will be evident at times. Still, this book is concerned with discoveries about linguistic and cognitive diversity that have been made worldwide, primarily with non-WEIRD cultures but also with WEIRD ones. Some of the discoveries come from experiments in laboratory settings or from computational research on new databases filled with linguistic data from hundreds and even thousands of cultures worldwide. My own research utilizing such methods, along with more traditional linguistic fieldwork, will be mentioned at various points in the book when relevant. Unsurprisingly, there is some personal bias in terms of the themes covered in this book because I do research on several of the topics discussed. That said, I have tried to avoid focusing too much on the work of any one scholar (including myself), in order to show the array of fascinating types of research on the world's linguistic diversity being conducted by many scholars, often with novel methods. These researchers are changing our understanding not just of how language works, but of how people think and behave while they speak. It is also worth noting that the researchers themselves represent an increasingly diverse group of scholars, which no doubt contributes to the growing breadth and quality of the work surveyed in this book.[7]

In contrast to the bulk of linguistics research conducted in the twentieth century, contemporary research on language is also becoming increasingly collaborative and geared toward replicability when possible. Instead of the introspections of individual linguists and philosophers at famous universities, data and methods are now taking their rightful places at the center of discussions of language research. This is another reason why the book avoids a focus on any particular scholar or set of scholars, though the research of some will make multiple appearances. The book partakes in a general shift toward collaborative and reproducible efforts, which has resulted at least partially from the greater integration of language research with other fields. The growing integration of the study of linguistic behavior with the study of other forms of human behavior is not, however, simply due to a clearer focus on methods and data. Many language researchers have come to recognize that we simply must rely on insights into other aspects of human behavior to truly understand language and associated thought. For an intense period in the late twentieth century, linguistics aimed to divorce language from nonlinguistic aspects of culture and from other cognitive processes, but linguists increasingly recognize that these phenomena cannot be separated. For example, in Chapter 1 we will see how we cannot make sense of how people in some cultures talk and think about time without also understanding how they gesture about time. In Chapter 6 we will see how the structure of languages can be influenced by the social environments in which they develop. Because of this increasingly integrated view of linguistic behavior, the book will often veer outside the strictly linguistic because, well, not much is strictly linguistic. For example, we will see in Chapter 4 how the interaction of some lifestyles with certain environments helps foster distinct terms for colors and smells that can in turn affect how people remember visual and olfactory stimuli. The growing recognition of the integration of linguistic and nonlinguistic thought and behavior means that those of us concerned with linguistic behavior have had to familiarize ourselves with other fields. My own work has become increasingly reliant on findings from fields such as cognitive psychology, data science, and respiratory medicine, and it has veered into such fields at times. My collaborators now include biologists, chemists, political scientists, and engineers. I am not unique in this respect: a growing number of language researchers are migrating toward cross-disciplinary methods and collaborations as we see that language cannot properly be understood in a silo. The more careful engagement and collaboration with such disciplines by numerous language researchers represent another undercurrent flowing through this book. Three examples of cross-disciplinarity in my own research may serve as helpful illustrations of this trend. My research on number words relies on experimental research as well as computational analyses of number words in thousands of languages. In other work, I am collaborating with medical researchers and chemists to better understand how people produce tiny aerosol particles when speaking, and how such particles can transmit airborne pathogens during conversations. As a last example, some of my research has suggested that extreme ambient aridity impacts how languages evolve because it places subtle pressures on how humans use certain sounds. This research, which is controversial and will be discussed a bit in Chapter 5, is reliant on previous experimental research in biomedicine. These examples from my own research are simply illustrative of how language research is potentially relevant to and impacted by findings in a wide variety of disciplines. Thus, while the findings discussed in the book are related directly or indirectly to language, most of them are noteworthy because they also relate to other aspects of how humans think and behave. In that sense, this is very much not a linguistics book per se. It is a book about how research on myriad languages is reshaping our understanding of how people think when they are speaking, and in some cases how they think when they are not speaking.

While this book examines findings from a number of academic disciplines, most of the work it discusses is nevertheless based in one way or another on the research of linguistic fieldworkers who have documented countless unrelated languages during the past few decades. In many cases linguistic fieldworkers have drawn attention to interesting cognitive phenomena, including nonlinguistic phenomena, simply because field linguists have spent a lot of time living with very diverse populations around the world. To study a particular language, one often needs to invest countless hours listening to and recording that language. The increased focus of linguists on studying unrelated languages has meant they have spent time with distinct peoples who, besides speaking disparate languages, often have varied lifestyles in diverse ecologies. In short, all the linguistic documentation of the last few decades has also yielded a broader awareness of human cultural and cognitive diversity. Many linguists have brought back accounts of such diversity, encountered while doing fieldwork. These accounts, sometimes only anecdotal, have often served to entice others to return with them to remote settings to investigate, with the linguists' help, the behavioral diversity in question. In this and other ways, linguistic documentation has ultimately yielded a large crop of findings on humans' cognitive and cultural diversity that extend beyond linguistic diversity.

This book focuses on a variety of findings that stem directly or indirectly from the documentation of non-WEIRD cultures, but some studies on English and other well-documented languages are also discussed. In fact, some new work on English has been informed by work on unrelated languages, and this work has led to new discoveries on English and other languages spoken by WEIRD cultures. The book highlights recent key discoveries from a variety of cultures, discoveries that are in one way or another tied to the growing realization that the ways people think and talk are more varied than we once thought. I use the word "recent" in a relative sense. Some of the work discussed in this book is already decades old, but keep in mind that people have been studying languages for millennia. And much of the research discussed in the book has only appeared in the last decade or so. As previously noted, this book does not aim to exhaustively catalog key discoveries on speech, which would require volumes. Instead I offer a survey of some particularly interesting findings that are meant to be indicative of the larger trends at work in language research, with an emphasis on the themes mentioned above. In Chapters 1, 2, and 3, we will look at how discoveries related to talking are changing our understanding of human thought associated with time, space, and relationships. In Chapters 4, 5 and 6, we will examine research that points to the interconnectedness of speech, thought, and the environments in which languages are spoken. Finally, in Chapters 7 and 8, we will examine findings that are changing our understanding of how we think in order to create words and sentences.

Somewhat paradoxically, the language-based discoveries I will discuss have surfaced during an ongoing decline in the world's cultural and linguistic diversity. By some estimates, as few as six hundred of the world's languages, less than 10 percent, will survive this century. The median number of native speakers of a language is only around ten thousand, and hundreds of the world's languages are spoken by one hundred or fewer speakers. Such figures hint at the ongoing extinction of languages, which is happening as younger speakers in less populous cultures migrate to hegemonic, more economically useful languages like English. Awareness of this ongoing extinction has motivated many scholars to investigate dying languages while they still exist. Many of these languages are unwritten and unrecorded, hence the urgency of the task of field linguists. The mass extinction continues largely unabated, due to a host of socioeconomic factors outside the influence of any language-conservation efforts, however well intentioned such efforts may be. We therefore stand at a captivating stage of our species' life span, an ephemeral nexus that is unrecognized by most. We stand at the intersection of two trajectories: the growth of the recognition of cognitive and linguistic diversity across human populations, and the unrelenting decline of the linguistic diversity that enabled that recognition. Unfortunately, the ineluctable disappearance of most languages is, by all measurements, a onetime receding tide that is much stronger than any efforts at fighting it. While the work of linguistic fieldworkers is certainly not holding the receding waters in place, it has served to pull incredible specimens out of those waters, holding them up for others to appreciate. In this book we will take a look at some of these data specimens, showing how they are essential to our understanding of how humans actually talk and think.[8]

Whether or not Eskimos really have that many words for snow, it becomes clear to me this snowy morning that I do not have many at the ready. I leave the coffee shop, walking quickly to my next refuge, a subterranean one where I will hop on a crosstown subway. The freshly fallen snowflakes crunch audibly underfoot. But "snowflakes" doesn't really seem quite right, not now that the snow has accumulated on the sidewalk. As I take another step against the prevailing wind of the blizzard, I conclude that the snow I am walking on is probably no longer *qana*. I guess now it is *aput*.

1

Your Future Is behind You

PAST, PRESENT, FUTURE. These domains of time seem so fundamental to life, almost tangible, at least once we are adults. Early in life, we begin learning that these three core components of temporal progression are reflected in the language we speak, and that verbs take different forms depending on when the actions occur. We learn that we say things like "I jumped" when the action happened in the past. That is, we learn that an "-ed" suffix gets added to many verbs to inform the listener that something already happened. An English-speaking child must also learn that when referring to a future jumping event, they should say something like "I will jump" or, more commonly, "I'll jump" or "Ima jump." These conventions represent a key challenge for a child or an adult acquiring English; it is not easy to learn how to convey with regularity the past, present, and future status of events. To further complicate matters, English learners must learn that the tense markings on verbs often vary in irregular ways. They must memorize, for example, that they *"ate* lunch earlier," but that they *"will eat* dinner later." As with much of the language-learning experience, these idiosyncrasies can be maddening at times.

Such word-level particularities perhaps obscure the more fundamental thing that we are learning about tense as we become language speakers. We are learning that there is precisely a past, a present, and a future. When we acquire English as kids, we are also meant to learn that these particular temporal categories exist in the first place, that they are almost tangible, or at least that they are the basic categories to which we should refer by default because that is how time works. Our language helps to reify these abstract categories of time. After all, *past, present,* and *future* are nebulous notions that are not perceived in the concrete manner in which, for instance, you perceive the physical space around your body. You cannot revisit the past or prove its existence by reaching out and touching it as you might an object in your physical surroundings. And we never actually reach the future. Meanwhile, the present is not capturable since any moment we recognize is gone by the time we recognize it. It is in large part through language that the categories of past, present, and future are made to seem natural to us. In this chapter we will see that some aspects of time that seem so "natural" to us English speakers may seem unnatural to speakers of many other languages. This does not mean that we actually experience time in unique ways. Yet the linguistic evidence suggests that we conceptually segment time in particular ways because of the language we speak, and that speakers of other languages, while they may experience temporal progression in similar ways, must come to think of other temporal categories—not necessarily past, present, or future—as basic if they are to become fluent in those languages. In this chapter, I will discuss a few ways in which, according to various strands of research, languages reflect and potentially affect the diverse ways in which people think about time.

Time and Tense

The place to start is with tense. When asked why English has three tenses, some of my college students seem flummoxed. It seems a bizarre question. To them, English has three tenses because there are three tenses in time. English grammar refers to the past, the present, and the future because, well, that is how the universe works. In actuality, though, there are other ways to demarcate time grammatically, and one could argue that the past, present, and future seem to be natural domains of our lives precisely because we speak a language that demarcates time according to these parameters. So the true causal association may be the reverse of that typically assumed—it may be that our language constrains our default way of referring to and perhaps even conceptualizing time, and not that time's inherent qualities constrain how we talk about it. Again, I am not suggesting that people around the world physically experience time in markedly different ways. The claim I am making, and that others have made before me, is less radical but still potentially counterintuitive: how we talk about time, as English speakers, impacts our default mental description of how time works. If this claim is true—that is, if a grammatical characteristic of English impacts how we conceptualize temporal progression, or at least dictates how we refer to time—we would expect that not all languages should break up time into past, present, and future. In fact, many of the world's languages do not require speakers to refer to these categories. Past, present, and future are not actually temporal categories in many grammars of the world's languages, as we will see with a language on which I have conducted field research.

Much of what we have learned about languages in the last few decades is based on research with indigenous groups all over the world. Contemporary linguistic fieldwork consists of a variety of tasks, which potentially include running basic experiments and analyzing acoustic data for quantitative patterns. But the methods of such fieldwork still include seemingly straightforward but deceptively complex old-school approaches like sitting with a fluent speaker of some language spoken in a remote corner of some jungle and asking that speaker questions. Ideally these questions are informed by years of prior study by the field linguist, in classrooms and libraries, on the sorts of phenomena evident across the world's languages. Ultimately, then, the fieldwork often requires simply talking to and recording individuals in far-flung locales. The bulk of my own fieldwork was on a language called Karitiâna, which is spoken by a group of people in southern Amazonia. Others had done research on this fascinating language before me, and others have since. For about two years in the mid-2000s as I worked on my PhD, my days entailed working with Karitiâna speakers to better understand the intricacies of their language. This fieldwork sometimes consisted of simply sitting across from those speakers in the uterine Amazonian air, asking them questions.[1]

As simple as this particular task may sound, it was also mentally exhausting. Linguistic fieldworkers almost uniformly agree that this sort of research is draining, though rewarding. If you have ever tried to learn another language as an adult, you know that it can be difficult to learn one well even when provided with books, YouTube samples, ChatGPT texts, or any other of the sundry helpful tools at your disposal. This is true even if one is studying a language that is closely related to your native language, such as when an English speaker learns German.

Describing and speaking an unrelated language without such tools can be trying. In my case, I benefited tremendously from the work of previous linguists, in particular some missionaries that had documented aspects of the Karitiâna language. Still, I often found myself befuddled, feeling as though I was trying to decipher a code in the tropical heat, with bountiful bugs and other distractions around.

Such fieldwork can also lead to exhilarating moments when one feels as if one has cracked the code and reached some insight that might prove useful to the wider understanding of language. This was true when I started to better understand the ways in which Karitiâna refers to time, which are in some respects "typologically unusual," or not common to other languages around the world. One way in which Karitiâna is only a little unusual, vis-à-vis the description of time, is evident in how the language uses tense, what we so often think of as "past, present, and future." Consider the way in which one says goodbye in Karitiâna, via an expression that means, literally, "I will go":

(1) *ytakatat-i*   *yn*
    "I will go."

Note that the verb in this case is **ytakatat**, meaning "I go." There is an **-i** suffix attached to the verb, which signifies that the denoted action has yet to occur. In contrast, here is the phrase that is used to say "I went":

(2) *ytakatat*   *yn*
    "I went."

As you can see, there is no **-i** suffix added to the verb in this case. So we might be tempted to say that past tense in Karitiâna is signified by not adding a suffix, that it is somehow the default tense. This is somewhat true, but this account does not hold up when we look at how one says "I go" in the language:

(3) *ytakatat*   *yn*
   "I go."

As we see, the Karitiâna phrase in this case is the same as it is for "I went." This is not an irregular verb either, and I could offer limitless examples like these. What we see for the verb "go" is simply an indication of how the basic Karitiâna tense system works. That system distinguishes events that happen in the future from those that happened in the past *or* those that are happening in the present. As far as Karitiâna tenses are concerned, then, the past and present are not distinguishable. Of course, its speakers still recognize that some events are happening now and others happened in the past, but like some other languages in the world, Karitiâna uses a binary future versus nonfuture system of tense. When I translate English (or Portuguese) sentences into Karitiâna, I am forced to push three tenses into two. Conversely, when a Karitiâna speaker learns Portuguese, as most of them do, they must recognize that Portuguese breaks one of their tenses, nonfuture, into two categories, past and present.

The point here is not that Karitiâna is strange. While many languages have three-tense systems, like that of English, there are also some that have two-tense systems; this includes some that have "past / nonpast" systems, rather than "future / nonfuture" systems. The exotic feel of Karitiâna's future and nonfuture tenses may say more about our own expectations of how a language should work, because of our familiarity with three-tense languages like English, than it says about Karitiâna itself. In general, our perception of the features of an unrelated language is going to be inevitably grounded in the features of the language(s) we actually speak well, a fact that field linguists are often forced to remember. We try to have our expectations of the features of any language grounded in what we know about language in a much broader sense, rather than grounded in our own native language. The native language of field researchers tends to be an Indo-European language spoken by WEIRD people, after all.

Not all languages employ just two or three different tenses. Some languages lack any grammatical tense, while others have more than three tenses. Let us consider some more points along this spectrum. Mandarin generally lacks suffixes and prefixes, so its verbs are not technically inflected for tense. But Mandarin has other words that potentially denote tense. Better examples of tenseless languages would be Yucatec Maya, Burmese, Paraguayan Guaraní (which is distantly related to Karitiâna), and various others. Here is a sample sentence from Yucatec Maya that is tenseless as evidenced by the ambiguous nature of its English translation:

(4) *túumben   lenaho'*
"The house is / was / will be new."

Here the verb of the sentence, *túumben,* means to "be new" and comes at the beginning of the sentence, the reverse order of its English translation. The key point here is that this Mayan sentence does not change regardless of whether the house was once new, is only now new, or will be new in the future. This pattern is typical of a tenseless language.[2]

At the other end of the tense spectrum are languages with more than three tenses. Perhaps the most extreme case is Yagua, an Amazonian language with eight tenses. Five of the tenses break apart the past in fine-grained ways. There is a "distant past" tense, another tense for events that happened between a month and a year ago, another for events that happened about a week to a month ago, another for events that happened about a week ago, and yet another for things that happened yesterday or earlier in the day of the moment someone is speaking. There is also a present tense, and there are separate tenses for events that are about to happen and those that are expected to happen further into the future. Consider these two examples:

(5) *sadíí-siymaa*
"He has died (between a week and a month ago)."
(6) *sadíí-tíymaa*
"He has died (between a month and a year ago)."

In these examples *sadíí* means, roughly, "he die." The different suffixes let us know approximately when the dying happened. These suffixes represent just two of the five past tenses in Yagua. Other languages make fewer distinctions with respect to when an event occurred in the past, but more distinctions with respect to when it will occur in the future.

These few examples are enough to demonstrate that languages vary quite substantially with respect to how their grammars refer to the "when" of events being described. Those grammars may or may not require speakers to use morphemes—meaningful chunks of words like suffixes, prefixes, or auxiliary verbs—to describe when an event occurred with respect to the utterance. Even languages that do have that requirement can vary in terms of the temporal categories to which they refer with their systems of tense.

Since languages vary so substantively in how their grammars refer to the passing of time, it is fair to ask whether the speakers of such languages think about time differently. For example, do Karitiâna speakers think of past and present actions as being temporally more similar than English speakers do, because their language treats all such actions as nonfuture events? The answer to such a question is difficult to arrive at, requiring careful experimentation that is not easy to perform in nonlaboratory settings. Some cognitive psychologists would likely be skeptical that such tense distinctions have a meaningful impact on humans' nonlinguistic perception of time. Humans, like other animals, have ancient biological and neurobiological hardware used for perceiving temporal progression in broadly similar ways. Yet this biological homogeneity does not imply that such linguistic disparities have absolutely no effect on the discrimination of time. As we will see in subsequent sections of this chapter, there is now evidence that the disparate ways in which languages treat time, in domains outside grammatical tense, influence their speakers' perceptions of time in subtle ways. So it is certainly possible that crosslinguistic variation in grammatical tense has some subtle cognitive effects on the speakers of the relevant languages.

Of course, the lack of data does not always stop scholars from speculating and hypothesizing, and much has been made of the fact that some languages are tenseless. The most famous case on which much conjecture has been based is that of the Hopi language. Hopi is spoken by about six thousand people today. The Hopi reservation sits on a desert plateau and is circumscribed by the larger Navajo reservation in northeast Arizona. Just a few hours from Phoenix, the Hopi reservation can be easily reached by driving along Interstate 17, out of the Sonoran desert and into the high desert country. As one reaches the reservation, a series of higher tabletop plateaus or mesas present themselves, and it is on these mesas that the Hopis have lived since at least the late seventeenth century, when battles with Spanish settlers forced them to retreat to their present locale. The sienna visage offered by the mesas, along with the crisp aridity of surrounding air, offers as stark a contrast as possible with the verdant, humid environment in which the Karitiâna reside. Nevertheless, on a visit to Hopi country I was struck by some similarities between the two cultures. Like the Karitiâna and many other groups speaking endangered languages in diverse ecologies worldwide, the Hopi have for centuries been forced into a reclusive and somewhat impoverished existence. Like the Karitiâna and so many other such groups, their economy benefits from the sale of culturally representative artifacts sold to tourists passing through or near their remote reservation. Many of the Hopi, also like many of the Karitiâna, actively preserve their linguistic and cultural heritage. While only a few dozen people are monolingual speakers of Hopi today, some remain fluent in the language while also being fluent in English. Many of the Karitiâna are also bilingual, speaking Portuguese well, and the bilingualism of such populations allows them to keep their native language alive as they are forced to interact with the economically hegemonic, monolingual populations surrounding them.

In the early twentieth century, a linguist by the name of Benjamin Whorf also passed through the Hopi reservation. Most of his understanding of the Hopi language was acquired in New York from a Hopi speaker who lived there. Through his studies, Whorf arrived at some radical conclusions about the way that Hopi speakers describe and, more controversially, think about the passing of time. Whorf's work ultimately led him to hypothesize that languages have strong effects on their speakers' nonlinguistic thoughts. I do not wish to revisit this hypothesis, nor the many debates it has sparked in the intervening decades in fields like linguistics, anthropology, and philosophy. But it is worth revisiting at least one of Whorf's famous claims:

> I find it gratuitous to assume that a Hopi who knows only the Hopi language and the cultural ideas of his own society has the same notions, often supposed to be intuitions, of time and space that we have, and that are generally assumed to be universal. In particular, he has no notion or intuition of *time* as a smooth flowing continuum in which everything in the universe proceeds at an equal rate, out of a future, through a present, into a past . . . After a long and careful analysis the Hopi language is seen to contain no words,

grammatical forms, construction or expressions that refer directly to what we call *time*, or to past, present, or future.[3]

Subsequent to Whorf's work, some linguists have documented ways in which the Hopi language does in fact allow its speakers to refer to time. Others, for instance psychologist and linguist John Lucy of the University of Chicago, have argued that such rebuttals miss the mark and caricature Whorf's position on Hopi temporal reference.[4] Regardless, it is hard to make the case that Hopi refers to the categories of past, present, and future as consistently as a language like English does. Whether, and how much, such crosslinguistic disparities of tense impact people's general perception of time is still an unresolved issue. But what is clear is that languages like English, Hopi, Yagua, and Karitiâna vary with respect to how they encode tense, requiring people to conceptually segment the passing of time in distinct ways as they speak. And as we will see in the following section, there is certainly evidence that other linguistic disparities related to the encoding of time, aside from tense differences, do in fact foster dissimilarities in how people think about time even when they are not speaking. The relevant linguistic disparities relate to the variant metaphors for time that recur within some, but not all, languages.

Where's Time?

While it remains unclear how much tense distinctions reflect or impact people's actual perceptions of time, it is clear that speakers of diverse languages think about time in different ways. While all people may experience time in broadly similar ways, different populations use varied cognitive strategies to make sense of the passing of time, and these strategies can be linguistically codified and thereby impact subsequent language learners. For instance, even the phrase "passing of time"—an English-specific expression, with analog expressions in many but certainly not all languages—encodes a particular spatial way of thinking about time. "Passing of time" depicts time as though it moves through us or as though we move through it, when neither of these possibilities holds in a real, physical sense. We do not move through time nor it through us. Our strategy of depicting time via movement- and space-based expressions like "the passing of time" is, at its core, metaphorical. The relevant metaphor is hardly a linguistic universal. In Karitiâna, for example, there is no way of referring to the "passing" of time.

Do divergent metaphors for time yield differences in how people discriminate time even when they are not verbalizing such metaphors? There is some debate surrounding this question, but the best answer at present seems to be a simple yes. The thornier issue is whether the linguistically and metaphorically motivated differences in how people across cultures conceptualize time matter all that much in day-to-day life. In this section I aim to give you some sense of the conceptual disparities that stem from linguistic differences in metaphors for time. More critically, though, I aim to underscore the simple and less debatable fact that discoveries made in places like Amazonia, New Guinea, and the Andes have critically reshaped the contemporary debates of cognitive scientists regarding the human construal of time.

Before delving into some of the relevant crosslinguistic data, though, please indulge a simple experiment. It requires three small objects, perhaps three pens (though you can also follow along with imaginary objects of your choice). Place one of the pens on a flat surface in front of you, perhaps a desk. Let us say that this pen represents daytime, since this is a concept with which all human cultures are familiar. Now take another of the pens, one that we will say represents sunset. Place that "sunset" pen down on the same surface as the "daytime" pen, so that it is located in a position that seems "later" than the daytime pen. Finally, the third pen will represent "nighttime." Place that pen on the surface as well, so that you now have all three pens, representing "daytime," "sunset," and "nighttime," laid out in a logical sequence from "earliest" to "latest." There is no correct sequence here, but there may be a sequence that feels more natural to you. If you are like most English speakers, that natural ordering will be one in which the "daytime" pen is placed to the left of the "sunset" pen, while the "nighttime" pen is placed to the right of the "sunset" pen. This ordering depicts time as though it moves from the left to the right. There is a clear cultural and linguistic motivation for this spatial projection of temporal progression: the direction in which English speakers read. As you read these words, future moments of reading exist to the right of your fixation point at any given moment, while past moments of reading exist to the left of the fixation point. Reading direction is one of the many language-associated factors that impact how we think of the passing of time. Readers of languages that are written from left to right tend to use the left-to-right ordering of pens and other objects to represent moments in time. More commonly, they order time as though it moves from left to right in basic symbolic depictions of temporal progression, for instance in calendars and timelines. Readers of languages like Arabic and Hebrew, which are written from right to left, tend to adopt the opposite ordering in tasks like the one I just gave you.[5]

Work by a linguist on an Australian language brought to the fore an unrelated way of discriminating time, one that is not centered around a person's body like the left-to-right or right-to-left models of time movement. These latter models are referred to as "egocentric" models, because they are centered around the person interpreting the spatial orientation of the "movement" of time. But models of the temporal progression need not be egocentric; they can also be geocentric, based around some feature of the natural environment. Alice Gaby, the Australian linguist in question, has documented a geocentric way of describing time evident among speakers of Kuuk Thaayorre, an indigenous language spoken on the Cape York Peninsula in northern Australia. Along with her colleague Lera Boroditsky, a cognitive psychologist whose research has opened new ways of testing the influence of language on thought, Gaby's work on Kuuk Thaayorre has helped to draw attention to an alternate way of thinking about the passing of time. As with many of the world's languages, Kuuk Thaayorre lacks several of the words or expressions for segments of time that may seem natural to many of us, like "weeks," "hours," and "minutes." In actuality, most languages do not refer to such concepts as they represent fairly recent innovations that are contingent on certain kinds of number systems, and they arose out of a narrow set of linguistic and cultural conventions, having spread to many languages only in the last century. Despite the absence of such terms, Kuuk Thaayorre does have words for temporal units that are related to natural phenomena and not culturally contingent. These include words for seasonal and diurnal cycles, along with words for some other basic concepts of time such as "today" and "tomorrow," "soon" and "long ago." More intriguingly, speakers of the language also speak of time through phrases that refer to the sun's movement. According to Gaby, they can say *raak pung putpun,* or "the time when the sun is at the top," to refer to late morning and noon. Or they might refer to sunset as *pung kaalkurrc,* "the time when the sun is cold." As with certain other languages, including one from Amazonia discussed below, references to time are tied to the sun's "movement" along its arc throughout the day. While this temporal reference is not as regular or quantifiable as our hours and our minutes, it serves a related function.[6]

What is perhaps most interesting about cases like Kuuk Thaayorre is this: how the language's speakers think of time appears to be related to how they talk about the space around themselves. Speakers of this language frequently refer to cardinal directions associated with the sun's movement. For example, -kaw is used to denote the eastward direction, while -kuw refers to the westward direction. This system even applies to the description of the arrangement of small-scale objects. Whereas you might refer to one object being, for example, to the "left" of another, a Kuuk Thaayorre speaker might say the item is to the "west" of another as Kuuk Thaayorre does not employ egocentric terms for "left" and "right" in the way that a language like English does. Such egocentric terms are not as common in the world's languages as many people assume, a point that we will return to in Chapter 2. Instead, cardinal directions and the sun's movement are critical to how Kuuk Thaayorre speakers describe the location of objects, and the movement of the sun is also relevant to how they refer to time. One could say that this language requires its speakers to be geocentrically, or even heliocentrically, focused.[7]

A cultural and linguistic geocentric bias can impact how people construe time even when they are performing nonlinguistic tasks. To test this, Gaby and Boroditsky conducted a simple experiment, one not that different from the brief thought experiment you just did with the pens. They ran it in the remote Pormpuraaw community in which Kuuk Thaayorre and other related languages are spoken, and they also conducted it with English speakers in the United States. There are a few variations of the experiment, but the basic task is this: Subjects are presented with a series of pictures that clearly represent time passing. For example, one series of pictures represents a man aging. The participants are shown four pictures of the same man at different points in his life. Another series of pictures might represent an inanimate object, for instance a banana ripening and then being peeled and eaten. Each series of pictures is given to the participants separately. While outdoors, they are then asked to lay the four pictures out in front of themselves, from the earliest / youngest to latest / oldest stage represented in the pictures. They are given no specific instructions on how to do so, so the strategy they adopt for orienting the pictures is completely at their own discretion. English speakers almost always adopt the same strategy: the images are ordered from left to right, with the one representing the earliest / youngest stage placed in the leftmost position and the one depicting the latest / oldest stage placed in the rightmost position. In contrast, the ordering of the participants in Pormpuraaw seems random upon first inspection. Some might order the images from right to left, others from left to right, and others according to distance from their bodies, so that the earlier / younger images are closer to their bodies and the later / older ones are farther away. The reverse is also possible, with some ordering the images toward their bodies, with the older images closer.

As you might have intuited given the preceding discussion of the prevalence of cardinal directions in the Kuuk Thaayorre language, the ordering adopted is actually far from random. In contrast to English speakers, the majority of the participants in Pormpuraaw typically order the objects from east to west, so that earlier / younger images are placed toward the east, while later / older images are placed toward the west. The ordering of the objects appears disorganized upon first inspection because it is not consistently left to right or right to left. Instead, it changes in accordance with the direction each participant is facing when they perform the task, which Gaby and Boroditsky varied during the experiment. If the participants are facing north, the ordering appears to be right to left; if they are facing south it appears to be left to right. If they are facing east, earlier / younger images are placed farther away from their bodies; when facing west, the reverse holds.

Such simple experimental findings, along with relevant ethnographic and linguistic data, suggest that speakers of Kuuk Thaayorre think about time differently than we do. This difference apparently reflects linguistic and other cultural factors, since English speakers raised in environments similar to the ones the Kuuk Thaayorre speakers grow up in adopt a left-to-right strategy, not a geocentric one. Clearly the Kuuk Thaayorre speakers' "cardinal" sense of time is not simply the result of ecological factors, for instance the fact that they grow up in an outdoor, sunny environment. Nevertheless, it seems unlikely that such a strategy would develop in certain regions of the world. Regardless of the ultimate motivations for thinking of the passing of time in terms of the sun's movement, though, it is clear that members of some cultures conceptualize time in ways that differ markedly from the default conceptualizations of time upon which most of us rely. These divergent conceptualizations would never have been brought to the attention of cognitive scientists were it not for the efforts of field-workers like Gaby documenting linguistic phenomena in places like the Cape York Peninsula.

Kuuk Thaayorre speakers may think of earlier events as occurring toward the east, but they do not say things like "that happened in the east" to refer to something in the past, nor do they say things like "that happened in the west" to refer to future events. In contrast, in many languages there is a more direct linguistic mapping of time onto space. In English, for instance, I can say, "I *went* through a tough time," or "I *made it through* that period of life unscathed." Whether we talk about ourselves moving through time or time moving through us, we continuously refer to time as a spatial entity. The future is located in front of us, and the past is behind us. Consider just a couple more of the ways English reflects this underlying and pervasive metaphor for time. "I'm really *looking forward* to next season." "I'm so glad that's *behind* you and that you can focus on all the good things *coming your way.*" "The best days of your life are *ahead of you*, I promise." And so on.

There are two primary motivations for such a spatial interpretation of time. One is that time is inherently abstract. Our minds have a tendency to make sense of the intangible via the tangible, and objects in space are concrete and tangible. So it is helpful for us to think of past and future events as discrete objects that we move past. In fact, not long ago it was believed that all human populations, and all languages, used metaphors through which time was mapped spatially. It was believed that humans could not think about time without referring to space somehow. As we will see later in the chapter, this assumption has been challenged by research with speakers of an Amazonian language. Aside from this general motivation for a spatial interpretation of time, there is a second motivation for the specific spatial metaphor for time observed in English, in which the future is located in front of a speaker and the past is behind the speaker. That factor is walking, or locomotion more generally. When we walk, we move forward, and so the temporal intervals of stepping can also be construed as being physically behind us. Conversely, the locations of our next steps are literally in front of us and represent future moments. The basic facts of locomotion thus give us a natural motivation for describing time metaphorically. But time does not actually move, we do not actually move through it, and future or past events do not actually exist in the space around us. If I walk backward, the "location" of the future remains unchanged.

English speakers refer to temporal progression through a front-to-back spatial metaphor in speech, or via the left-to-right spatial metaphor evident in nonverbal semiotic tools like writing and calendars. Some tentative experimental evidence demonstrates that our verbal and other linguistic strategies for representing time impact how we think even when we are not using symbols or words to describe time. Perhaps my favorite bit of experimental evidence comes from a simple task undertaken by a team of psychologists led by Lynden Miles. The team looked for evidence of the effects of *chronesthesia,* the subjective movement through time that is likely unique to our species. To do this, they had twenty English-speaking subjects take part, one at a time, in a simple experiment. The subjects were blindfolded and fitted with a motion sensor that could detect any forward or backward bodily sway. The subjects' anterior or posterior sway was then measured as they were asked either to imagine what their life would be like four years into the future or to recall what their life had been like four years prior to the experiment. The results of the experiment were straightforward. As people thought about the future, they leaned forward in a very subtle manner. As they thought about the past, they leaned backward slightly. The amount of leaning would have been impossible to detect without the motion detector, so it is not as though this sort of behavior is perceivable in everyday interactions. In fact, the amount of body sway did not exceed three millimeters in most cases. Further, this finding has not replicated well in subsequent research, which is why I noted that the evidence is tentative.[8]

Findings based on English alone may give the impression that the future-is-forward metaphor represents the natural way to think about time. But evidence gathered among speakers of diverse languages disproves the latter conclusion. It turns out that languages vary substantially in how they describe time in terms of space, if they do so at all. Let us consider the case of Aymara, an Andean language spoken by nearly three million people in Bolivia and Peru. It is one of the most widely spoken indigenous languages in the Americas, though it is still much less utilized in Peru and Bolivia than Spanish. Rather than the future being in front of you, in Aymara the future is behind you and the past is in front of you.[9] As evidence of this, consider these two expressions in which the word *nayra* (meaning either "eye" or "front" or "sight," depending on the context) is used to describe a past time:

(7) *nayra mara*
    "last year"
(8) *ancha nayra pachana*
    "a long time ago"

The first expression is easy to understand, given the meaning of *nayra* and the translation of *mara,* which is "year." It might be literally translated as "the year I can see," while meaning "last year." The second expression includes the words *ancha* ("a lot"), and *pachana.* The latter word consists of a root *pacha,* meaning "time," and a suffix *-na,* meaning "in," "on," or "at." We might loosely translate this expression as "a time way in front of me." These translations reflect the underlying logic of the Aymara perspective on time. Since we have already experienced the past, we can "see" it and know it. In contrast, we cannot really see or understand the future with the same clarity. It is undetermined and opaque, whatever plans we might have for it. Yet the perspective on time that English takes also has a clear grounding in our physical lives, as noted previously. Simply put, there are multiple ways to construe the progression of time through space, and languages reflect those alternatives.

This Aymara metaphor for time, in which the future is behind you, is also reflected in the ways its speakers gesture while they speak. This is further evidence that the metaphors in people's native languages have nonsuperficial effects on their thought processes and are, at the very least, evident in their co-speech nonverbal behavior. English speakers routinely point (or otherwise gesture) forward when discussing future events, and routinely point backward when discussing past events. In contrast, Aymara speakers do the reverse. Rafael Núñez and Eve Sweetser, two cognitive scientists, published a study in 2006 demonstrating this pattern of co-speech gestures. They filmed hours of Aymara conversations, as well as conversations among Spanish speakers in the same geographic region and representing the same culture (broadly defined) as that of the Aymara speakers. When they analyzed the resultant videos, they found that some speakers pointed forward when speaking about the past and / or pointed backward when speaking about the future. These participants were always fluent Aymara speakers. This gesturing appeared to be the result of their native language. The Spanish speakers native to the same environment pointed forward when referring to the future and gestured backward when referring to the past.

Aymara is not the only language to exhibit this sort of perspective on time. Lisu, a Tibeto-Burman language spoken by about one million people in the mountainous Yunnan and Sichuan provinces of China, utilizes the same metaphor. In that language, the expression best translated as "in front of" can be used to refer to events that happened in the past. Conversely, the word for "behind, at the back of," can be used in a spatial sense but can also refer to the future. This metaphor is found not only in Lisu but in some other languages of the Tibeto-Burman family. The fact that this space-time association exists in languages on the opposite side of the globe from Aymara demonstrates that unrelated languages and cultures have arrived at this space-time mapping independently. In the case of Lisu and other Tibeto-Burman languages there is, to my knowledge, no experimental evidence demonstrating that the future-is-behind-you metaphor surfaces in other behavior or thought. But in the light of the evidence that has been gathered among the Aymara, it seems plausible that this perspective on time also surfaces in nonverbal cognition among the Lisu.[10]

The Yupno are a group of people indigenous to another distant land with mountainous terrain, like the Aymara- and Lisu-speaking lands.

The Yupno live in the highlands of eastern New Guinea and speak a language that, like Aymara, utilizes a completely different pervasive metaphor for time when contrasted to the recurrent metaphor of English. The future in Yupno is located neither in front of nor behind the speaker. In fact, temporal progression is not spoken of as though it were egocentric (centered around the speaker) at all. Yupno refers to future events as though they are "uphill" and past events as though they are "downhill." This exotic topographic basis of temporal reference is evident in phrases like the following:

(9) *omoropmo bilak*
    "a few years ago"

The word *omoropmo* means (roughly) "down the hill," and *bilak* means "year." In this phrase we see that "a few years ago" is actually translated as "the year that is down the hill." What are we to make of such an unusual expression? The case of Yupno time reference, like that of the Aymara, has also been brought to the attention of the scholarly community via the work of Rafael Núñez and his colleagues. In a 2012 paper they shed light on this fascinating language and its roughly five thousand speakers. They pointed out that Yupno speakers also gesture in ways that reflect the cognitively pervasive nature of their terrain-centered timeline. They demonstrated this point by recruiting twenty-seven native Yupno speakers to help them in a task. The task consisted of video-recorded interviews in which the speakers were asked to discuss some of the features of their language and culture. The speakers were not aware that the researchers were primarily interested in gestures, for instance in how they point when discussing past and future. Critically, the speakers were recorded both indoors and outdoors, while facing a variety of different directions. The net result of this was almost nine hundred recorded gestures made while the Yupno spoke, gestures that were then analyzed by independent coders who were unaware of the motivation for the study. The coders analyzed the directions in which Yupno speakers pointed while talking about time. A clear pattern emerged in the interviews recorded outdoors. When people gestured about the past, they generally pointed downhill. When they gestured about the future, they pointed uphill, more precisely in the direction of the closest mountain range. For example, one speaker produced the Yupno word for "yesterday" and simultaneously pointed forward when facing downhill. But when he produced the same word for "yesterday" while facing uphill, he pointed backward. This despite the fact that most time words and temporal expressions in Yupno, including the word for yesterday (*apma*), do not have a literal connection to the surrounding topography. The data suggested that, at least when they are outdoors, the Yupno speak and gesture about time as though it flows upward, from the bottom of a valley toward the peaks of the nearby mountain range. Their perspective on time is mapped onto space, but onto three-dimensional space rather than a horizontal two-dimensional timeline that transects the individual, with the future in front of or behind a given speaker.[11]

The extent of the implications of such findings remains a matter of some debate, but it is certainly well established that the Yupno refer to time as flowing uphill, in terms of both speech and co-speech gestures. While cognitive scientists have demonstrated this point via video recordings, experiments, and the like, it should also be noted that linguistic fieldworkers brought the point to the attention of such researchers. In this case, one of the coauthors of the 2012 paper, Jürg Wassmann, was a field linguist whose work about twenty years prior had documented features of the Yupno language that eventually drew the interest of scholars in other disciplines. This is a story that has repeated itself time and again in the language and cognitive sciences: Field linguists who are, by the nature of their vocation, forced to learn an endangered language unrelated to their own come across a remarkable feature of the language in question. Eventually, their finding percolates through academic circles and reaches those in related disciplines. Finally, a team of researchers ventures into the field to follow up on the pathfinding work of the linguists who spent extensive time in the remote locale learning and documenting the language in question. This sort of symbiotic relationship has yielded a host of key findings on human cognition over the last few decades.

Yet another mountainous region of the world has played a role in delineating the extent of variation in the spatial bases humans use when construing time. The Mayan Tzeltal, who live in the rugged forested region of Chiapas, are known to refer to the location of objects or animate beings as being "uphill" or "downhill" from each other, where uphill referents are located to the southeast (roughly) since the elevation of their surrounding landscape generally increases as one proceeds in that direction. The Tzeltal do not refer to things as being to the "left" or "right" of each other, as we typically do in English. As we will see in Chapter 2, this way of referring to objects in space is actually common to many groups worldwide. Consider this Tzeltal sentence:

(10) *ja' y-anil   abril   te   marzo=e   ja' y-ajk'ol   abril*
"March is downwards (*anil*) of April; April is upwards (*ajk'ol*)."

The meaning of all the words and suffixes in this example is not relevant to this discussion. The key point is that April is referred to as being *ajk'ol*, "uphill" with respect to March. Conversely, March is referred to as being *anil*, "downwards" with respect to April. Given such landscape-based temporal reference, we might predict that the Tzeltal similarly think of time as proceeding uphill, like the Yupno, and that such thought surfaces when they gesture about future or past events. As with so many predictions related to human language and cognition, though, this one does not hold. To test this possibility, researchers conducted a variety of tasks with the Tzeltal, including some similar to those conducted with speakers of Kuuk Thaayorre, in which participants were asked to arrange pictures from earlier to later events, in a spatial configuration of their choosing. The responses to such tasks suggest that Tzeltal speakers do not consistently think about time as flowing uphill, as the Yupno appear to do. There are numerous potential reasons for this, including the fact that Tzeltal speakers talk about time in many ways. Given that their language maps time onto space in multiple ways, maybe it should be unsurprising that they do not consistently think of time as moving uphill. Still, a few decades ago it was not even known that some populations spoke of time as proceeding in accordance with the local topography. Now we know that at least two groups do so: the Yupno do so consistently, while for the Tzeltal it is just one way in which speakers can refer to the passing of time.[12]

Spatial reference to time in the world's languages can also be literal. In contrast to languages like Yupno or English, in which there is a physically grounded metaphor guiding references to temporal progression, speakers of the Amazonian language Nheengatú use a direct spatial representation when communicating about time. Nheengatú speakers point to various locations in the sky when talking about time. This pointing is not optional like it is in Aymara, however, and field linguist Simeon Floyd has presented extensive evidence that speakers of this language are required to point to locations in the sky that are associated with specific times of day. Although Nheengatú has no words for the hours of the day, the language requires that people point to the sky when telling someone about an event, in order to describe when it happened or will happen. With Nheengatú's manual tense system, if I said something like, "The men arrived at 11 A.M.," I would be required to point to a specific point in the sky that approximates where the sun would be at 11 A.M. This pointing is not an optional clarification but an essential component of the phrase. The language requires visual reference along the east-west celestial axis to denote when events occurred. The visual component required of temporal language is, according to Floyd, "a point indicating the position of the sun at reference time, sometimes indicating two solar positions and the path between them." For example, if I am trying to tell someone, "I'll be back at noon," I have to communicate that "I'll be back" while pointing directly up into the sky, where the sun will be at noon.[13]

The Nheengatú system of time-telling is noteworthy for three reasons. First, it underscores how integrated gestures are with speech. This point is evident in reference to time in many languages since, as we have already seen, speakers often point in the "direction" of the time they are referencing. But the Nheengatú case is a particularly clear illustration of how intertwined gesture and speech can be, since the language *requires* that one communicate about times of day via gestures. To be fluent in Nheengatú, one must be fluent in pointing to solar positions. Second, the Nheengatú case illustrates how people can gesture about time in ways that are not body-centered. Unlike Aymara speakers or English speakers, the flow of time does not pass through the speaker. Like the Yupno, time "moves" in the same direction regardless of which way a speaker is facing. Unlike the Yupno, however, the movement of time is grounded in the perceived movement of the sun, and Nheengatú speakers point to locations in the sky that have physical associations with the time of day they are conveying. Third, the Nheengatú findings suggest a way in which language is subtly shaped by environmental factors. The time- telling system of Nheengatú is only effective in equatorial or near-equatorial regions and would likely not have developed at very high latitudes in which the position of the sun varies substantially throughout the year and some months are characterized by limited sunlight. Since Nheengatú speakers live near the equator, they can learn a more constrained set of celestial positions for time-telling, positions that hold with a high degree of constancy throughout their lives and throughout language acquisition more specifically.

While Nheengatú does not refer to time metaphorically, like the vast majority of the world's languages it refers to time spatially. Some researchers have claimed this is a universal of human temporal cognition. As is often the case with universalizing claims about human thought or language, however, it turns out that there is at least one exception. In a 2011 study, a group of linguists documented via extensive recordings the absence of spatially based depictions of time in Tupi-Kawahíb, another Amazonian language that is distantly related to Karitiâna. The linguists observed that Tupi-Kawahíb lacks any words or expressions in which time is talked about via reference to the human body, cardinal directions, or any other spatial cues. Also, while there are time-related words in the language, such as words for "today," "past," and "future," the language has no word for "time" itself and does not afford a critical role to temporal references. This fact may help to explain the complete lack of spatially based references to time in Tupi-Kawahíb. Through a series of simple experiments, the authors of the 2011 study also showed that the language's speakers do not map the passing of time onto any spatial axes such as left to right, front to back, east to west, up the hill, and so on. When they are asked to order objects representing the seasons of the year, for example, they do so in an idiosyncratic manner that is completely unlike that of speakers of other languages. As of now there is simply no evidence that the speakers of Tupi-Kawahíb talk about or think about time in spatial terms.[14]

These findings on languages like Nheengatú and Tupi-Kawahíb are illustrative of how much we are learning about how time is represented in human speech and cognition. I have focused on cases I think are particularly compelling, but there are certainly other interesting cases not covered here. (See, for instance, work on the Mian and Yélî Dnye languages of New Guinea for other interesting results related to this topic.[15])

Conclusion: Time and Numbers

Studies of the world's languages have helped to reveal just how nonrepresentative the forms of time portrayal in WEIRD cultures are of the bulk of the world's cultures, and just how nonrepresentative they are of the bulk of our species' history. As further illustration of this fact, just think about how many of the world's most populous cultures describe time through numbers. For many of us, time can also be described as passing by in discrete measurable units. Most people now measure time in seconds, minutes, and hours, and do so without realizing that such measurable units are the by-product of specific features of languages and cultures that no longer exist. A base-60 number system evolved in ancient Mesopotamia, and the vestiges of that base-60 system still live on in our minutes and seconds. While such facts have long been noted by those interested in the history of time-telling, studies of endangered languages have now underscored just how arbitrary this system of time-telling is. Such studies have revealed that some languages have few numbers or no numbers at all. Thinking of time in measurable, quantifiable units is bizarre in the first place to those who speak such languages. Numberless or nearly numberless languages include Pirahã and Munduruku, both spoken in Amazonia. Many other languages have only a few numbers or use number systems quite dissimilar from the decimal system that we use to measure tiny durations like milliseconds, or longer durations like decades, centuries, or millennia.

To speakers of such languages, learning the units of time we all take for granted is an entirely foreign endeavor for which they have no conceptual analogs.[16]

Time is discriminated in culturally and linguistically contingent ways, only some of which have been touched on in this chapter. Here I have focused on some of the key kinds of variations in temporal description and thought that have become known due to linguistic fieldwork, but there are plenty of other divergent ways in which languages refer to time. Nevertheless, the linguistic variation that has been surveyed in this chapter highlights the extent to which the depiction and construal of time is culturally and linguistically mediated. This is not to suggest that there are not universal components to the way in which humans experience time. We are all *Homo sapiens* with circadian rhythms and with the capacity to appreciate temporal progression and natural cycles like day and night. Nevertheless, it is increasingly easy to point to profoundly distinct ways in which humans conceptualize and describe time.[17]

Apart from their relationship to time, the findings considered in this chapter illustrate a methodological point that was elegantly encapsulated in a paper by Rafael Núñez, whose work among the Yupno and Aymara I discussed earlier. He notes, "Only by careful investigation of different cognitive domains, in radically different linguistic, cultural, and ecological circumstances, can the study of the mind take the true measure of human conceptual diversity."[18] When you look at a calendar on your smartphone and notice that you have a meeting "coming up," on a day that is "ahead of you," or when you think about how many minutes there are before your next meal, or count the seconds you have to wait at a traffic light, your thoughts are influenced by characteristics of English and its ancestral languages. And when you talk about time, you routinely rely on seemingly basic temporal referents that are not actually found in many of the world's cultures and languages. Consider a sentence as simple as "Last Monday I went on a half-hour jog, like I do every week." Now consider all the temporal concepts in that sentence alone that are not found in many of the languages discussed in this chapter: *Monday, week, went* (past tense), *half-hour,* and *do* (present tense). One short sentence can present a panoply of lexical and grammatical features impacting how we talk and think about time. As the detailed documentation of endangered languages like Karitiâna, Yupno, and so many others has now shown, these lexical and grammatical factors are hardly found in all human populations. Karitiâna, for instance, has no native terms for Monday, week, half-hour, or hour, nor does it have the same tenses evident in this simple English sentence. (There is no word for "jog" in Karitiâna either, but that's another matter entirely.) As should be clear by now, this is not because Karitiâna is somehow aberrant. Rather, the ways of referring to and conceptualizing time that seem natural to many of us may not be so natural after all.

2

Turn to Your West

ON AN UNCHARACTERISTICALLY sultry Italian day, I am slowly chasing shadows along the perfectly straight roads of the ancient city of Pompeii. With an approach that remains influential today, the Romans established cities like this one with easy-to-navigate grids. They were not the first to use the grid, but they were its foremost ancient purveyors. Pompeii's city grid was famously well preserved by Vesuvian ash for the better part of two millennia, and so the careful work of the city's planners still benefits tourists like me, wandering along its corridors and alleys. I am tracking shadows because my smartphone is inoperative and I was asked to meet up with my friends in another part of town, near the forum that once served as the city's social hub. Because of Pompeii's grid, I know that if I follow the stone streets in a generally westerly direction, I will end up at the forum. My journey began at the city's amphitheater, once used for gladiatorial entertainment, in the eastern part of town. But without my phone working at the moment, every intriguing detour takes me off course, and each *domus* courtyard tour disorients me a little. I find myself continually focusing on the shadows in the afternoon heat, to ensure they are cast in (roughly) the opposite direction from the one in which I am walking each time I return to my course. It is not exactly hard to do, but it requires concentration. The fact that it takes any concentration at all strikes me as a poor reflection of my navigational skills.

When I am reunited with my group and my smartphone troubles come up, the way-finding strategy I used strikes some as peculiar. How did the direction of shade help me locate the forum? "Chasing shadows" strikes others as a convenient direction-finding strategy even if it is not one they employ regularly. While they may not use the sun's trajectory to tell time, like the Nheengatú (see Chapter 1), they are certainly aware of the predictability of the east-to-west path of the sun's relative movement, even if that path does not follow an east-to-west route in Italy as neatly as it does in equatorial regions. Most of us Westerners, including English speakers like me, tend not to rely on cardinal directions when we need to find our way, unless we have access to a map, a compass, a GPS-based app, or the like. Our internal compass is typically poorly calibrated. What should be a trivial navigation task, crossing a grid-like city on a sunny day, actually requires some concentration.

It is tempting to say that all or most humans have weak internal compasses, but looking at a truly representative sample of the world's populations may prove this untrue. Consider another brief anecdote, this one taken from my fieldwork in Amazonia. Several years ago I followed a young indigenous mother, infant on her hip, from a jungle village to a location several kilometers away, where there was a clearing at which

I was to meet someone else for a journey out of the jungle. This woman and I did not share a language, so clear communication was impossible, yet she had been tasked by a third party with escorting me out of her village. I struggled to keep up with the adolescent woman (and her baby) along a labyrinthine jungle route as we made our way through the dense undergrowth. There was no visible trail or stone road in this instance. Save for the sporadic vertical shafts of light that pierced the emerald canopy about thirty meters overhead, we walked in shadows. It was midday in any case, so even if I had had a clear view of the overhead sun it would not have helped me all that much. My compass was the jungle guide who patiently led me to the meeting point. It was unclear then, and remains unclear to me now, how exactly she did so. How was she keeping track of our whereabouts, as we made our way toward a precise destination, without an obviously visible path, marks on trees, or other way-finding accessories? How did she know where we were going when there were no sight lines longer than a few dozen meters throughout the course of our journey? While the answer remains uncertain to me even now, her navigational acuity was likely the result of a combination of factors, including her intense familiarity with the particular stretch of rainforest we traversed. I suspect, for instance, that she used many of the towering Brazil-nut trees (*castanheiras*) that we passed during our journey as waypoints. The castanheiras were likely unique landmarks to her, arboreal skyscrapers. To me they were confusable large trees, homogenous. Regardless of the particular strategy she relied on, clearly it was not one to which I had access.

Human navigational abilities vary from individual to individual. But judging from the behavior of Romans, Americans, and others like the Amazonian adolescent I followed, the navigational strategies that humans use vary substantially across cultures and eras. In the last few decades and in particular the most recent one, this point has been driven home by linguistic fieldwork conducted with various populations in Amazonia, Central America, Africa, Australia, and elsewhere, which suggests that not just navigational strategies but also conceptualizations of space vary in profound ways. This chapter will offer a glimpse of some of the variation evident in the ways people think about, and orient themselves with respect to, the space and landscapes that surround them. This variation became evident not in transcriptions of speech, but as researchers listened to and watched people talk about space in diverse habitats.

Frames of Reference: Orienting the Things around Us

As field linguists documented the languages of Australia in the latter half of the twentieth century, they recorded interactions with native peoples. Some of the interactions suggested that those people perceived and described spatial relationships in very different ways than one might have expected given the dominant paradigms on spatial cognition that existed at the time. These paradigms, influenced in large measure by the work of some prominent psychologists and philosophers, suggested that human spatial reasoning was naturally biased toward egocentric and anthropomorphic approaches to making sense of space. People naturally make sense of the space around their bodies, and of the spatial orientation of other entities, by referring to their own bodies. We think of space as being centered on our person, and we think of spatial coordinates in terms of imaginary planes that transverse us from left to right, front to back, and top to bottom. The supposedly universal bias toward these strategies is evident in the way many of us give or follow directions when we are not utilizing maps or smartphones. For instance, the other day as I was walking across my university's campus on my way to lunch, a new student passing by asked me how to get to one of the main buildings. I informed her that she needed to "walk past the bookstore, turn right, walk past the lake, and then make a left across the bridge." Alternatively but still accurately, I could have said the following: "Walk west past the bookstore, turn south, walk past the lake, and then turn southeast to cross the bridge." But I suspect this would have been a completely fruitless strategy. It would have required some concentration on my part, maybe even some consultation of the shadows around me, and would almost certainly have confused the student. In contrast to such a geocentric strategy, I opted for the more culturally acceptable, and more natural-seeming, egocentric strategy. Note that I say "more natural-seeming" rather than "more natural" since the latter choice would imply a biologically grounded bias of some sort. Increasingly, it is unclear that the culturally appropriate "egocentric" strategy I used is actually more natural to all humans. It is now clear that some human populations do not rely on the egocentric strategy as a default way of giving directions or, more broadly, of making sense of their surroundings.[1]

In his detailed descriptions of the Guugu Yimithirr language spoken in Far North Queensland, Australia, linguistic anthropologist John Haviland has noted that speakers of that language often describe directions not in an egocentric manner but in a geocentric manner that relies on cardinal directions. The work of Haviland and other field linguists drew the attention of a number of scholars fascinated with the way these populations talk about, and think about, directions. These scholars included linguist Stephen Levinson. Here is a telling anecdote, based on Levinson's interaction with a Guugu Yimithirr speaker named Roger, who informed him that "in a store 45 km away there are indeed frozen fish, and it's here, 'on this side' he says, gesturing to his right with two flicks of the hand. What does he mean—not it turns out what I thought, namely that standing at the entrance to the store, it would be to my right. No, what he means is that it would be to my left. So how to explain the gesture? He gestured north-east, and he expected me to remember that, and look in the north-east corner of the store. This makes me realize just how much information I am missing each time he says anything." Roger expected Levinson to refer to the cardinal directions he was highlighting when Levinson made it to a store dozens of kilometers away. If someone like me needs to see the sun or its shadows to make sense of cardinal directions in a grid-like city such as Pompeii, how could Roger expect such an "unnatural" aptitude from a foreign linguist? One potential answer lies in the Guugu Yimithirr language, which requires that people constantly familiarize themselves with cardinal directions. The language does not utilize egocentric spatial terms like left or right, whose meaning varies depending on the direction in which a person is facing. Instead, the language relies on absolute and geocentric terms that are not dependent on the direction being faced. Consider another brief anecdote taken from Levinson's work: "Old Tulo, Guugu Yimithirr poet and painter . . . tells me to stop and look out for that big army ant just north of my foot." Judging from these and the many other experiences of linguists familiar with the Guugu Yimithirr language, its speakers refer to directions and space in a geocentric manner whether referring to small scales (foot-sized ones) or large scales (ones dozens of kilometers in size).[2]

The illuminating fieldwork experiences of Levinson were not limited to Australia. His research on human spatial cognition, and on its relationship to language, was conducted in other locales, such as an island off the coast of New Guinea and, perhaps most notably, among the Tzeltal Maya. Levinson and his wife, Penelope Brown, published a paper in 1993 in the *Journal of Linguistic Anthropology* that proved seminal to research on this topic and helped to deconstruct the then-popular hypothesis that human spatial cognition was fundamentally egocentric. What they learned from the Tzeltal also did not mirror neatly the solar-based cardinal-direction way of talking about space that Haviland and others had observed among the Guugu Yimithirr. Instead, the Tzeltal findings added a whole new dimension to linguists' understanding of how people talk about space, and eventually to cognitive scientists' understanding of how humans think about space. More specifically, the findings helped to alter the way we think about human "frames of reference." Frames of reference are the varied strategies available to humans as they conceptualize and describe the spatial orientation of objects with respect to each other and with respect to their own bodies.[3]

The default Tzeltal frame of reference that Levinson and Brown described was far from egocentric. Tzeltal speakers do not describe the spatial orientation of things in terms of left, right, or some other set of directions centered on their bodies. It is this nonegocentric spatial reference that apparently yields their nonegocentric interpretation of time passing, discussed in Chapter 1. Conversely, the egocentric spatial bias evident in many WEIRD populations seems to promote our egocentric depiction of time. While there is now extensive linguistic and experimental evidence supporting the claim that Tzeltal Maya speakers use geocentric spatial reference, the initial support for the claim was anecdotal. The Tzeltals' way of speaking of spatial relationships surfaced in informal interactions that left an impression on people like Brown and Levinson. No doubt many other foreigners who interacted with the Tzeltal had previously been impressed by their strategy for making sense of space and for giving directions, but here again it was the work of field linguists who brought this strategy to the attention of the academic community. In their 1993 paper, Brown and Levinson offered some intriguing anecdotes regarding the way in which the Tzeltal used the local terrain, rather than oppositions like left / right or east / west, to frame the spatial orientation of objects in their surroundings. For example, they described how they took a Tzeltal woman to a nearby town for medical care. The place where they slept had hot- and cold-water taps. The woman asked her husband which tap was for the hot water. Rather than asking whether the hot-water tap was the one on the left or right, as you or I might, she asked her husband whether the hot-water tap was the one that was *ta aijk'ol* or "uphill." She oriented the taps not with respect to her own body but with respect to the surrounding landscape, even though she was indoors and the taps were on the same horizontal plane as each other and the woman. To understand how and why she might do so, a little background on the Tzeltal is in order.

The Tzeltal community in question lives in the Chiapas highlands of Mexico, near the Guatemalan border. (Coincidentally, as an infant I spent time with my parents and two sisters in a Tzeltal village in the Chiapas highlands, but I have no recollection of that time that could offer direct insights into how the Tzeltal use spatial language.) The surrounding rugged terrain, traversed principally by foot, stretches a few miles along downward-sloping land. In the southern portion of the terrain, the altitude reaches almost three thousand meters, while the northern section is lower than one thousand meters. This southern-facing incline of about two thousand meters is associated with a host of ambient effects on the flora and fauna of the Tzeltal ecology. Ridgelines border the descending landscape in the east and west, giving it a somewhat enclosed feel. Whereas a precipitous drop in altitude has pronounced effects on local biology anywhere, this seems particularly true in regions like Central America, where higher elevations may be covered in pine trees while lower elevations are covered in tropical forests. From an early age the Tzeltal orient themselves according to the incline of their surrounding landscape, and that landscape helps to reinforce the orientation concretized in their language. When giving directions or speaking about object locations more generally, they consistently describe the positions of objects as being either *ta alan,* or downhill, or *ta ajk'ol,* uphill. Such terms can be used to metaphorically describe the passing of time, as noted in Chapter 1, but more fundamentally they are literal descriptors of spatial relationships. This is true whether they are describing objects with respect to each other, or with respect to speakers and those they are addressing. Consider this simple sentence:

(1) *ay*   ***ta***   ***aijk'ol*** *a'w-u'un / k'u-un*   *te*   *lapis*
     "The pencil is uphill from you."

In this case, the speaker can describe the location of a pencil (*lapis*) as being "uphill" (*ta aijk'ol*) from either themselves or their interlocutor. The critical point is that the pencil may be on a desk when this sentence is uttered, or on any other flat surface for that matter. The speaker could also say that the pencil is *ta ajk'ol* from some other object on a table, perhaps a bottle.

The fact that such utterances are used even when both objects are on a flat surface is perhaps puzzling. When the speakers refer to *ajk'ol* and *alan,* they are not literally referring to uphill or downhill terrain, respectively, at least not in an immediate sense. One could even argue that these are poor translations for the terms, though there really are no perfect translations. If someone says a particular object is *ajk'ol* from you, for instance, you do not need to be standing literally downhill from it. The two referential terms are not based on the immediate surrounding terrain, but on the wider landscape in which the Tzeltal are ensconced. If you and I were there, I would be *ajk'ol* from you if I were further toward the higher elevation or, roughly, to your south.

What is fascinating about this Tzeltal case of spatial orientation is that it is the principal way in which speakers of the language communicate about directions, from the relatively large-scale descriptions of space like "your house is downhill from the school," potentially used in direction giving, to small-scale descriptions of space like "the pencil is uphill from the bottle." In neither type of description do the referents have to be on an inclined plane with respect to each other, but in both cases they must be located in the appropriate directions with respect to the surrounding landscape of the Tzeltal speakers. This is the critical frame of reference for conceptualizing the spatial orientation of animate and inanimate things. Communicating spatial descriptions with alternate strategies like our own basic egocentric one, which relies so heavily on the body-centered notions of "left" and "right," is a foreign enterprise to the Tzeltal. This fact would make it difficult for them to give accurate spatial directions to those of us unfamiliar with their system, and vice versa. If you or I were to visit one of their villages, imagine how our lack of awareness of the surrounding landscape would make communication about basic tasks difficult. That awareness is apparently critical not just to their day-to-day communication but also to many other essential behaviors from a very early age. Because if basic communication requires a constant awareness of the surrounding landscape, then one must obviously have that awareness ingrained through consistent practice and habituation.

Maybe this is better understood if we think of a reverse situation. Imagine if a speaker of a geocentrically biased language, perhaps the member of a community that does not even use terms like "left" or "right," were to help you host a dinner party in your home. If they were assisting you with table settings, and presuming for the moment you were the punctilious sort that cared about things like silverware ordering, you might find yourself perplexed that your guest could not keep track of which sides of the plate are to the "left" and "right." As they looked at the place settings on different sides of the table, they would likely be particularly confused by the strategy you wished them to adopt. You would need to tell them to put the fork to the west of the plate. Or the east. Or maybe *ta ajk'ol*.

Since the publication of Brown and Levinson's seminal work, there have been dozens of studies on this topic carried out with indigenous groups worldwide. Much of this work was conducted by Levinson and his students and colleagues in the nineties and aughts. He and others have prominently advanced the position that language impacts what we once assumed were deep-seated, universal facets of human spatial cognition. Much debate persists around this claim, though even skeptics now generally acknowledge that language plays some role in helping to shape the default spatial strategies on which people rely. Such skeptics might suggest that the motivating factor in these cross-cultural disparities is not so much language, but other things like behavioral differences and ecological factors—for instance, a culture being embedded in a unique landscape like that of the Tzeltal. Regardless of one's position in such debates, what is clear is that the work of field linguists in places like the Chiapas highlands of Mexico has shattered some once strongly held notions of the supposedly universal ways in which people talk about and orient themselves and other entities with respect to their surroundings. For example, in the nineties, research was undertaken on the spatial-cognition strategies employed among speakers of Mopan and Yucatec Maya, as well as speakers of Totonac in Mexico.

Much work on this topic was also conducted outside Central America. The spatial cognition of speakers of many languages has been investigated, including speakers of Hai‖om in Namibia, Belhare in Nepal, Arandic in Australia, Longgu in the Solomon Islands, and Yupno in New Guinea. Work on spatial cognition carried out primarily by field linguists, and always with at least the assistance of such linguists, has now been undertaken in dozens of diverse regions with speakers of completely unrelated languages. It is impossible to succinctly summarize all the findings that have resulted from this work, but the pithiest assessment might be that people vary substantially in terms of how they describe space, and in terms of the spatial frames of reference on which they rely. Through this work it is now known that there are at least three basic frames of reference observed in the world's languages, including the egocentric sort most of us rely on by default and the geocentric type relied on by the Tzeltal.[4]

During the course of these investigations, conducted over the last three decades, methods were refined in order to more clearly test for cross-cultural differences in spatial thought without needing to rely too heavily on ethnolinguistic anecdotes like those related above. While such anecdotes are illuminating, they also leave some questions unanswered. Most critically, they do not answer the question that has long been the source of discussion in linguistics and anthropology: Do people think differently, even about basic things like the space surrounding them, when they are not speaking? Stories that are centered around people speaking cannot address this question directly. Consider the anecdote about the Tzeltal speaker who asked whether the hot-water tap was *ta alan:* When she walked into the bathroom, was she really looking at the water taps and perceiving one to be *ta alan* and the other *ta ajk'ol?* Or was she forced to think of the taps in these terms in order to communicate? Surprisingly, perhaps, some cognitive scientists still adhere to the belief that people think about space in fundamentally egocentric ways, and that geocentric frames of reference like the one used by the Tzeltal reflect something merely about their language, not about their basic nonlinguistic spatial cognition. According to such views, a geocentric frame of reference is a patina covering a deeper egocentric spatial way of thinking. Such a perspective is problematic to many of us who consider it (a) difficult to falsify, when theories of cognition (like all other theories) must be falsifiable and testable, and (b) biased by the commonality of egocentric frames of reference among WEIRD people. Yet proponents of this perspective do raise an important point, which is that we cannot assume that just because people speak and behave differently they also think in fundamentally different ways.[5]

One experimental task that has been used and adapted in dozens of populations, in order to test the default frame of reference people use even when they are not speaking, is called a rotation task. The particular variant of the task I will outline was used in a study comparing the way in which speakers of Dutch and Hai‖om, in Namibia, think about space. Dutch speakers, like speakers of English and most other European languages, generally rely on an egocentric frame of reference that involves reference to *links* ("left") and *rechts* ("right"). In contrast, speakers of Hai‖om generally refer to two main cardinal directions, west and east, when giving directions or describing the spatial configuration of things. Their term for west translates literally as "where the sun goes in," and the term for east translates to "the warmth." Here is how the task worked. Each experiment participant stood outside, facing a table. On the table was a linear array of plastic toy cows of different colors. The table was located next to a rectangular school building about twenty meters long. The school building was not the same for everyone, since the researchers ran the experiment separately in Holland and in Namibia. The toys were the same in both cases, however. Each participant looked at the table and tried to silently memorize the order of the toys. It was a simple memorization task. After they memorized the order, they were taken to the other side of the school and placed in front of a table, in a direction that differed by 90 degrees from the original direction they had faced while memorizing the order of the toys. Now they were given the toys again, in a randomly ordered pile, and asked to place the toys in the same sequence as the one they had originally seen on the other side of the school. The order they used reflected whether they had memorized the spatial configuration of objects in an egocentric or geocentric manner.

This may all be a bit confusing, so let me break it down step by step while you pretend you are a participant in the experiment. You look at the toys—say, four plastic cows of different colors. You try to memorize the order of the line of toy cows in front of you, laid out across the length of the table that is parallel to your waist. How would you memorize the order? If you are like nearly all Dutch- or English-speaking people that have undertaken this task, you would make mental and unspoken observations that rely on the fact that some toys are to the left or right of each other. Perhaps the white cow is the leftmost cow, the black cow is to the right of the white cow, a brown cow is to the right of the black cow, and a spotted cow is all the way to the right. You might take a mental picture, paying attention to this relative ordering. Then, when you are on the other side of the school and rotated 90 degrees, you would place the cows in the same order—white all the way to the left, spotted cow all the way to the right.

Now imagine how this experiment would have played out if you had used a geocentric strategy that relied on cardinal directions like east and west, much like the Kuuk Thaayorre speakers when positioning pictures with respect to their temporal order. (See Chapter 1.) When you took the mental picture of the plastic cows, you would not have paid attention to their left-to-right positioning. Assuming for the moment that the table was to your north, you would have observed that the white cow was the westmost cow and the spotted cow was the eastmost cow. This is where the 90-degree rotation required for the task becomes really useful, for it reveals which strategy participants initially used when taking their mental picture of the objects on the table. If you were facing north when first examining the toys, then after a 90-degree rotation you would be facing east, though on the other side of the school. If you had memorized the order of the toys as proceeding from west to east, you would maintain that ordering on the other side of the school. You would place the white cow to the west and the spotted cow to the east, but since you would now be facing east, the line on the table would look quite different. You would place the white cow closest to your body with the other cows in a line projecting away from you on the table. If you had been rotated 180 degrees (a variant of the task), so that you were now facing south, you would actually place the white cow to the right of the other cows and the spotted cow all the way to the left. To most Europeans or Americans it might appear that you reversed the order of the objects, when in actuality you had just been using a completely different frame of reference, one untethered to your body. Again, this calls to mind the performance of the Kuuk Thaayorre on the temporal-reasoning task, discussed in Chapter 1.[6]

This rotation type of experiment, along with many variants, has now been employed in many cultures. Time and again consistent cross-cultural differences have been uncovered, and it is by now clear that people vary with respect to how they conceptualize and organize the configurations of objects in their surroundings. Perhaps this is not all that surprising given the stories that linguists and others have been telling for decades, stories pointing to varied spatial-cognition strategies used in far-flung cultures worldwide. Nevertheless, it is comforting to know that we now also have experimental data to support this claim, even if debate persists regarding the depth of the cognitive diversity hinted at by such stories and simple experiments.

Some researchers now believe that language is the principal determining factor that shapes how people think about space. If you grow up speaking an egocentric language, you will think about spatial relationships in egocentric terms. If you grow up speaking a geocentric language, you will think about spatial relationships in geocentric terms. Some evidence suggests that human spatial reasoning, along with that of other primates, may have a default nonegocentric bias, and that only those of us who speak egocentrically biased languages like English are likely to conceive of space in egocentric ways. That is, if you are not repeatedly exposed to words like "left" and "right" from an early age, the associated concepts will not mature.[7]

Another key factor suggests that the kind of language you speak plays a prominent role in shaping the kind of spatial reasoning you rely on, even when not speaking: language is ubiquitous. Humans produce an average of about sixteen thousand words per day, though individuals vary a lot, at least in cultures in which this has been measured. The ubiquity of speech implies that we are constantly referring to culturally specific concepts like *ta alan* and *ta ajk'ol*. So, although the way we refer to space may stem from other ecological and cultural phenomena, our behavior can be reinforced by language—just as certain kinds of behavior can reinforce the use of certain kinds of language. Furthermore, language is the key facet of culture through which ideas get transmitted. Even if language is not the ultimate source explaining why people think about space in a given way in a particular culture, that way of thinking about space must be transmitted from individual to individual, including from parent to child, through language. As Tzeltal children grow up, they hear phrases with *ta alan* and *ta ajk'ol* all the time, likely multiple times a day. Although they are not initially aware of what concepts those common words refer to, they are aware that they must learn certain concepts in order to understand and use those common words. Languages create pressures compelling people to learn the concepts associated with particular labels they must wield in order to be fluent speakers, but also so that they can conduct the most basic spatial tasks of reasoning and object manipulation and get others to do so. English-speaking children are also exposed to pervasive spatial terminology: the labels they must use are words like "left" and "right." Learning the proper meaning and use of such spatial labels becomes an integral part of growing up, as we learn to orient ourselves to the spatial surroundings in which we are embedded.[8]

People necessarily become very experienced with particular frames of reference in speaking their native language. The experience of speaking then helps to foster certain cognitive habits that lead to conceptualizing one's surroundings in particular ways. It is not that human populations that speak geocentric languages cannot learn to speak or think egocentrically, but they lack the experience to do so with ease. Conversely, most of us that speak a language with default egocentric reference lack the experience to speak easily in geocentric ways. This perspective implies that different ways of thinking about space are transmitted linguistically from generation to generation as each new set of kids in a population learns cognitive habits associated with the default way of talking about space in its community. Language transmission yields patterns of thought, even if it does not constrain thought in deterministic ways.

This lack of deterministic constraints on thought is reflected in a point that was largely ignored in much of the research of Levinson and colleagues: the way speakers of a given language talk about space may actually vary substantially. A host of studies produced in the last several years suggests that spatial language can vary within communities according to factors like gender and vocation. Using "speakers of English" as one data point and "speakers of Tzeltal" as another is an oversimplification. While speakers of English may be much more likely to think and talk about space egocentrically when contrasted to speakers of Tzeltal, Guugu Yimithirr, or any other of a number of languages, speakers of all these languages can adopt different strategies depending on a number of factors. For example, some research has found that spatial reasoning is heavily influenced by language, but also by nonlinguistic culture and ecological factors like the local topography.

Research with speakers of the Dhivehi language, on the Laamu Atoll in the Maldives, suggests that vocation plays a major role in how people conduct spatial reasoning tasks. On the islands in the atoll where the dominant subsistence strategy is fishing, about 80 percent of responses in such tasks suggest geocentric reasoning. On the islands where the dominant subsistence strategy is small-scale farming, only about 40 percent of responses are geocentric. This makes sense, as the fishers are well practiced with geocentric navigation. It is critical to both their short-term and long-term survival. One suspects that similar patterns, though perhaps less pronounced, might be found among many populations. For example, American fishers and pilots are probably more likely to think geocentrically after years of being trained to do so, even if most Americans use egocentric reference most frequently.[9]

Among the Maya, researchers have now observed striking variations. For speakers of Mopan Maya and Yucatec Maya, for example, it has been noted that men are much more likely to rely on geocentric directional terms, while women are less familiar with the terms. The most likely explanatory variable here is that men in these communities tend to work in the fields, while women tend to work at home. The daily lives of the men seem to foster a greater reliance on the geocentric way of talking about space. Yet the language they happen to speak is still critical in all this, as Mayan languages offer their speakers geocentric expressions and words that facilitate geocentric speaking and reasoning. If you speak a language in which expressions like *ta alan* and *ta ajk'ol* do not exist, there is no reason you will necessarily come to think of the space around you in terms of the directions they denote. This point can be taken a step further. If the Tzeltal did not live in the geographic context they do, they would never have developed a directional system that relies so heavily on "uphill" and "downhill." The fact that they live on a sort of inclined plane, rising to the south (roughly), is obviously critical in all of this. This very salient feature of their surroundings eventually promoted a way of talking about space, a way of talking that now helps to enforce a default way of thinking about space. Nevertheless, while it is tempting to conclude that the origins of this kind of thinking about space are determined solely by the surrounding landscape, this would not be completely accurate either. The landscape does not *determine* how the Tzeltal or others speak about space, because many other populations live on inclined planes without developing directions like *ta alan* and *ta ajk'ol*. Yet while a particular sort of landscape is not a sufficient criterion for the development of a particular way of talking about space, it is clearly a necessary criterion. No group living on a flatland would come to refer to space in terms of uphill / downhill like the Tzeltal, Yupno, and some other populations. Yet groups living in flat terrain may come to use other geocentric terms to talk about space, as evidenced by the fact that the Guugu Yimithirr use cardinal directions so pervasively. The use of solar-based geocentric terms like those of the Guugu Yimithirr does not require mountainous terrain, but it does require an environment in which the trajectory of the sun is visible most days. People are more likely to use directions oriented according to the sun's movement if that movement is readily discernible. This point is related to one made in Chapter 1: the Nheengatú of Amazonia would likely not have developed a gestural system for telling time by pointing at the sky if they did not live in an equatorial region. Equatorial sunshine allows for much greater ease of "time pointing." More broadly, such simple observations illustrate that languages encode concepts in ways that are affected probabilistically and nondeterministically by environmental variables.[10]

This discussion has focused on a few specific cultures and spatial frames of reference, but as with everything else human, there is always greater complexity to be found. Other cultures and languages do not rely on any of the frames of reference described so far. As mentioned above, at least three basic kinds of frames of reference have now been uncovered. In addition to the egocentric and geocentric frames of reference, some cultures use what are called "object-centered" frames of reference, in which they orient themselves spatially according to features not of their bodies or of regional landscapes, but of smaller things like buildings. Most of us do this on occasion. For instance, I can talk about a lectern being at the "front of the classroom," while perhaps the door is at the "back of the classroom." Rather than referring to one student's desk as being to the left / right or north / south of another's, I might say that the desk is "closer to the front" of the class. As an English speaker, I use this object-centered way of talking about space in specific circumstances, like being in a classroom or in a vehicle. Most of these circumstances involve enclosure in a relatively small space, but not all of them. On a large ship, even when outdoors, I might say something like "Your cabin is aft of mine" to mean it is closer to the stern. In nautical contexts we can even refer to the spatial orientation of smaller points of reference. A ship crewmember could quite likely tell someone to place "the chairs aft of the table" to organize a dining room. I have heard this sort of instruction on numerous occasions on shipboard journeys.

While object-centered directions are not the norm for most of us, they are the norm in certain cultures. This seems to be true among some of the Karitiâna. While Karitiâna has words for "right" and "left," these terms do not appear to be commonly used when people are describing the spatial orientation of objects or giving directions. And the Karitiâna do not seem to think (at least not traditionally) about space primarily in egocentric terms or in geocentric terms. Consider again the toy-organizing experiment that I described above. Speakers of primarily geocentric languages like Hai‖om generally memorized the order of the toys according to cardinal directions, like "the black toy cow is to the west of the white cow." Speakers of primarily egocentric languages like Dutch and English memorized the ordering with strategies like "the black cow is to the left of the white cow." These different strategies became clear when the participants were rotated and placed on another side of a building. Speakers of Karitiâna, on the other hand, would do something completely different. They would memorize the order of the objects by thinking that "the black cow is closer to the school building than the white cow." Then, when placed at the other side of the school, they would once again put that black cow on the side of the table that was closer to the school, regardless of other factors. In fact, when I conducted similar nonlinguistic experiments with Karitiâna speakers about ten years ago, this is exactly what I observed for the majority of them.

Another type of spatialization strategy is closely tied to the local environment. Inhabitants of some islands refer to things according to directions like "seaward" and "landward," where the latter direction points to the island's center, regardless of one's location. If you were on the north side of the island, "landward" would be south and "seaward" would be north. The opposite would be true if you were on the southern part of the island. A number of studies on endangered languages have led to the documentation of various sorts of island-specific directional systems. In Amazonia and elsewhere, some related systems of direction giving and spatial orientation are tied to the direction of a major river's current. For instance, consider the phrase *Piibooxio xigahapaati,* meaning "go upriver," which is common in the Amazonian language Pirahã. Pirahã has become well known among language scholars over the last decade due to the research of my father, Daniel Everett. He observed that *Piibooxio xigahapaati* is used not just at the river's edge, but deep within the heart of the jungle. The Pirahã use the current of their local river—the black, serpentine Maici, which flows in a northerly direction—as the basis for their default system of spatial reference. This kind of spatial reference requires that Pirahã speakers constantly keep track of where they are with respect to the southerly "upriver" direction, a difficult thing to do for those unfamiliar with this system, as attested by both of my parents, who have spent many years studying the Pirahã language and culture. As a result of my parents' missionary work in the eighties, my sisters and I visited and lived with the Pirahã intermittently during our early childhoods. I have spent more evenings and afternoons than I could count swimming *Piibooxio xigahapaati* and downriver in the cool waters of the Maici.[11]

In the Amazonian region in which I have spent much of my life, many Brazilians also speak of the locations of towns and villages in terms of *pra cima* ("upriver") and *pra baixo* ("downriver"), even when the speakers are not on the river or at the river's edge. They would not, however, say that a fork is *pra cima* or *pra baixo* of the dinner plate, as this frame of reference is not used at small scales. Still, the point holds: humans have different kinds of directions and basic frames of reference at their disposal, and a variety of factors influence the way they think and talk about space. This chapter has touched on only some of these, but enough to show that neither landscape, nor language, nor nonlinguistic cultural factors, nor native characteristics of our brains completely determine how people think and behave with respect to the space around them. Instead, all these factors are interrelated and help to inform human spatial reasoning and associated behavior. The most extensive recent experimental work, across a variety of populations, supports this conclusion. Humans are a wildly variable bunch.

When wandering around a grid-like city like Pompeii, whether today or two thousand years ago, a person might rely on cardinal directions to find their way. The likelihood that someone would do so, and the ease with which they would do so, would depend on the person's cultural lineage and the default frame of reference used in their language. Interrelatedly, their spatial reasoning might depend indirectly on the landscape characteristics of their native homelands, the consistency of the sun's arc in those lands, their occupation, gender, and so on. What is clear from the now enormous body of research on human spatial reasoning is that people can talk and think about space in varied ways. Some of these ways are egocentric, some geocentric, some object-centered. Languages encode highly varied spatial concepts. This degree of variation would have been surprising to most cognitive scientists not that long ago. Now, although debate still exists as to just how profound the variation is, it is impossible to deny its existence. Such variation tells us something critical about human thought and behavior: how we orient ourselves to our surrounding space differs cross-culturally in ways that were once considered impossible given basic assumptions about the homogeneity of humans. The discovery of that variation ultimately owes itself to the work of linguists in places like the Chiapas highlands who paid attention to what people actually do and say when talking about space.

Landscapes: What's a Hill, Really?

So far, this chapter has focused on the ways people talk and think about the spatial orientation of themselves and of other entities, orientations grounded in particular frames of reference. But there is more to talking about one's surrounding space than referring to particular frames of reference. Much more, actually, but here I will focus on a topic that relates indirectly to the frames of reference: how people talk and think about surrounding landscapes. As I stressed in the previous section, features of the local environment can play a critical role in helping to shape how people talk about space. The fact that the Yupno frame space and the passing of time with respect to "uphill" or "downhill" owes itself in some measure to the steep hills they live on. We might phrase this observation as follows: being surrounded by hills leads to an increased likelihood that people use a geocentric type of spatial reference. But this, too, is an oversimplistic assessment, for a reason that might surprise you. Not all people talk about "hills" or even conceptualize hills as distinct entities.

Consider Lao, a language spoken by dozens of millions of people. Nick Enfield, a linguist at the University of Sydney, has spent years studying Lao. His work demonstrates that speakers of the language refer to the surrounding Southeast Asian landscape with terms that do not translate neatly into English or other European languages. For instance, Lao does not have a word for "mountain." Instead, the word *phuu2* (the symbol "2" refers to a particular tone) is used to refer to mountainous terrain.

Here are some of Enfield's observations: "A land form which in English may be called an individual mountain . . . can be referred to in Lao by using a complex numeral classifier phrase. Thus *phuu2 nuaj1 nii4* means 'this mountain' (literally 'this unit of mountainous terrain'). This suggests that in the Lao imagination, there is no 'thing' corresponding to the English *mountain*." Nor is there a straight translation for "hill" in the language. There is a Lao term that refers to very small hills, but it also refers to small mounds of earth and even to termite mounds. Perhaps this strikes you as odd, but think about what we call "mountains" and "hills" for a moment.

Mountains in a given range are not exactly distinct from each other: they are geographically interwoven. There may be one summit with various lesser peaks around it, all on the same conical landmass. Each mountain does not descend down to a flat surrounding plain, and the profiles of individual mountains vary significantly in terms of their salience. In some cases, many volcanoes for instance, mountains may appear as solitary individuals, cast against a flat terrain. This is not really the case in the Laotian landscape, however, nor in the case of most mountains in ranges, wherein bases and summits represent interlinked wrinkles on the earth's surface. The point at which a "mountain" becomes a "hill" is not well defined in the first place, nor is the point at which a hill becomes a "mound." Landscapes themselves lack clear divisions in physical space, so some cultures have terms like *phuu2* that refer to mountainous terrain as opposed to separable mountains.[12]

Languages also refer to other elements of the surrounding landscape in diverse ways. In Lao, for instance, there are two words for jungle: a *khook4* is a jungle with trees that are spaced apart, and a *dong3* is a term for tropical forests with densely packed trees. Clearly languages refer to their geographic surroundings in disparate ways, and this disparity can affect how people learn about the space that surrounds them. Consider a Laotian child living on the plains next to mountainous terrain. They see a clear difference in altitude between the plains and the interlaced peaks. They can distinguish the peaks, but perhaps the more salient distinction is that between the dark green forested peaks and the bright green grassy plains used for farming. At some point they hear the word *phuu2* spoken. They have no way to distinguish what that term means; all they have is a label. During language acquisition, they realize how that label is used in interactions, and they construct its meaning from those interactions. They grow to realize that the core concept of the term refers to the surrounding mountainous terrain, much as a learner of Tzeltal must gradually work out the concepts referred to with labels like *ta alan* and *ta ajk'ol*. Similarly, English-speaking children grow to work out the concepts for "left," "right," and "mountain." While our senses, shared across all populations, may predispose us toward certain ways of deciphering our spatial surroundings, the labels of our native language help to concretize particular spatial and physical concepts that come to seem natural to children as they age. We can learn other concepts or adapt our language to refer to slightly different concepts. I can say "mountainous terrain" and convey, at least roughly, what is meant by *phuu2*. A speaker of Lao can say *phuu2 nuaj1 nii4* to refer to an individual mountain. But such lexical adaptation does not change the fact that the fundamental lexical building blocks of communication about landscapes differ in languages like Lao and English.

This point has been driven home by other studies in the last decade and a half. For instance, in a special issue of the journal *Language Sciences* published fifteen years ago, a large collaborative team of scholars reported on the series of findings they had obtained after years of inquiry into the terms for landscapes in a number of endangered tongues. These languages were chosen not at random, but to represent a variety of language families and ecologies. The languages were Marquesan (spoken on a Pacific island), Kilivala and Yélî Dnye (both spoken on separate islands east of Papua New Guinea), Seri (spoken in Sonora, Mexico), Chontal and Tzeltal Maya (spoken in Central America), Jahai (spoken in Malaysia), Lao, and Hai‖om.

Spoken by cultures indigenous to islands, rainforests, and deserts, these languages reveal distinct ways of talking about landscapes. They reveal that many seemingly basic landscape notions, including "mountain," may not be neatly translatable into other languages. In the words of two of the authors of that journal issue, "'Mountain,' 'cliff,' and 'river' presume the existence of such things. They seem real enough that one might reasonably consider universal concepts here. But one of the central messages of this collection is that we are in for a surprise—there are no direct equivalents for these terms in, e.g., the language Yélî Dnye." For example, in Yélî Dnye the word *mbu* means a "conical elevation" and can be used to refer to a mountain or a hill but also a mound of sand or dirt. While in English we might metaphorically refer to a "mountain of dirt," "mountain" itself cannot refer to conical shapes that are very small. *Mbu* is not perfectly translatable with any one English landscape term.[13]

This is true of other key landscape words in Yélî Dnye, for instance some water-based terms. Terms like "river" and "lagoon" have no clear translations in Yélî Dnye, which has myriad basic words for forms of water. These forms vary in accordance with, for example, the depth of the water in question, in addition to factors that are relevant to English, like whether the water is flowing (as in the case of "lake" versus "river"). The basic word-level distinctions for different waterscapes are particularly elaborate in Yélî Dnye. It is tempting to suggest that such distinctions are due simply to the kinds of waterscapes that exist on Rossell Island, where Yélî Dnye is spoken, and the central relevance of those waterscapes to the way of life of Yélî Dnye speakers. While these factors obviously play some role, it should be stressed that there is no straightforward relationship between particular environmental types and particular ways of referring to landscape features in a given language. In other words, the local geography is of course relevant to how people talk about landscapes, but it does not neatly determine how the words in a language evolve. As evidence of this, consider that Kilivala, a language spoken in an ecology similar to that in which Yélî Dnye is spoken, has many words for various waterscapes. However, the words do not match up very closely with those in Yélî Dnye, despite the similar geographic contexts in which the languages are spoken.[14]

Intriguingly, languages can also use different verbs, not just different nouns, to integrate culturally salient landscape concepts. Speakers of Yélî Dnye have verbs such as *paa,* which means "walk along a flat surface." This sort of verb has no translation in English or most (perhaps all) other languages. It illustrates the fact that languages integrate landscapes in sometimes unexpected ways. The pronounced elevations on Rossell Island seem to help motivate intransitive verbs such as *paa, kee* ("ascend"), and *ghii* ("descend"). The latter two terms are neatly translatable into many languages, including English. The Yélî Dnye language also has transitive verbs that incorporate landscape objects, terms like *vy:uu* ("climb a slope") and *'nuw:o* ("descend a slope"), as well as *km:ee* ("carry something up a slope") and *ghipi* ("carry something down a slope"). The terrain of Rossell Island, and the surrounding landscape more generally, is integrated into the Yélî Dnye language in unique ways. Languages often encode locally relevant landscape concepts.[15]

A few years ago a paper came across my desk in my capacity as an associate editor of the *International Journal of American Linguistics,* a journal that has offered many interesting findings on the endangered languages of the Americas since it was founded by Franz Boas in 1917. The paper outlined the way a particular South American population speaks about the surrounding landscape. The language in question, spoken by the Lokono in the savannahs of the Guianas north of Amazonia, distinguishes between nouns that refer to objects and those that refer to places. The Lokono language uses one word to refer to all landforms, and this cover term is modified in various ways to denote particular kinds of landforms. The word is *horhorho,* and while it is best translated in English as "landform," it has no true translation. What we know is that the term is modified in various ways. For instance, *horhorho diako* refers to the top of a landform while *horhorho bana* refers, simply, to the surface of a landform. The former expression might be used to describe something located on a hilltop, the latter to refer to various kinds of surfaces. *Horhoro* can be modified in ways that reflect nuanced distinctions in the shape, the function, and even potentially the material of the landscape being described. It is a required term whether one is describing jungle, steep hills and ridges, savannahs, swamps, or various other geographical features surrounding a speaker. Furthermore, *horhorho* can be used to refer to the landscape at very large and very small scales, serving to unify diverse elements of landscape that are treated as completely separate entities in languages like English.[16]

Many more examples could be offered here, but those presented so far should give you a sense that how people talk about basic characteristics of their surrounding landscapes, and therefore how they distinguish particular features of those landscapes, differs markedly across populations. Members of diverse cultures can think of landscapes in very distinct ways, much as they differ with respect to how they give directions or how they describe the spatial arrangement of objects.

Conclusion: Nonuniversal Spatial Concepts

When I was first conducting research on Karitiâna, I did what many field linguists who have been trained with old-school methods do: I tried to find definitions for basic words that are traditionally considered common to all languages. (Some field researchers avoid this approach these days, as it faces plenty of limitations, but it does offer certain advantages for initial analyses of basic word types.) Such words, including "sun," "moon," "cloud," "blood," and the like, refer to entities found in all populations. They exist in every earthly ecology. The words for such entities are referred to collectively as the Swadesh list, after a linguist by that name. Some of the words on this basic list are not really so basic, though they may seem that way. For instance, the list includes words for "one" and "two." Some languages have words that represent "one" and "two" perfectly, but in a few languages the word for "two" is imprecise, better translated as something like "a couple of." In even rarer cases, a similar imprecision holds for an apparent translation of the English word "one." Some languages lack most or all precise number words, hinting that "basic" words are not always basic across cultures. The latter point has been observed time and again through linguistic fieldwork over the last few decades, and the case of landscape terms helps to drive it home further. I confronted this point when trying to figure out the word for "mountain" in Karitiâna. When I asked a Karitiâna friend what the word for *montanha* (Portuguese for "mountain") was in his language, he said it was *deso*. At some point later I asked him what the word for "hill" was and was again offered *deso*. In fact, it turns out that the word *deso* does not mean mountain, or hill, or hillock. It has no perfect analog in English, nor does it neatly match the word *phuu2* from Lao. It seems to be used for large protuberances in the earth, anything as large as a hill. From a functional perspective, this is not all that surprising. The usefulness of a separate word for "mountain" would be limited for the Karitiâna, whose surroundings contain no mountains for hundreds of kilometers in any direction. It took me some time to figure out that *deso* did not match up neatly to any words I knew in Portuguese or English. And in that lag time rests a methodological point. People, even trained researchers aware of such variation in word meanings across unrelated cultures, often try to force the circle peg of a word in one language into the square hole of the word in their native language. We seek translations for *our* words, often without realizing that our words do not necessarily correspond neatly to the words in a little-documented language. This is even true of words like "two" or "mountain" or "left" or "right," words that might seem universal. But they seem universal precisely because we have so much practice using them and handling the concepts with which they are associated. The words and associated concepts are not actually evident in all human populations.

The cross-linguistic differences in how people refer to directions, landscapes, and other spatial phenomena point to the interaction of people with their environments. But it is not as though environments completely determine how people talk about space. Within similar environments around the world, people talk about space in sometimes unpredictable ways. A fair amount of experimental evidence suggests that talking about space in divergent ways can foster different ways of thinking about space, even if the linguistic differences were once motivated by how useful those ways of talking were in particular environments. If your language requires that you frequently distinguish between hills and mountains, or between "left" and "right," the distinctions between these referents will likely become ingrained in your head. They will become integrated into your cognitive habits.

Toward the beginning of this chapter I talked about my experience following an indigenous woman through the dark jungle, awed by her navigational abilities. It is impossible to know how much of her superior navigational ability was due to cultural, linguistic, or ecological factors. Much research now suggests that some populations are generally adept at that sort of navigation—she was not necessarily a navigational savant. The study of diverse languages in non-WEIRD populations in very distinct habitats has revealed that people talk and think about space in ways that differ from the ways that seem natural to many of us. As a result, human behavior associated with space, including default navigational strategies, can vary markedly cross-culturally. In Chapter 3 we will see how other findings from linguistic research in non-WEIRD populations has further challenged some of our preconceived notions about human thought and behavior.

3

Who's Your Brother?

PORTO VELHO, the city in which I spent much of my childhood and have conducted some of my research, is spread out along the northern bank of the Rio Madeira, a mile-wide tributary of the Amazon. By itself, the Madeira is one of the world's largest rivers. Porto Velho remains something of an urban island in southern Amazonia, connected to northern destinations largely by the expansive riverine highway that flows past it toward the equator. In the jungle surrounding Porto Velho there are many reservations belonging to various indigenous populations. Many of their languages, like Karitiâna, have been spoken in this jungle for millennia. The diversity of languages in the Brazilian state of Rondônia, of which Porto Velho is the capital and largest city, actually tells us something important about the history of South America. First of all, this is the region wherein Proto-Tupí, the ancestral tongue from which all Tupían languages like Karitiâna descended, was likely spoken long ago. When the Portuguese and other Europeans arrived on the beaches of what is now Brazil, they encountered speakers of Tupían languages up and down the coast. This means that, in the centuries prior to their arrival, Tupían cultures and languages had somehow expanded eastward from southwestern Amazonia, where Rondônia is located, across much of the South American landmass. I point this out to underscore the fact that languages like those spoken by the Karitiâna offer us all sorts of insights that are not related strictly to language or thought.

As you might imagine, the life of indigenous people living in a Brazilian Amazonian city is fraught with challenges. Like many small populations worldwide, they confront severe prejudices from some people in the larger cultures in which they are embedded. The Karitiâna are referred to as *indios* ("indians"), a name that ultimately owes itself to Columbus's mistaken belief that he had landed in India when he had actually landed in the New World, which humans had inhabited for over twenty thousand years prior to his inadvertent "discovery." The terms used to describe the lower socioeconomic classes around Porto Velho include *indios* and *ribeirinhos* ("riverine people"). Of course the local middle- and upper-class Brazilians are hardly unique in having such terms to signify social groups outside their own to signify "others." In fact, all cultures have labels that can be used for "foreigners" to denote people that are, well, foreign to the in-group. This is even true among the native Amazonian populations like the Karitiâna. In their case, the terms they traditionally used to refer to themselves include *pyeso*, meaning "the people." Non-Karitiâna were traditionally referred to as *opok*, which might best be translated as "foreigners."

These terms for people—"citizens" versus "foreigners," *pyeso* vs. *opok*, etcetera—have wide-ranging effects and are hardly trivial labels.

The category one falls into can have a profound influence on your life. Not long ago I was driving through one of Porto Velho's many *bairros*, speaking to a close Karitiâna friend as I gave him a ride across town. He, like a few other of the three hundred or so remaining members of the Karitiâna nation, lives in the city. This choice is forced upon him by strong socioeconomic pressures. While my friend acknowledges that he would prefer to live in the main Karitiâna village, located several hours from Porto Velho by off-road vehicle, that preference is somewhat irrelevant given the absence of sufficient game and fish needed to maintain the traditional Karitiâna way of life on their reservation. The Karitiâna must interact regularly with Brazilian culture, learning Portuguese as they attempt to supplement their incomes by selling artifacts to tourists. This sort of interaction is not unique to them and repeats itself all over Amazonia and in the other world regions in which many languages are becoming endangered.

As we drove, I was asking my friend about what it meant to be part of *pyeso* or an *opok* in a place like this, in this new milieu. It was my friend's grandparents' generation who were likely the first Karitiâna to have constant contact with the outside world, so "new" is not an exaggeration. The economic and social challenges of being a member of *pyeso* are, as you might imagine, numerous. But my friend also shed light on the importance of this linguistic distinction to the Karitiâna prior to their consistent contact with the outside world. The Karitiâna sometimes practiced cannibalism of non-*pyeso,* of *opok.* In fact, he assured me that there is an elderly woman in the village who would be willing to discuss this with me. She could, he told me, apprise me of the tastier parts of the human body, a topic on which he claims she has strong opinions. (I passed on the offer.) While I was unaware of the woman's experience, I had long been aware that the Karitiâna, like some other Tupían and non-Tupían groups in South America, once practiced cannibalism.

This practice terrified European colonists. Conversely, Tupían groups and many other South American indigenous groups were terrified by the Europeans' habit of torturing their enemies which, one could argue, is a much more objectionable practice since victims of torture actually suffer the ordeal. (This does not mean that torture was entirely absent in the Americas prior to the arrival of Europeans, of course.)

The Karitiâna belief system once focused in large measure on the spiritual and physical power of human blood, *nge* in their language. The consumption of the *nge* of the *opok* was seen as energy-giving, a literal lifeblood. This may sound quite unusual, but consider that Christianity, which has now replaced traditional beliefs for many of the Karitiâna, emphasizes blood too. It is centered around the crucifixion and general torture of a person to his death. Consuming that person's blood, in a literal sense to those who believe in transubstantiation, is essential to some practitioners of the Christian faith, separating the "believers" from the "nonbelievers." At some point in history, *pyeso* and *opok* separated people into critical categories that related to, among other things, whose blood might be consumed.

All this is to say that the way humans categorize other humans culturally and lexically, with their acts and their words, can matter a great deal. People consider it essential to linguistically categorize others as being either a member of their own culture (or some other group they are a part of, perhaps based on physical appearance), or as a foreigner. Languages consistently reflect and reify the powerful social divisions that exist across cultures. What we call people matters immensely. It affects how we treat them and may even reflect whether or not those people fall into the edible category of humans. Just as critically, though, the words we use for people reflect the divisions and structures within cultures, not just across them. They reflect our mental categories of people whom we can live with, for instance, or marry. They reflect patterns of kinship.

Descriptions of kinship term systems have begun to alter our understanding of how people think of others within their own societies or bands. Unlike some of the other topics covered in this book, there is a long history of studying the kinship systems of the world's languages, and such systems have served as fertile ground for generations of linguists and anthropologists. Rather than retreading all that ground, let me illustrate just how different kinship systems can be by contrasting some key characteristics of the kinship terms in Karitiâna and English.

When people consider differences in kinship systems they often focus on distant relationships, like the terms for parallel cousins and cross cousins across the world's languages, or the terms for second and third cousins, and so on. Such terms are trivial, though, at least in the sense that many if not most English speakers are unfamiliar with these distinctions or are hazy on the details. To clarify the distinction between "cross" and "parallel": cross cousins refer to the children of a sister and to her brother's children, while parallel cousins are children of two sisters, or of two brothers. This distinction is not particularly relevant in our culture, and we really only use the term "cousin." Yet the cross / parallel distinction is consequential in many languages, and distinct terms are used for these kin types in day-to-day speech. More surprising, perhaps, is that languages can differ in how they categorize genetically tighter relationships like those between parents, children, and siblings. Let us take a brief look at the Karitiâna kinship system and how it treats some of the categories that we think of as basic or nuclear.

One of the traditional kinship terms in Karitiâna, *'et,* means a "woman's child." Another, *it,* means a man's child. Note that the gender distinction here is not based on the child, as in the English words "son" and "daughter," but on the parent. Immediately we see a major way in which Karitiâna kinship terms differ from those in many other languages, including English. The term used to refer to a relative may depend on the gender of the person speaking, not just on the gender of the person to whom the speaker is referring. There are also ways to refer to the gender of the child via kinship terms, so a gender term can reveal both the gender of the speaker and that of the relative to whom it is referring. In this sense Karitiâna kinship terms are more symmetrical or reciprocal than English terms, which only refer to the gender of the person being referred to.[1]

Consider another foundational term in our English kinship system, "sister." Any speaker refers to a female sibling by this term, meaning the only factors that motivate the use of the term are (a) the female gender of the person being referred to, and (b) the shared parentage of that person with the person who is using the kinship term. In contrast, in Karitiâna those two factors plus two others determine the use of terms that might be translated from the English word "sister." The first of these factors is the gender of the speaker, and the second is the speaker's relative age. As a man I would refer to my sister as *pat'in*. In contrast, a woman would refer to her sister as *kypeet* but, and this is where it gets even trickier, only if her sister were younger than herself. To refer to an older sister, a woman would say *haj*. More precisely, she would say *y-haj* since, as noted above, the *y-* prefix denotes "my." "My sister" has three Karitiâna translations, then: *y-pat'in, y-kypeet,* and *y-hai.* In a similar fashion, "my brother" is translatable with three Karitiâna terms. A woman or girl would say *y-syky* to refer to any of her brothers. In contrast, a man or boy would say either *y-keet* or *y-hai.* The first of these terms refers to a male's younger male sibling, the second to an older male sibling. These are also used as terms of endearment with non-kin. For instance, my closest Karitiâna friend refers to me as *y-hai,* while I call him *y-keet.*

The complexities of Karitiâna kinship terms do not stop there, of course; they extend to cousins and more distant relatives. It is clear, though, that even with respect to one's closest relatives, Karitiâna kinship terms present distinct complexities, at least when contrasted to those in English and other European languages. Your gender is relevant to the kinship terms you use, not just the gender of the person to whom you are referring. Your age and the relevant relative's age also affect how you refer to that person. These two factors, relative age and gender of both the speaker and the person being described by a given term, are not pertinent in most kinship systems and certainly not in most WEIRD languages. Karitiâna is not unique in this respect, however. Instead it merely illustrates that languages' terms for family members can vary in key ways. I should stress that crosslinguistic differences in kinship terms correlate with all manner of cultural phenomena, such as incest taboos. For instance, it is generally considered taboo to have sex with your cousin among speakers who use that English term. In Karitiâna, incest taboos are also relevant, but not in ways that match those of most English-speaking cultures. Karitiâna men were traditionally expected to marry their *saka'et* relatives. This is a male's sister's daughter, one of the relationships referred to by our less precise term "niece." In contrast, a male's brother's daughter, his *tiogot,* was off limits when it came to marriage. One kind of niece was once considered an ideal marrying partner, while marriage or sexual relations with another were considered incestuous. (These days most Karitiâna do not marry nieces of any sort, nor do they practice polygamy, as they once did.) Kinship terms do not simply denote relationships arbitrarily; they effectively convey critical components of a culture, including incest taboos. Much as one's status as *opok* or *pyeso* may once have affected how edible they were, a woman's status as *saka'et* or *tiogot* impacted whether they were the source of attention and desire from the men that referred to them with those terms. Sometimes these linguistically reified cultural categories reflect a kind of complexity that we might not expect to find were we only aware of the kinship systems of the world's widely spoken languages.

This is not to imply that the world's disappearing languages, like Karitiâna, only exhibit complex kinship systems. On the contrary, some of them exhibit quite simple kinship systems. One of the simplest kinship systems described in the anthropological and linguistics literature is that of Pirahã. (This language was mentioned in Chapter 2 and will be discussed again in Chapter 8, as it has some unusual characteristics.) One of the most puzzling features of the Pirahã language is that it makes no distinction between terms for mother, father, aunt, uncle, and grandparent. Everyone from a generation older than the speaker is referred to as *màíʔi*. Having spent some of my childhood in Pirahã villages and having visited them many times as an adult, I can confirm that this term is ubiquitous, uttered by children day and night as they talk to their elder relatives. The only other kinship terms in the language refer to daughter, son, and sibling. The gender of the sibling is not relevant, nor is the gender of the speaker. There are no words for cousins, much less specific terms for cross cousins and parallel cousins. The ages of the speaker's siblings, like their genders, do not affect the terms with which they are referred.[2]

The Pirahã and Karitiâna kinship systems differ in extreme ways, and despite their relative geographic proximity (the two languages are spoken just about 250 kilometers apart), they represent distinct points on the continuity of complexity exhibited by languages' kinship systems. Extensive surveys of the world's words for kin types have demonstrated that the ways in which humans refer to the most critical relationships in their lives vary substantially. However, there are some striking patterns. Charles Kemp and Terry Regier, researchers at the University of Melbourne and UC Berkeley, respectively, conducted a careful survey of kinship systems across 566 of the world's languages for which basic kin terms have been described by field linguists and others. This survey was only possible because linguists and anthropologists have now collected extensive data on kinship systems worldwide. Regier and Kemp's analysis of the surveyed kinship systems led them to a simple conclusion: languages tend to use kinship systems that strike a neat balance between functional usefulness and complexity. What does that mean, exactly? Consider this. No two kin-based relationships are actually identical, genetically or socially. You likely have two people you can call "grandmother" (or some variant), for instance, but these are obviously not the same person, and their relationship to you is not identical. One is your father's mother and one is your mother's mother. You also have two "grandfathers," at least biologically, so your four grandparents are referred to with only two terms. In Mandarin, Swedish, and many other languages, on the other hand, each of these four relatives is labeled with a different kinship term. But despite such variations in complexity, all the world's kinship systems group some relationships together. While Mandarin and Swedish do not group "grandfathers" or "grandmothers" together, as English does, they do group other relationships together. For instance, all your female siblings are referred to via a term translatable as "sister" whether you speak English, Mandarin, or Swedish. In these three languages, the female sibling is not referred to differently based on one's own gender, or based on their age, as in Karitiâna. Kemp made the following observations in an interview: "A kinship system with one word referring to all relatives in a family tree would be very simple but not terribly useful for picking out specific individuals. On the other hand, a system with a different word for each family member is much more complicated but very useful for referring to specific relatives."[3] Kemp and Regier's rich survey of the world's kinship systems revealed that those systems almost always strike a useful blend of simplicity and effectiveness at distinguishing critical relationships. Kinship term variation is constrained by basic cognitive and communicative pressures. The communicative pressure is clear: people need to distinguish the basic relationships in their lives effectively and precisely. But this communicative pressure is counterbalanced by a cognitive pressure: it is easier to learn just a few kinship systems describing simple relationships, and harder to learn, remember, and pass on terms that describe complex relationships and that have limited usefulness within a culture. An exceedingly complex set of kinship terms would start to feel more like a set of names for each of the countless individual relationships that exist within a family group and would not be generalizable or easily learnable. There is clearly a trade-off between simplicity and complexity, as with many aspects of life, and such a trade-off is not wholly unexpected. What is unexpected is the nature of the key relationships referred to via basic kinship terms in some languages, when compared to the relationships denoted by kinship terms in languages like English. Some kinship terms reflect profoundly divergent cultural norms regarding core practices like marriage. The terms may reflect, for instance, the fact that it is alright to marry some nieces but not others.

Inanimate Pineapples: Categorizing Things in Fuzzy Ways

In addition to being critical to many kinship terms in the world's languages, gender is also fundamental to another type of word used to describe people, namely pronouns. In English, we say *her* or *him,* or *she* or *he,* depending on a person's gender. This seems necessary, as though we were conveying pivotal information. Yet a person's gender may actually be irrelevant at the time a speaker is using a pronoun to refer to someone. Or someone's gender may simply be unknown. In such cases we English speakers are forced to choose a gendered pronoun, and until recently the default option was the masculine pronoun. There has long been debate about this androcentric default and whether better options are available. Many people have pushed for more egalitarian pronouns, but no gender-neutral third-person pronouns have had uniform acceptance as of yet. One option that is often employed in instances where gender is irrelevant or unknown is the use of third-person plural pronouns like *them* or *they,* even when only one person is being referenced. I might say something like "If a student attends all the lectures and does all the reading, they are likely to do well in the course." Note that this strategy is only possible because English does not make gender distinctions on third-person plural pronouns. Some languages do, however. Portuguese, for instance, uses *eles* or *elas* depending on whether the speaker is referring to a group of males or females. (And if the group is mixed? Well, here again the traditional default is the masculine *eles.*) While English enforces the pronominal gender of people in some contexts, in others it is less gender-enforcing than languages like Portuguese. On the other hand, some languages do not enforce gender on speakers' pronoun use in any contexts. Here again Karitiâna is a useful example. In that language, none of the pronouns denote the gender of the people or person being referenced. There is just one third-person pronoun in the language, *i* (pronounced "ee"), which may refer to "she" / "he" / "her" / "him" and also "they" / "them." It is, unsurprisingly perhaps, a very common word in the language.

Clearly, languages vary with respect to how they incorporate gender into their pronouns. How people are categorized varies crosslinguistically, and gender is one of the key factors in this nonuniform process of categorization. The influence of gender also creeps into the categorization of nonhuman and even inanimate entities. This is a familiar concept if you have ever learned a widely spoken language like Spanish, German, or any other language that groups objects according to their "gender." The gender of objects must be memorized in frequently painstaking ways since, of course, the objects are not biologically gendered. In Spanish you must learn that *mesa* ("table") is female, for instance, while in German you must memorize the fact that *Tisch* ("table") is masculine. Some phonetic tendencies may assist in this memorization process, for instance the fact that Spanish words for "feminine" objects often end in *-a,* and words for masculine objects often end in *-o.* There are many exceptions to such tendencies, though, and ultimately the language learner, child or adult, must simply memorize the grammatical gender of many nouns since it affects other things, like, for instance, the definite article used with the nouns in question. It is, after all, not *"el mesa"* but *"la mesa."* And it is *"der Tisch,"* not *"die Tisch."* The use of the wrong article is a telltale indicator of a lack of fluency, as many learners of Spanish, German, and other languages can attest.[4]

Grammatical gender is a phenomenon that categorizes not just people, then, but animals and objects into categories. And not just two sex-based categories, necessarily, but multiple categories. In some languages, including Romance languages like French, Spanish, and Portuguese, there are two gendered categories of things: masculine and feminine. In some other languages, including the aforementioned German, there are three categories: masculine, feminine, and neuter. In others like Karitiâna, Mandarin, and Japanese, there is no grammatical gender. We might expect that languages are limited to having zero, two, or three grammatical genders, as in the cases cited so far. This is a reasonable expectation given that languages could reasonably not use biological sex categories as any basis for grouping inanimate things, or they could use the two major biological sex categories to categorize referents, or they could use these two categories plus another neutral category for referents that are not classifiable according to sex. In short, languages could be limited to three grammatical genders: one for feminine things, one for masculine things, and one for everything else. Yet, as you have already seen, languages are not particularly eager to meet our expectations. In fact, some languages have more than three grammatical genders. Consider the case of Dyirbal, an Australian language well known to linguists. Several decades ago field linguist Bob Dixon wrote a paper demonstrating how Dyirbal categorizes people, animals, objects, and other entities. To give you a sense of how "gender" works in that language, consider the following categories treated in distinct ways by Dyirbal grammar:

> Category one: Men, and many other animate entities

> Category two: Women, a few animal types, water, fire, violence

> Category three: Vegetables and fruit, presuming they are edible

> Category four: Miscellaneous items

Aside from the surprising ways in which these four categories group some entities, this system is intriguing because it appears to consist of four genders, not three. Perhaps the fourth category might be thought of as a neuter gender, but then what do we make of category three? Is it an edible gender? Categories one and two are also obviously not just structured according to any simple sex-related distinction. Yet sex is not irrelevant either, as men and women are placed in different categories. And bear in mind that gender systems in other languages hardly represent clear reflections of sex categories. For instance, "girl" in German is famously neuter, being preceded by the neuter article: it is *das Mädchen*, not *die Mädchen*. Since objects are quasi-randomly assigned genders in languages that have grammatical gender, it is perhaps misleading to think of them simply as systems of "gender." Instead, what we find is that the world's grammars often categorize people, objects, and other entities along fuzzy lines that are motivated, in some cases but not in others, by associations with biological sex. Dyirbal illustrates well the fuzziness of such patterns of categorization.[5]

As field linguists have documented non-WEIRD languages in greater detail, they have uncovered myriad grammatical systems for classifying things. These systems have been found in some languages in Australia, like Dyirbal, but the two major regions in which unexpected noun classification systems have surfaced are Africa and Amazonia. Some of the languages in these regions have many more classes of nouns than the four evident in Dyirbal. Note that we no longer use the term "gender" in languages with more than three categories of nouns but instead refer to noun "classes." Systems of grammatical gender arguably represent very simple types of noun classes.

Entities are categorized in all sorts of different ways by the world's languages. The semantic factors motivating noun classes include biological sex, of course, but also factors like whether the classified thing is animate or not. Many noun classes are based in part on an object's function. Edible items may be placed in a different class than inedible ones, for example. Shape is another prominent factor that helps structure noun classes in many languages. For instance, some languages place round objects in one class, square ones in another, and so on. These categorization decisions have wide-ranging effects on grammatical patterns in the languages.

Linguist Thomas Payne makes an accurate observation based on surveys of the noun class systems that have been described in the world's languages to date: "In every case, there are items that seem as though they should belong in one class, but for some apparently idiosyncratic reason, are placed in another class." He notes that in Yagua, a Peruvian language, pineapples are classed as inanimate objects just like rocks, while other plants are categorized as animate. There is no natural reason to group pineapples with inanimate things and other plants with animate ones, but this sort of inconsistency is evident whenever one digs deep enough into noun class systems.[6]

Setting aside such idiosyncrasies, it is fair to say that there are clear semantic bases for the noun classes in many languages. The precise historical origins of such bases are unclear in most cases. Another thing that is unclear is whether the meaning associations of some noun classes have any effect on how speakers of a given language actually perceive or mentally categorize the items in their surroundings. Consider the case of a language in which objects fall into different noun classes according to the objects' shapes. Say, for instance, that most round objects fall into the "round" noun class. Does this fact impact in any way how speakers think about shapes like circles and squares? Are they more likely to pay attention to the shape of objects than speakers of English, for example? There is much debate on this topic, as it is difficult to demonstrate a causal link between linguistic patterns and patterns in thought. Still, some research has offered suggestive data pointing to "linguistic relativity," according to which such linguistic factors do have subtle effects on nonlinguistic thought. (Note that evidence for such relativistic effects is not the same as evidence for the stronger claim that languages *determine* how people think.)[7]

Research with speakers of Yucatec Maya, conducted by anthropological linguist John Lucy, has offered evidence that noun classification systems do impact how speakers construe the objects associated with the categorization system. Almost unbelievably, Yucatec Maya has about one hundred noun "classifiers." Classifiers, not the same as noun classes, typically refer to a grammatical phenomenon in which numbers are given some prefix or suffix during counting. This prefix or suffix helps to categorize the object being counted.

Meanwhile, in languages with true noun classes each noun belongs to a particular class and has a fixed category membership that surfaces in all sorts of grammatical ways. (However, the line between noun classifier systems and noun class systems is blurry in some languages.) Consider the following phrases in Yagua:

(1) *tin-kii*   *vaturu*
   "one married woman"
(2) *tin-see*   *vaada*
   "one egg"

The word for "one," *tin,* has a different suffix, *-kii* or *-see,* depending on whether a person is counting animate objects or inanimate objects, respectively. This kind of number-suffix variation is quite common in languages that have classifiers.[8]

In Yucatec Maya, classifier suffixes are attached to number words as in Yagua and many other languages, including some widely spoken ones like Mandarin and Japanese. These classifiers are used to denote whether a counted noun refers to plants that are agricultural in nature or have some other social significance. Many of the noun classifiers help to specify the shape of something, and this is a common tendency of noun classifiers in the world's languages. In the next two examples, we see that the Yucatec suffix *-tz'it* is attached to counting words like *un,* "one," which lets a hearer know that the counted object is long and thin. In a way, this suffix describes the shape of the amorphous material that is being counted, wax (*kib*) in this case.

(3) *un-tz'it*   *kib*
   "one long thin candle"

(4) *k.'a-tz'it kib*
"two long thin candles"

Because the work of defining an object's shape is often done by the classi-fiers in Yucatec Maya, Lucy has suggested that the meanings of nouns in the language are more likely to be based on the material of the object to which they refer. So rather than saying "candle" in Yucatec, one uses a classifier to delimit the shape of the wax being described. Lucy hypoth-esized that, as a result of this characteristic of Yucatec Maya, its speakers should be relatively attuned to the material of objects, when contrasted to speakers of English. He conducted numerous experiments with fellow linguist Suzanne Gaskins, the results of which were generally consistent with this claim. These nonlinguistic experiments required that partici-pants categorize objects according to shape or material. English speakers generally categorized objects according to shape, while Yucatec Maya speakers generally used material as their basis of selection. Here is one example of this simple sort of experiment: Subjects were given a wooden comb, a plastic comb, and a piece of wood, and then asked to group to-gether the two most similar objects. English speakers generally chose the two combs, while Yucatec Maya speakers generally chose the two wooden items. This sort of grouping task was conducted with many types of stimuli. Lucy and Gaskins also offered the following anecdote about how Yucatec speakers grouped objects: "The Yucatec speakers were constantly evaluating the material composition of the test items before sorting them: feeling how heavy they were, poking their nails into them to test for mal-leability, scraping the surface to see what the material under the paint was, smelling and tasting the objects, and generally questioning or com-menting on their material properties—and all this with familiar objects. The English-speaking Americans showed none of this sort of reaction—they could get all the information they needed by sight alone."[9]

Of course it is hard to establish that this difference across populations is due simply to the linguistic factors in question, as opposed to the alternate hypothesis that some underlying cultural factor is motivating both the linguistic differences and the differences in how the two populations group things in such simple experiments. Still, Lucy and other scholars have offered some data hinting that noun classes and noun classifiers play a role in how people think about the objects being classified. This includes research on a host of languages besides Yucatec, research involving a variety of methods that have been refined since Lucy's pioneering work. Japanese psychologist Mutsumi Imai has been at the vanguard of such work. Her lab has produced a number of influential studies on the ways in which cultural and linguistic factors impact how people mentally categorize things.[10]

Regardless of the potential role of classifiers, noun genders, and noun classes in impacting nonlinguistic thought, what is uncontestable by now is that languages differ profoundly with respect to how they categorize things. Some types of noun classes have only been documented in Amazonia. One interesting case is that of the Miraña language, spoken in Colombia. There are about four hundred people remaining in the Miraña culture, but only about one hundred of them still speak the language well. (Critically, the language is no longer acquired by children, who speak Spanish instead.) The noun classes in this language have a variety of effects on the suffixes used in the language, including so-called agreement markers. The latter are suffixes that are attached to words that are not nouns in order to show consistency with the class of the noun. In Miraña, agreement markers are used on adjectives, verbs, and numbers, so the class of a given object really has pervasive effects on speech. You cannot speak Miraña with any degree of fluency unless you are aware of how nouns and their associated objects are categorized. This is much more extreme than the challenge faced when learning grammatical gender in Spanish, for instance. In Spanish if I categorize a noun into the wrong gender, it affects the article I use, as in saying *el mesa* instead of *la mesa.* The gender of adjectives also must agree with the gender of the noun, so miscategorizing a noun might result in something like *el mesa rojo,* "the [masculine] red table," instead of the correct *la mesa roja,* "the [feminine] red table." In a language like Miraña, on the other hand, the situation is exceedingly more complex. Many word types agree with a given noun, and instead of two noun classes that we might call genders, there are dozens of noun classes. Memorizing these noun classes is an onerous affair. Linguists Frank Seifart and Collette Grinevald have described in some detail the fascinating noun classes of languages like Miraña. To get a sense of how great an effect the class of a given object has on sentences in the language, consider the following example. In this sentence, the object in question is *ubi,* "basket," which falls into the "container" class of things in Miraña. This class of items is denoted by a suffix, *-ba,* which is attached to four of the five words in the sentence.[11]

(5) *o-di* *ihka-ba* *tsa-ba* *muhu-ba* *ubi-ba*
"I have one big basket."

All those *-ba* suffixes simply serve to let the hearer know that *ubi* falls into the container category. Imagine how difficult it must be to learn the noun classes of Miraña well if there is a class as specific as "things that serve as containers," and how hard it must be to learn the effects of all such classes on the language's grammar. Such classes are not unique to this language, however, and related phenomena exist in many languages. Anyone who has struggled learning such a language can tell you how frustrating and foreign such noun categorization systems can seem, presuming one speaks a language like English that lacks them. To be clear, though, it is not that English is "basic" in this respect and languages like Miraña are exotic in some language- neutral, objective way. They simply feel exotic to speakers of languages that lack such nuanced noun classes.

Given that there are dozens of noun classes in Miraña, I will not explore all of them here. Yet the language is a useful indicator of how complex noun class systems can be. This table depicts ten of the Miraña noun classes, each with a sample noun and the associated suffix that is used on nouns, adjectives, verbs, and numbers, as in example (5).

Some noun classes in Miraña:

Class Meaning	Example Word / Object	Suffix Used
Oval things	*uhkaaj,* "beard"	*-aj*
Trees, bushes, plants	*koohue,* "avocado tree"	*-e*
Oblong things	*aao,* "maraca fruit"	*-o*
Clearings	*jaahtsy,* "patio"	*-ahtsy*
Powders	*bajiihu,* "ash"	*-jiihu*
Hard shells	*kuumuhymyyo,* "turtle shell"	*-myyo*
Liquid	*ajbehpajko,* "liquor"	*-hpajko*
Pack of things	*umehtsuuo,* "pack of salt"	*-htsuuo*
Corner of something	*hatohko,* "corner of a house"	*-tohko*
Thin part of something	*umeemehkei,* "thin part of a tree"	*-mehkei*

From the example classes in the table alone, we can get a sense of the complexity of the Miraña system of categorization. We can also begin to understand the historical origins of at least some of these noun classes. In general, suffixes are just shortened forms of separate words that once followed the nouns in question. With enough time, the separate words are shortened and attached to preceding words. They become suffixes that signify something that is only weakly associated with the original meaning of the separate words from which they were derived. This common pattern of "grammaticalization" is evident in some of the noun classes in Miraña, which still use the original words from which the relevant suffixes are derived historically. For example, take the word *kaamee-ha,* which means "shirt." The suffix in this word, *-ha,* signifies that the noun in question refers to something that serves as a cover or shelter. Not coincidentally, the word for house in Miraña is *ha.* This word apparently served as the historical basis of the suffix now used to categorize all members of the "shelter" class. Or consider the longer word *mutsyytsyba-tuhke,* meaning "the stem of a pear apple." This word contains the suffix *-tuhke,* which is used for the class of objects that include fruit stems. Not coincidentally, there is also a distinct word in Miraña, *tuhkenu,* that is similar in form to the suffix *-tuhke.* The word *tuhkenu* means "beginning," and it is easy to see a metaphorical relationship between "beginning" and a plant's stem. The rest of the fruit originates or begins at the stem, after all. This metaphorical use of "stem" is also evident in the English idiom "to stem from."

In many of the world's languages with complex noun class systems, the historical origins of some of the noun classes are apparent, as in the case of *-tuhke* and *-ha.* Meanwhile, the origins of other noun classes are lost to time. Speakers are often left with loose semantic categories that have a somewhat coherent but very fuzzy set of admission criteria. These categories often include exceptions that do not seem to fit the criteria at all. Language learners are therefore forced to simply memorize the set of nouns belonging to each individual noun class in the language being learned. This is a challenging affair. Speakers of English often struggle learning just the two noun classes in the grammatical gender system of languages like Spanish. In a case like Miraña, or in many African languages with elaborate noun classes, these classes often have a pervasive effect on the grammar. Consider that, were you to miscategorize the word for "basket" in Miraña, you would make mistakes in four of the five words in example sentence (5).

Languages like English have no noun classes, but they do have traces of such categories. For example, we English speakers make distinctions between nouns that can be counted and those that cannot. I can speak of "two clumps of dirt" or "three barrels of petroleum" or "five buckets of sand" or "two sticks of butter" and so forth. This is reminiscent of how Yucatec Maya speakers say things like "two long, thin pieces of wax" to refer to "two candles." However, I cannot usually say "two dirts" or "three petroleums" or "five sands." That is because diffuse liquids and solids, without predefined shapes, are typically not countable on their own. Instead we need to add words like "clumps," "barrels," and "buckets" that serve a similar function to the classifiers we find in many languages. They help define the shape of the counted material. The fact that in English there are countable nouns and uncountable "mass" nouns implies that nouns fall into two major categories. Still, English exhibits a very modest kind of noun categorization, even compared to many other European languages. After all, many of those languages categorize all nouns into two or three grammatical genders. Yet, overall, the ways that European languages categorize their nouns are relatively simple. In contrast, many languages in Amazonia, Africa, Australia, and elsewhere rely on intricate ways of grouping nouns and the entities they describe. Speakers must learn to categorize entities in the ways required by the grammatical intricacies of such languages. We have only scratched the surface of those intricacies here.

Conclusion: Common (Un)natural Classes

In our brief foray into the ways in which languages classify people, objects, and other entities, we have focused on a few languages to illustrate more widespread patterns. A natural question you might have is just how representative our sample cases are. Is the kinship system of Karitiâna, for example, representative of kinship patterns in the world's languages? Is the noun class system of Miraña illustrative of more pervasive global tendencies? The answer in both these instances is no in some ways, yes in others. For example, as we saw for Karitiâna, the world's kinship systems do vary in terms of their complexity. But this complexity is constrained, as evidenced by the work of Regier, Kemp, and other cognitive scientists. That is, languages do not just randomly assign distinct labels to each unique relationship. Still, cases like Karitiâna and Miraña demonstrate that languages are capable of categorizing people and things in very complex ways that are unfamiliar to most of us. Crucially, researchers are only discovering these complexities as they sound the depths of the world's linguistic diversity with greater care.

While noun class systems as elaborate as that in Miraña are not widespread, they have now been documented for a number of language families. Furthermore, many of the world's languages have basic noun classes, perhaps a simple two-way or three-way gender contrast, or perhaps something more elaborate like the four "genders" of Dyirbal. Linguist Greville Corbett conducted a survey of 257 of the world's languages across many geographic regions and language families. He concluded that just under half those languages had some means of categorizing nouns into basic groupings. Most of the languages with noun classes had simple gender systems with two or three categories. Yet about 14 percent of the languages surveyed had four or more noun classes, so robust categorization systems are not that rare.[12]

Elaborate noun classifier systems, which surface primarily in counting, as in the Yucatec Maya examples presented earlier in this chapter, are also not infrequent. In a study of four hundred languages, linguist David Gil found that seventy-eight of them had obligatory noun classifiers that speakers must use when counting items, while sixty-two of them had optional noun classifiers. Judging from Gil's large sample, over one-third of the world's languages have noun classifier systems. These systems, like noun class systems, are found across diverse geographic regions and language families. Based on surveys like those conducted by Corbett and Gil, about half the world's languages have rigid systems of noun classes and / or noun classifiers that surface in contexts like counting. And all languages have kinship systems, though the complexity of those systems varies in pronounced ways.[13]

Debate exists regarding the extent to which a language's kinship system or noun categorization system impacts how native speakers of that language think about the people and things found in their social and physical environment. What is clear is that the profound differences in such systems reflect very distinct ways of categorizing things and people. To native speakers of the languages we have considered, their respective noun classes feel natural, and the absence of those classes in languages like English may feel odd or impoverished conceptually. Imagine if you spoke a language like Miraña as a child and then learned English as a second language later in life. Perhaps you would wonder where all the nuance and subtlety of object categorization went as you were forced to brutely lump together seemingly unrelated items via the coarse tools of English grammar. It might feel odd that you had no grammatical means of distinguishing between, for instance, oval things and trees. You would of course recognize that English speakers do not think trees are oval, but it might feel strange that this distinction is not evident in the grammar. Ultimately, the study of noun classes, like the study of kinship systems, illuminates how some languages encode conceptual categories that feel natural and familiar to their speakers, while potentially feeling unnatural and unfamiliar to the speakers of other languages.

4

The Sky Is *Grue*

DUE TO THE PREVAILING westward winds, flights departing from Miami International Airport typically take off toward the east, over Biscayne Bay. If you are seated next to a window on an outbound flight on a sun-drenched day, and the days in this part of the world are typically sun drenched, you will be presented with a dazzling array of hues reflecting off the waters below. The shallow waters in the bay are various shades of green, with patches of blue coloring in the deeper areas. After quickly traversing the bay and then the narrow island that holds the city of Miami Beach, the ocean waters come into focus. They extend into the distance, over the horizon to the nearby islands and atolls of the Bahamas. They are bright green near the shore but transition to darker blues as the ocean floor below them descends to the continental shelf.

Terms like "green" and "blue" hardly do justice to the dazzling spectrum that reflects back to the plane on such days, and I have caught myself searching for adequate descriptors on more than one flight (much as I found myself searching for better descriptors for snow on that cold day in Manhattan). Such searches are fairly unsuccessful. Some of the hues could be described as turquoise, some aqua, maybe even teal or cyan. Frankly, though, the precise colors delimited by such terms are not always clear to me, and even if I were more confident of their meanings I would only use them as modifiers anyway, in word pairs like "turquoise blue." If I were to use such terms by themselves, without the help of the more basic terms "blue" and "green," that terminological choice might seem a bit too deliberate or poetic for natural conversation. In practice, I would likely tell someone that the waters are various shades of green and blue, from bright green to dark blue, as I just told you. There is a straightforward reason for this, namely that green and blue are so-called basic color words in English.

In this chapter we will see how basic color words vary across the world's languages, and what this tells us about how people describe and recall certain stimuli like those ocean waters. Our focus will not be restricted exclusively to color words, however, as we will also examine new insights into other types of sensory terms, particularly terms for smells. While color terms have been the most thoroughly investigated sensory words in the world's languages, new research on how languages encode sensory stimuli has uncovered unexpected findings across several sensory domains. In this section of the chapter we will focus on color terms, and in the second section we will restrict our attention to words for odors. In the third section we will widen our scope to other, less investigated sensory domains.

In linguistics and related disciplines, basic color words are known to have a special status within a given language. In an influential global study of such words first published in 1969, linguists Brent Berlin and Paul Kay outlined a set of characteristics shared by basic color words like green and blue, as opposed to terms like cyan or teal. Here are those characteristics, paraphrased:[1]

a) Basic color words are single words, not combinations of modifying words and other color words (not, e.g., "navy blue").

b) Their meaning is not describable as part of the meaning of another color word. In the case of "crimson," for example, the term is used to denote a part of the visible spectrum we call red. So it is perfectly alright to say one has a dress that is "crimson red," but it does not make much sense to say that the same dress is a "red crimson."

c) They are used to describe any object, without restrictions. Many nonbasic color terms are restricted to describing certain objects. I have heard a car's color referred to as "sunset orange," for instance, but I would not use that compound term to refer to most objects. Some hair colors and wood grains may be referred to as "blonde," but that term is not extended to many items. So blonde and sunset are used to denote colors in restricted contexts and do not qualify as basic color words.

d) Basic color words are cognitively salient for the speakers of a given language. If you give an English speaker who has normal vision a red poker chip and ask them what color it is, they will easily recognize its redness and label it immediately. It will be the first term used to describe the item by all or nearly all of those questioned. Ask them to name the color of a ripe banana, and they will say yellow. In short, they can easily distinguish basic colors and, critically, have some term in their native language to refer to that color. In contrast, not everyone knows terms like cyan, teal, or periwinkle, and the colors those words denote are less salient and recognizable.

There are other criteria that help establish which terms in a given language are basic color words, but the above list is sufficient to establish why "green" and "blue" are basic color words in English. They are not the only ones, of course. English, like many languages, actually has eleven basic color words: white, black, red, green, yellow, blue, brown, purple, pink, orange, and gray. On the color spectrum, green hues bleed into blue hues, with no clear physical demarcation between them. The fact that English has only two basic color words for this portion of the spectrum enforces a binary choice between those interbled hues: they must be categorized as blue or green. This sort of enforced lexical choice helps promote the phenomenon cognitive scientists refer to as categorical perception. Essentially, we are likely to conceptualize green and blue hues as either green or blue, even when the witnessed colors fall along a nonbinary continuum. This point matches my intuitions on a flight over the multihued waters surrounding Miami. Yet intuitions are hardly a sufficient replacement for experiments, and in a bit we will consider some of the experimental evidence suggesting that color words help to foster the categorical discrimination of hues.

Is English's system of eleven basic color terms typical or atypical? Systematic research by linguists over the last few decades, working with the same methods applied to over one hundred languages, has helped to answer the question. This work, part of the World Color Survey that Berlin and Kay initiated, has shifted our understanding of color terms in a variety of ways. For one thing, it has demonstrated that some languages have very few basic color words. Languages tend to have between two and eleven basic color words, according to both the World Color Survey and most other research on this topic. There are exceptional cases, however. Some languages have more than eleven basic color words. Korean has fifteen. At the other end of the color-word spectrum, a few languages arguably have no terms that meet the criteria required of basic color words. Languages present striking variation in the domain of color description, yet the variation is not all random. It is intriguing, for instance, that languages generally have a modest number of basic color words, given the incredible variation evident in the visible color spectrum, not just with respect to hues but also with respect to brightness and saturation and other qualities that we might associate with color.[2]

The World Color Survey had a simple methodology that was implemented by fieldworkers in diverse locales. The survey utilized an array of paint chips representing the color spectrum. The array consisted of 330 distinct, separated colors. There were two simple tasks required of the survey's respondents. The first was a naming task, in which each respondent was provided a basic color word from their native language. They were then asked to denote all the color chips that they believed could be represented by the word in question. The responses to this task could then be used to determine the hues represented by each of the respective basic color terms. The second task was a "focal" task. For this task, the participants were provided with a basic color word in their language and then asked to choose the best exemplar of that color from among the 330 options. Via this simple two-task method, dozens of linguists helped conduct the World Color Survey and greatly improved our understanding of how people describe colors. The method was not perfect, of course, and was very much oriented according to hues as opposed to other visible qualities.

Scholars like John Lucy at the University of Chicago, whose work was mentioned in Chapter 3, have pointed out that some languages refer to hues in ways that are inextricable from other physical characteristics, like the luster, reflectance, and texture of described objects. For instance, the word "golden" connotes a shininess, not just a hue. Yet in English and many other languages, hue is typically separated from other factors like shininess. According to Lucy, however, it is unwise to assume that all languages separate these factors, and so he and others maintain that the World Color Survey's data are inherently limited in terms of what they can tell us about the overall system of colors in a given language. As an example of this, consider the case of Hanunóo, a language spoken on the Mindoro island in the Philippines whose terms for colors were described in detail by anthropologist Harold Conklin. In an article based on his fieldwork there in the mid-twentieth century, Conklin noted the following: "First, there is the opposition between light and dark . . . Second, there is an opposition between dryness or desiccation and wetness or freshness (succulence) in visible components of the natural environment which are reflected in the terms *rara* ['red'] and *latuy* ['green'] respectively. This distinction is of particular significance in terms of plant life . . . A shiny, wet, brown-colored section of newly-cut bamboo is *malatuy* ['green'] (not *marara* ['red'])." Color terms in Hanunóo are apparently more about a general opposition of visible qualities that include things like visible wetness, not just hues. Similar points have been made for other languages, so it is important to note that when we talk about "colors" in the cognitive sciences, those colors represent only some of the terms for visual qualities encoded in the world's languages. Some of the "color" terms in non-WEIRD languages may relate to visual qualities in ways that are not evident in, for instance, English color words.[3]

Nevertheless, the findings obtained in the World Color Survey are still an excellent source of data on how humans perceive and talk about hues. When surveyed, speakers of a given language are consistent in the words they use to label color chips. The general consistency of responses within populations suggests that, with some notable exceptions, the methods of the color survey tell us *something* about how people perceive and talk about colors. Those data may not speak to how factors like luster and reflectance or texture are interrelated to hues in some languages. Yet it is also clear that the perception of hues is a critical component of humans' visual apparatus, an apparatus selected for over millions of years. Exploring the ways that people talk about hues is a pretty key part of understanding how people talk about basic physical stimuli in their environment. It is fair to say that the World Color Survey has yielded very useful findings on how people talk about colors and, in so doing, has also yielded insights into human cognition. The survey has ultimately pointed to intriguing similarities and disparities across the world's basic color words.

What are some of these similarities and disparities, and what do they tell us about language, thought, and, perhaps, human vision? Well, for one thing, they tell us that languages exhibit strong tendencies in how they encode hues. While scholars have pointed to exceptional languages that have no clear color words according to the criteria I listed above, we can at least state confidently that the vast majority of languages have basic color words. This is not surprising, perhaps, given how salient hues are to vision, and how critical they are to distinguishing the objects in our environments. People often need to talk about colors much like they need to distinguish shapes, and this functional need puts pressure on languages to develop color terms. Interestingly, shape seems to play a more foundational role in the world's languages in that, as we saw in Chapter 3, shape types are often the basis for different kinds of noun classes. The same cannot be said of color, but still, basic color words pervade language. More to the point, there are some intriguing patterns evident in the basic color terms of the 110 languages studied in the World Color Survey. For instance, the focal color task of the survey revealed that speakers of different languages choose similar color chips as the best exemplars of certain colors. In other words, while speakers of two different languages may differ in terms of how many color chips they refer to as "yellow" (that is, the closest translation in their language to English's "yellow"), the best example of yellow in their eyes will often be taken from a very small range of the 330 color chips.

Another finding from the World Color Survey is that, as mentioned before, languages use a relatively small number of basic color words. Whereas 330 color chips were used in the survey, as mentioned above languages typically use between two and eleven terms that match the criteria of basic color words. Even more interestingly, there are easy, reliable ways to predict the color terms in a given language. If I know that a language has only two color words, for example, then I can predict with confidence that those two words describe "white" and "black" separately. In the case of two-color-word languages, the two words are really best thought of as distinguishing "warm" and "cool" colors. If a language has three basic color words, then one can predict that those three terms will separately denote white chips, black chips, and red chips. If it is a language with four basic color terms, the terms will separately denote white, black, red, and yellow or green chips. However, the color term used to refer to green chips is often also used to describe blue chips. This common color category combining reference to greens and blues is often referred to as *grue* by linguists and anthropologists. If a language has six basic color words, only then are there typically separate terms for green and blue. And if a language has seven or more basic color terms, these will include terms separately denoting brown, purple, pink, orange, and gray. Such tendencies hint that six focal hues are particularly critical to human communication. In descending order of importance, these would be (1) black and white, (2) red, (3) green and yellow, and (4) blue. Why might these be so essential to human communication? The simplest answer, perhaps, is that we are biased to have words for such colors because human vision is better equipped to distinguish certain hues. There is some innate bias shared by all human populations toward speaking about colors in our environments that we can easily discriminate with our vision systems. This is the traditional answer, anyway, and it is supported by how visual neurons operate, as the vision of humans and many other primates seems to be biased to certain color contrasts like red versus green. Perhaps this bias ultimately owes itself to the usefulness of distinguishing brightly colored fruits from the foliage that surrounds them in nature, bearing in mind that primates are typically herbivorous. Yet while innate biases in color perception are likely responsible for some of the patterns in basic color terms worldwide, it is important to stress that they are relatively modest biases. Furthermore, some research suggests that the biases may not be due simply to the characteristics of the human visual hardware, but to specific tendencies in the colors encountered by humans in their natural environments beyond brightly colored fruit. One incarnation of this basic idea, suggested by linguist Anna Wierzbicka, is that the basic color terms owe their primacy to the human experience with phenomena including daytime, nighttime, fire, the sun, vegetation, the sky, and the ground. We will return to the notion that environmental factors help shape color terms.[4]

Given that languages do vary a fair amount even with respect to their basic words for hues, it would be a gross oversimplification to say that human vision solely dictates the color systems of human languages. For this reason, many scholars have long stressed that cultural factors must also play a role in how color words evolve. After all, humans have the same visual apparatus worldwide, but there is clearly variation in terms of how essential basic words for hues are to communication in their cultures. Perhaps the fact that languages almost always have terms for red, regardless of whether they have terms for blue, for instance, is due to the fact that people need to communicate about red things more often than blue things. Relatedly, bright red is universal to all environments and populations since humans and their prey have red blood. The English word "red" can even be traced back to the Sanskrit word for "blood." Blood naturally exposes us to bright red, and similar etymologies exist in many language families. In contrast, brightly colored blue objects are comparably rare across the diverse environments in which humans live. Deep in the Amazon jungle, for instance, bright blue is not prevalent in things that people focus on and is typically restricted to the ecological background, in the sky perhaps. Even in the case of the sky, though, it is not blue most of the time, varying between black, orange, pink, white, light blue, purple, and so forth. It exhibits countless shades throughout the day and night. Referring to the "blue sky," or even the *"grue* sky," is a cultural norm more than a statement of physical reality.

According to one new hypothesis, the prevalence of red in the world's cultures could owe itself not just to visual biases, but to the particular usefulness of having a word to describe the color of blood and other items with bright red pigments. Such red pigments are common worldwide. For instance, the *urucum* plant in Amazonia has been used to dye people's skin bright red, across many cultures and in many contexts like battles and celebrations. In contrast, there are not many easily obtainable blue dyes in nature. While indigo dyes have been used for millennia in a few parts of the world, often in textiles, the plants from which they are extracted are restricted to the tropics and subtropics and relatively difficult to process into dyes. Blue dyes were something of a rarity in

Europe until trade routes with India were established. Given the relatively recent introduction of bright blues into artifacts in many of the world's cultures, but the ancient status of red in the form of blood, the fact that many languages have words for "red" but not "blue" is at least partially attributable to factors distinct from the nature of human vision. As a particular bright object enters a culture and is referred to with greater frequency, the object's name may come to refer to the characteristic color of the object, and then that name may be extended to other things with that color. As I have noted, the word for "red" may come from the word for "blood." Sometimes the relationship between a color and an object is more obvious, as in "orange." One can imagine how, depending on the fruits, flowers, and natural pigments present in a population's natural environment, certain colors may not need to be referred to much. As people began creating dyed products, from textiles to pottery to plastics to metals, the functional use of many colors may have increased markedly. While human vision may be identical worldwide, the World Color Survey results may also owe themselves to the fact that some colors are just more prevalent in nature, while others have become prevalent only in some cultures. As cultures adopt new colored objects, new color categories may crystallize.

Perhaps a high rate of occurrence of a particular color in a given environment increases the likelihood that people in that environment will create a word for the color. This is intuitive: languages will naturally develop words for concepts whose expression meets a common communicative need. If you see a color often, you are more likely to need to refer to that color when communicating with others, especially if you need to refer to the color to accomplish things in your day-to-day life. It's true that intuition can lead us astray, but a groundbreaking study offered some very intriguing evidence in support of the idea that color words develop in order to meet the different communicative needs of speakers across cultures and are not simply the indirect result of biological biases in human vision. Led by Ted Gibson, a linguist and cognitive scientist at MIT, a team of researchers offered a few pieces of evidence that color terms have evolved to more efficiently encode hues people talk about often, particularly bright or "warm" hues. The first piece of evidence for this, found in the languages in the World Color Survey and three others tested in the study by Gibson and colleagues, was that color-term inventories across languages vary substantially in their precision. For instance, if two languages have the same four color terms of "black," "white," "red," and "yellow," those terms can still differ with respect to how consistently they are used to describe particular color chips. When Gibson's team analyzed the World Color Survey data, they found that some languages' color-term systems are much more efficient and precise than others, at least with respect to naming the hues of color chips. The speakers of some languages use their color terms in really consistent and predictable ways. For example, a word for "red" might be used by speakers to describe only certain color chips, with little variation across speakers. In contrast, speakers of languages with more inconsistently applied color terms may also have a term translatable as "red," but this term may be used to describe hues in more unpredictable ways, depending on which person is being asked to name the color chips.[5]

Gibson and his collaborators also found that terms for brightly colored hues like red, yellow, and orange are generally more precise and efficient than those for cool colors like green and blue, across all the tested languages. This was something nobody had noticed before about the results of the World Color Survey, and it is not predicted by the commonality of the six color words listed earlier in the chapter. Another way to see this is that if a language has a word for both red and green, the former is typically used more precisely. This may help explain my terminological challenges on flights out of Miami. In some languages, a given speaker may use a term roughly equivalent to "green" in order to refer to more hues than another speaker of the same language, or to fewer hues, or to a slightly different set of hues. This imprecision is describable if the data for all the speakers' responses to the World Color Survey are quantified in careful ways. Gibson and colleagues undertook that quantification with a novel computational method. The methodological details of their study are not critical here, but the general conclusions arrived at via their analysis are: While most languages use color terms pretty efficiently, terms for warm colors are generally used more precisely and consistently than terms for cool colors. Also, languages vary with respect to the overall precision of their color terms; some languages consistently denote narrow ranges of hues with their color terms, while others are more variable and unpredictable in their use of color terms. Two languages, each with six basic color terms, might employ them with different degrees of precision; that is, speakers of one language may use the terms more consistently than speakers of another while referring to a more constrained portion of the color spectrum.

The more interesting discovery may be that languages tend to more efficiently encode brighter, warmer colors than they do cooler colors. Why might this be? Our native visual propensities, some might say. That, however, is not the case that Gibson and colleagues make. Their study offers an intriguing correlation that could identify the true cause of this pattern: warmer colors are relatively more common in foregrounded objects. Foregrounded objects in visual scenes include many items that people are more likely to communicate about when compared to backgrounded items. Via an analysis of twenty thousand images, the authors found that the pixels of foregrounded objects in the images tended to be warm colored, full of reds and yellows, while the pixels of objects and items in backgrounds were generally cooler colored, full of brown, greens, and the like. The authors concluded that color terms have evolved to more efficiently encode information about the colors in the objects that humans tend to be more likely to focus on and talk about. This hypothesis shifts our understanding of why basic color words have evolved the way they have. Two other interesting pieces of data support the hypothesis. The first is that European languages like English and Spanish have very precise color-term types, which could be because these languages are spoken by cultures that typically have many artificially dyed artifacts. English and Spanish speakers frequently use basic color words to refer to artificially dyed things like bedroom walls, clothing, cars, and so on, items that are often foregrounded and focused on during conversations. The vast colorization of objects enabled by dyes, paints, and industrialization has yielded more bright and warm colors in our day-to-day lives, to a degree that is anomalous when compared to most cultures in history and even most cultures represented in the World Color Survey.

Perhaps, then, the color terms in some languages have become more consistently applied over the last few hundred years as a greater need for consistency and efficiency of communication about colors has arisen. As brighter, warmer colors have become more and more common to the human experience, such oft-foregrounded colors have become more prevalent in speech and thought. This greater prevalence has, it seems, created a communicative usefulness for more terms like "orange" and "pink" to be consistently applied to a precise range of hues. According to this hypothesis, color terms are shaped by their usefulness and frequency in speech. While the hypothesis is supported by the color terms of English and Spanish, however, these are related Indo-European languages. It is difficult to establish a causal connection between linguistic and nonlinguistic variables like industrialization and the increased use of dyes, even when clear large-scale correlations link the relevant factors.

This point will surface in Chapter 5, when we discuss findings suggesting that languages evolve to adapt to their speakers' physical environments. Yet it is promising that Gibson and colleagues' hypothesis is so well supported by the innovative computational approach they employed, which ultimately relied on the work of field linguists that, over many years, contributed data to the World Color Survey.

Setting aside for a moment *why* languages' color-term systems vary, it is clear that they do vary markedly. Even if there are certain observable regularities that constrain this variation, the variation is real. A number of linguists, anthropologists, and psychologists have long puzzled over the question of whether variation in color-term language impacts how people actually think about colors even when they are not speaking. For instance, does the lack of a word for a color in a given language have some sort of negative effect on speakers' ability to visually distinguish that color from others? Many researchers have sought to answer these questions empirically. The work of such researchers has shown that crosslinguistic differences in color terms do affect how people conceptually discriminate and recall colors, though the extent of this effect is still debated. Some of the relevant work has demonstrated that people tend to, for example, recall color differences better if their native language has distinct terms for the relevant colors.

One of the most famous studies offering evidence for this kind of color-recall difference across populations is now over twenty years old. Published in *Nature,* the study described the color terms of the Berinmo language of New Guinea as well as some experiments carried out among speakers of the language. Berinmo has only five basic color terms used to describe the Munsell color chips generally used in this work. It has a *grue* category, since its speakers use the same word, *nol,* to refer to most color chips that English speakers label "green" and "blue." However, Berinmo speakers also have a word, *wor,* which they use to refer to yellows and bright greens. In other words, Berinmo makes a distinction that is not made in English between yellowish greens and other greens, since these colors are referred to with *wor* and *nol,* respectively. Yet Berinmo does not make the green / blue distinction that is evident in English. Given these points, the researchers conducted an experiment to test whether speakers of the two languages differed in how they recalled the various associated color chips. The method was simple: subjects were presented with a color chip and then, thirty seconds later, were asked to choose which of two color chips they had been presented. Speakers of English were found to generally choose the correct color chip if the two chip choices differed in terms of their color labels in English. If they saw a green or blue chip and then thirty seconds later were asked to choose between two similar chips, their recall was more accurate when choosing between two chips from different sides of the blue / green boundary. In contrast, they were less accurate picking out the correct color chip if their choices fell on different sides of the *nol / wor* boundary. The reverse pattern was evident in Berinmo speakers' recall of color chips: they were more accurate when picking out the correct color chip if their two choices fell on different sides of the *nol / wor* boundary, and less accurate when the choices were on different sides of the English blue / green boundary. This seems to be a clear example of categorical perception, the cognitive phenomenon mentioned at the beginning of the chapter. Categorical perception occurs when people discriminate stimuli more neatly because the stimuli fall into distinct conceptual categories (e.g., the categories reflected by color terms), or when they discriminate stimuli more poorly because they fall into the same conceptual category. There are numerous examples of categorical perception, and many have nothing to do with color perception. Here is another linguistic example: speakers of English distinguish *l* and *r* sounds as either *l* or *r,* even when played artificial sounds that are equally similar to both *l* and *r*. This is because these sounds fall into separate categories in English and are used to distinguish word meanings, so English speakers have a lifetime of practice perceiving such sounds in categorical, binary ways. In contrast, speakers of Japanese do not distinguish *l* and *r* sounds in such neat, binary ways because there are not separate categories for those sounds in their language.[6]

The interesting thing about cases like the Berinmo color-recall experiments is that they suggest that one's native language significantly impacts very basic categories associated with vision. It is notoriously difficult to establish that linguistic differences actually cause the observed cross-population differences in categorical perception. After all, Berinmo speakers live very different, nonindustrialized existences when contrasted to WEIRD populations of English speakers. As the research of Gibson and colleagues demonstrates, Berinmo speakers' experiences with hues may differ from our own, during both childhood and adulthood. Perhaps such nonlinguistic factors help explain the results obtained with Berinmo speakers and some other indigenous populations.

Yet linguistic factors appear to be the most likely motivation for differences in color discrimination that have been observed in other cultures. For example, speakers of some languages, ones with different basic color terms for "dark blue" and "light blue," have been shown to discriminate between hues that cross this divide better than speakers of English. This includes speakers of Russian, Korean, and certain dialects of Spanish. Given that these languages are all spoken by large, industrialized populations, the relevant linguistic differences more likely explain the color-discrimination differences than, say, how much the members of the relevant cultures have been exposed to the relevant hues. Tellingly, studies have now demonstrated that such color-discrimination differences across populations are more evident in experimental tasks that involve the presentation of hues in the right visual field (for instance, when the colors are presented to the right of a fixation point in the middle of a screen). One key bit of background here is that the right visual field is processed first by the left hemisphere of the cortex, while the left visual field is processed first by the right hemisphere. Another key bit of background is that most language processing happens in the left hemisphere. The relevant studies have demonstrated, for example, that when people see differences between colors that cross color boundaries, say green versus blue for English speakers, they are quicker to pick up on this difference than they are to pick up on differences between colors that do not cross color boundaries, say dark blue versus light blue for English speakers. Critically, the greater speed of distinguishing hues that cross color-term boundaries is only evident when the hues are viewed by the right visual field as opposed to the left. Since most language processing happens in the left hemisphere, the fact that this phenomenon occurs with the right visual field but not the left suggests that linguistic factors motivate the categorical perception of colors perceived by the right visual field.[7]

The preceding discussion reveals a recurring difficulty associated with the interpretation of cross-cultural studies on perception or memory: establishing the causal factors that yield the cross-cultural differences in question. The differences may be due to linguistic differences, other cultural factors like the extent of industrialization, some combination of these factors, or to some completely unrelated factor. In the case at hand, it is difficult to establish with certainty whether differences in the perception and recall of colors are primarily due to linguistic differences or another factor. Within some academic circles, debate has raged about this issue for a while. Two psychologists at the University of Wisconsin have presented strong evidence that color terms impact, to some extent, the nonlinguistic perception of colors. The two researchers, Lewis

Forder and Gary Lupyan, showed that merely hearing a color word before being presented with a particular color stimulus will affect a person's discrimination of colors. More specifically, categorical perception of colors is enhanced after hearing color terms. In the experiment, people became more accurate at visually discriminating colors that were labeled with different basic color words, and less accurate at visually discriminating colors that were labeled with the same color word. Participants were presented with four circles, three of which were filled with the same color and a fourth that was filled with a color of a slightly different hue. They were asked to pick which of the four colors differed slightly from the three other colors. In some of the trials, the participants heard a relevant color word about one second before being presented with the color circles on a computer screen. The authors summarize one of their key results as follows: "Immediately after hearing a color name (e.g. green), participants were more accurate in discriminating between targets and nontargets when they spanned a color boundary, for example, a green among blues, and in distinguishing typical greens from atypical greens." The increased accuracy of color discrimination across color boundaries was not minor; in fact, participants were about 10 percent more accurate after being verbally cued with a relevant color word. This suggests that people's actual accuracy of color discrimination is affected by color terms themselves. Forder and Lupyan's study was conducted entirely with speakers of English from the same culture, so the results were not due to nonlinguistic cultural differences. Given that basic color terms vary so much across the world's languages, it is reasonable to assume that speakers of languages with distinct color-term boundaries would differ with respect to how their color discrimination would be affected in this task. Future work with speakers of diverse languages will hopefully test whether this reasonable assumption is accurate.[8]

Let us return to my challenge of faithfully describing the dazzling array of colors in Biscayne Bay, described in the chapter opening. A few points are now worth stressing, based on the literature on this topic. First, the basic labels I struggled with depend largely on my native language. I might have only one basic color word to describe the waters (something like *grue*), two terms ("green" and "blue"), or three terms if I speak a language like Korean or Russian ("green," "blue," and a word for a darker "blue"). The poverty of options for basic color words stems, it would seem, from the fact that languages are generally poor at labeling cooler colors than they are warmer colors. This fact owes itself in turn to the very ubiquity of cooler colors like *grue* in the backgrounds of natural settings, backgrounds including ocean waters, and to the greater likelihood that warmer colors are more common in foregrounded artifacts that have become so common in the last few hundred years, at least to members of WEIRD societies. According to some research, my native language may affect my actual recall of some of the colors I have viewed from planes departing Miami. Finally, perhaps if the passenger behind me had said "green" repetitively while we flew over the bay, it would have affected in subtle ways how my mind discriminated the colors I was seeing below.

Smells Are More than Pungent

As the dry season turns to rainy season in Amazonia, the rains often come in short bursts while the sun is still shining. This phenomenon is hardly unique to that part of the world, of course, and many of the world's languages actually have expressions referring to rainfall that is happening alongside sunshine. (In the southern states of the United States, one puzzling expression for the phenomenon is "the devil is beating his wife.") I have many childhood memories of playing outside in such microbursts of rain. Some of these memories are tinged with a distinct olfactory sensation, the smell of rain being absorbed by dry soil. I suspect you know the particular odor in question. That smell is actually referred to with a term in English, "petrichor," defined as the earthy scent we experience when rain falls on dry soil. It is a relatively new word in the language and appears to have been coined in the 1960s. Many English speakers are wholly unfamiliar with the term, and it is hardly common in conversations. If I told a friend, "Petrichor brings me strong feelings of nostalgia," she or he would probably be confused by my odd word choice, even if they knew the term. In a way, then, petrichor is the exception that proves the rule: the English language does a pretty poor job of naming distinct smells, and we do not use words for specific odors like petrichor in conversation. Additionally, our words for smells are not abstract. Even petrichor is used only for petrichor; it is not a term that refers to a broad olfactory sensation that occurs in myriad contexts. In contrast, think of the basic color words we discussed in the previous section. We can talk about blue skies, blue jeans, blue cars, or a multitude of other unrelated objects with some visual commonality that we can draw from each of them, and it is this abstract quality of *blueness* that we are labeling with the color term. Petrichor, on the other hand, is not abstract. It is a specific odor existing in a particular context, and even then we have difficulty naming it.

The impoverished language of smells, particularly when contrasted with the richly abstract language of colors, has long been known. Consider this quote by German scientist Hans Henning over a century ago: "Olfactory abstraction is impossible. We can easily abstract the common shared color—i.e., white—of jasmine, lily-of-the-valley, camphor and milk, but no man can similarly abstract a common odor by attending to what they have in common and setting aside their differences." Why are smells so hard to name, and to name abstractly? There has actually been a fair amount of debate about this in the scientific literature. One potential reason is simply that humans are relatively poor smellers. For example, when tested on odors associated even with common items like peanut butter or coffee, many people struggle to name the item associated with the smell. Even for such common smells people can only name the source of the odor roughly half the time. Such facts have led some researchers to conclude that humans have a severe neurological deficit when it comes to smell, in contrast to their other senses and to the smelling abilities of many of our mammalian cousins. This is likely true. Yet it remains unclear just how large our species-wide olfactory deficit is. When you consider that humans have about four hundred distinct kinds of receptors for detecting smells, it seems a bit more puzzling that we are so poor at naming abstract odors.[9]

While no researcher would likely contest the claim that humans are relatively poor at distinguishing and labeling odors, we must also be careful not to fall into the trap of assuming that all people are awful at naming odors just because, say, English and German speakers are. We should be very cautious when extrapolating strong claims about all humans from observations made with WEIRD populations. In fact, as studies in cognitive science have cast a wider net on the world's cultures and languages, they have (seemingly inevitably) found that members of certain other cultures talk about smells in very different ways than speakers of English and other WEIRD languages seem to. A flurry of studies, many of them led by Asifa Majid, a linguist and cognitive scientist at Oxford University, have changed our understanding of how people talk about smells. The studies have also helped shed new light on the human olfactory sense.

The studies of Majid and her collaborators have focused on the members of cultures in different locales, primarily in Mesoamerica, the Andean highlands, and the jungles of Southeast Asia. The studies followed up on claims of linguistic fieldworkers that some of the languages in these regions had many more terms for smells than languages like English. Such claims had not been verified by, for example, presenting speakers of these languages with distinct smells to test their vocabulary for odors. One telling case is that of Jahai, a language spoken by a group of hunter-gatherers who live in the rainforests along the border of Malaysia and Thailand. The Jahai language, it turns out, has a number of basic terms for odors that are analogous to basic color words. Speakers of the Jahai language are familiar with the terms and use them in conversation, so they are not simply esoteric words used by specialists of some kind. Critically, the Jahai use the basic odor words in abstract ways that are not associated with one object only. In contrast, consider how we describe smells in English, even smells more commonly encountered than petrichor. If I walk into a movie theater I might observe, "It smells like popcorn in here." Yet I have no distinct or abstract word to refer to that smell, regardless of the object that I associate it with. If I arrive in some other place with a similar but distinct oil-based smell, I might say, "It smells like popcorn in here," even if I know the reason for my olfactory sensation is not because someone made popcorn in that place. I say, "It smells like popcorn" because I am lexically limited, but it probably does not smell just like popcorn, and this phrasing is a bit messy. I do not possess a term for the specific smell-based similarity between the movie theater and the other place. I am restricted to what researchers refer to as a "source- based" reference to smell, one that is always tied to the same source object. If I were similarly color-term challenged, I might describe the chromatic appearance of the noonday sun by saying it "looks like a banana." Our linguistic limitations vis-à-vis olfaction are so mundane that we do not even notice how much we appeal to specific objects, as opposed to abstract smells, to describe the odors we sense.

In contrast, speakers of Jahai have an arsenal of odor terms they can wield in such situations. As Majid and her colleague Niclas Burenhult observed about Jahai, "The term *Itpit* is used to describe the smell of various flowers and ripe fruit, including intense smell of durian, perfume, soap, *Aquillaria* wood, and bearcat (*Arctictis binturong*), which, according to Wikipedia, smells like popcorn."[10] Note that the abstract term *Itpit* is a verb in Jahai, so rather than saying, "It smells like popcorn in this movie theater," I might say something akin to "It sure *Itpits* in this movie theater." I could then use that abstract term in any similarly smelling room. Another term, *Cnes,* is used by Jahai speakers to refer to the smell of smoke, the smell of a particular species of millipede, and the smell of the wood of the wild mango tree, among other uses.

Majid and Burenhult tested Jahai speakers' ability to name smells and found that, in contrast to a control group of English speakers, they were very likely to use abstract terms for the odors they perceived. The experimental procedure they employed was quite straightforward. They simply presented English and Jahai speakers with different basic hues, like those used in the World Color Survey, and asked them what colors they saw. They also presented speakers of both languages with different odors via a basic sample kit of odors that emanate from a scratch-and-sniff card. The twelve odors were based on objects whose smells are familiar to most people, though arguably even more familiar to people in industrialized societies since the odor array included smells based on paint thinner and chocolate. Despite such a potential disadvantage, however, Jahai speakers named odors much more consistently than English speakers. The ten Jahai speakers tested were more likely than English speakers to use the same term, like *Itpit,* when describing a particular odor.

They were also more likely to stick to the inventory of abstract odor terms at their disposal. English speakers generally stuck to source-based descriptors, for instance, "smells like a banana." The reason is simple: with very few exceptions, like "musty," that are useful only in limited contexts, English speakers simply do not have abstract odor terms at their disposal. On the other hand, we do have more precise color terms at our disposal than Jahai speakers. This was evident in Majid and Burenhult's simple experiment: English speakers generally used the same basic color terms to describe the color stimuli, while Jahai speakers exhibited greater person-to-person variability in the color words they chose.

Maniq, which like Jahai is a language spoken in southeast Asia, has also been a focus of Majid and her collaborators, including Ewelina Wnuk, a specialist in the language. This language, spoken by roughly three hundred people in the mountainous jungles of Thailand, has very complex smell terms. They do not belong to a single word class as they do in Jahai, in which the smell words are verbs. Some of the Maniq smell words are verbs, but others are nouns. There are at least fifteen smell terms in the language, each of which describes the odors associated with a variety of objects. When Maniq speakers were asked to list the kinds of objects associated with a specific smell term, they generated an impressive assortment of items. For example, when asked to list the objects associated with the smell term *cane,* several Maniq speakers suggested that "tubers" smell like *cane.* Yet this smell is not associated simply with tubers but also, as some responses suggested, with the smell of rice, wild pig, cooked wild pig, and even animal hair. Similar patterns hold for the other fourteen smell terms in Maniq. While the smell terms of Jahai and Maniq are quite different, they all exemplify a relevant point: people in fact use odor words like *ltpit* and *cane* to describe smells abstractly, rather than being tied to describing smells in terms of individual objects. In that way, their odor terms can resemble our color terms.[11]

What motivates the fundamentally distinct odor-naming systems that have evolved in the world's languages? Why do speakers of languages like Maniq and Jahai have more abstract odor terms at their disposal than we (and speakers of countless other languages) do? The short answer is that we do not know, but potential factors include environmental characteristics and lifestyles. With respect to the former, it makes sense that speakers of Jahai might typically experience distinct odors when contrasted to, for example, populations living in the arctic circle. Among other factors, the jungles of Southeast Asia have many floral and faunal species that do not exist at higher latitudes. It is hard to imagine how environmental factors like these would not impact the olfactory terms used in particular languages. After all, if the people in a given environment never encounter a particular kind of smell, why would they need to create a word to refer to it? Such a word would be communicatively useless to them. Yet other nonenvironmental factors may also be at play in the evolution of smell terms, including the aforementioned lifestyle differences across cultures.

To try to get some sense of which causal factors directly influence terms for smells, and perhaps bias some cultures to use abstract smell terms, Majid and colleagues examined groups that live in similar physical environments but have distinct lifestyles. Like the Maniq, these groups reside in the rainforest of the Malay Peninsula. The two populations, speakers of the distinct but related Semaq Beri and the Semelai languages, differ in terms of their lifestyle. The Semaq Beri people are hunter-gatherers, while the Semelai subsist on horticulture. In a simple set of experiments, the researchers tested the consistency with which the members of these two cultures name smells and colors.

They found that Semelai speakers predictably used the same terms for colors but used fairly unpredictable terms for odors. This is the similar pattern that has been observed in WEIRD populations: colors are more abstractly codable than odors. In contrast, though, the Semaq Beri described colors and odors with equal predictability and consistency across speakers. This is perhaps surprising given that the Semelai and Semaq Beri live in the same general environment and, it would seem, consistently encounter many of the same smells. Furthermore, their languages are closely related, so the differences in their naming patterns cannot simply be attributed to linguistic diversity. The glaring difference between the two populations is their subsistence strategy, so Majid and her coauthor, Nicole Kruspe, interpret the results to suggest that hunter-gatherers like the Semaq Beri may have particularly attuned olfactory capacities that are reflected in the words they use for odors. Why might this be the case? Perhaps because the lifestyle of hunter-gatherers is so intimately tied to experiencing the rainforest, as opposed to transforming the rainforest, people like the Semaq Beri spend more time thinking about, distinguishing, and discussing odors within the forest. Majid and Kruspe point out, for example, that the Semaq Beri men "readily move around alone in the forest, but the Semelai are reluctant to do so without company."[12]

Distinct lifestyles may in fact represent a key factor impacting how terms for odors evolve in languages. We have no unequivocal evidence as of now that hunter-gatherer populations worldwide exhibit similarities in odor naming due to shared lifestyles. However, the results obtained in the Malaysian Peninsula are certainly consistent with such a lifestyle-based interpretation. Our understanding of smell naming and thought about smells will be refined as more populations are investigated in diverse regions. Such investigations are now underway, and some results have already been obtained in the Americas via the work of Majid and colleagues. A study of the language of the Seri, who live along the eastern shores of the Gulf of California and traditionally relied on hunting and gathering, demonstrated that the terms for odors in that language are very robust when contrasted to European languages. Consistent with the work among some languages on the Malay Peninsula, there is a rich smell lexicon in the Seri language. There are even a few similarities between the smell terms in Seri and Maniq. Both languages have dedicated terms for the "smell of rotting wood" and for the "smell of wet clothes."

Another similarity between the Seri smell terms and those studied on the Malay Peninsula is that lifestyle appears to play a role in how commonplace certain words for smells are in speech. In the case of the Seri, the older speakers who were raised as hunter-gatherers are more likely to use certain terms when asked to describe specific odors. The younger speakers, who apparently do not have as much familiarity with some of the flowers and plants once encountered in day-to-day Seri life, are less likely to use some of the odor terms. All of this is consistent with the idea that lifestyles can impact people's experiences with smells, and that those experiences can in turn impact how they conceptualize smells during speech. This is certainly congruent with my own intuition as someone who lives in a semitropical urban environment but has occasion to visit hunter-gatherers in tropical Amazonia. At times in various Amazonian villages I have felt awash in olfactory impressions that are missed in an urban environment. The lifestyle of hunter-gatherers in that region requires that they constantly be exposed to a variety of smells that have become largely unfamiliar to most of us today. Since they are exposed to such smells regularly, they may have a more common communicative need to talk about the smells with others in abstract ways.

In the study of the Seri lifestyle and odor terms, the authors offer the following conclusion: "It is certainly not the case that only hunter-gatherer communities have smell lexicons—olfactory lexicons exist in non-hunter-gatherer communities, too—but it does begin to appear that there is something about the hunter-gatherer lifestyle that promotes attention to, and talk about, smells."[13] Assuming that a lifestyle like hunting and gathering does impact the evolution of odor terminology in a given language, it is worth underscoring that this lifestyle effect ultimately owes itself to the degree of interaction of individuals with particular stimuli in their natural environments. The case of the Seri drives home this point. While all the people live in the same general environment, the older Seri once spent their days hunting and gathering and interacting with their natural environment in a way the younger Seri do not. They may reside in the same environment at a geographic level, but they do not really live in and communicate about the exact same environmental features. Similarly, speakers of European languages today do not have hunter-gatherer lifestyles like our ancestors. If we did, we would interact with our environments in completely different ways than most of us do now. We would have much greater motivation to decipher certain odors, for instance when paying attention to scents while tracking animals or gathering berries. And so the hunter-gatherer lifestyle would motivate a greater need for communicating about such odors. In a way, "lifestyle" in this case is essentially a proxy for the degree of interaction that people have with their native natural environments. As that interaction has diminished, the usefulness of many odor terms has likely diminished as well. Note that this is the reverse pattern as that observed for colors: as dyed objects have become more prevalent in industrialized societies, the usefulness of abstract color terms has increased as the need for talking about such colors has grown. To be clear, such technological pressures on the evolution of color terms do not imply that elaborate color language cannot develop without such technologies. In some cases it clearly has; however, the pressures in question do help to explain some of the tendencies evident in how the languages of some cultures encode terms for basic hues.[14]

Another language native to Mexico has been shown to include robust terms for smells. That language, Hehuetla-Tepehua, casts further doubt on the traditionally held assumption that odors are not thought about in abstract ways. It has almost four dozen terms dedicated to smells. Most of them are ideophones, or words based on sound symbolism. For example, in the language Upper Necaxa the word *kimkimkim* represents the repeated flashing of a firefly. (Ideophones are discussed at length in Chapter 7.) The repetition of the same *kim* syllable three times in a row represents the repetition of light flashing. In Hehuetla-Tepehua, many ideophones are also based on the notion of reduplication, where a repetition of some sound sequence represents the repetition of some physical entity. In this language, though, the entity in question may be an odor. For instance, the word *ɬkak* is used to refer to a spicy odor (or taste), but the word *ɬkakak* is used to describe something that has such a spicy-smelling odor (or taste) that will make one sneeze. This and other terms were discovered after researchers presented Hehuetla-Tepehua speakers with a series of odors via Sniffin' Sticks. These sticks look like markers, but instead of ink, distinct and reproducible odors emanate from their tips. They are increasingly used in research on olfactory terms as they allow researchers to test speakers' abilities to provide consistent terms for the relevant smells. As researchers use such tools with greater frequency, they are discovering that we may have grossly underestimated the olfactory terms in some little-documented languages. This is perhaps not so surprising. From a methodological standpoint, it is much easier to ask speakers to name color chips than it is to get them to name smells. A researcher need only take a set of two-dimensional chips and ask people to name those chips in order to elicit a particular color word. Introducing smells is a trickier matter. Even the sets of Sniffin' Sticks certainly do not exhaust all odors that might be named. We can divide the visible light spectrum into nifty sections, according to hue and brightness, and present them to individuals. While this is also a somewhat artificial task, it fairly comprehensively depicts the hues with which people are familiar. On the other hand, how do we present a comprehensive set of odors? We do not even know what it would mean to exhaustively describe smells, and there is no "smell spectrum" that parallels the color spectrum. Another difficulty is that smells are so often associated with specific sensations. For example, consider again the supposedly abstract smell word "musty." Is "musty" really just a term for a particular odor, or does it connote a smell plus a feeling? Even if you smelled a musty odor outdoors on a sunny day, perhaps via an artificial smelling stick, would it be accurate to say, "It smells musty out"? When we derive cross-cultural smelling tests based on stimuli like the Sniffin' Sticks, we might inadvertently oversimplify the labels for the overall sensations associated with the relevant odors by eliminating some of the relevant factors. Recall from the previous section that anthropologists have made similar points with respect to colors. In some languages a word for a given color encodes much more information than, simply, the hue of an item. It may also denote the item's luminosity, or perhaps even its texture. So presenting speakers around the world with a basic set of color stimuli may artificially reduce the amount of linguistic diversity that exists with respect to color-term reference. Analogously, we must be careful not to assume, simply because speakers of a language can refer to Sniffin' Sticks with varied odor terms, that those terms only encode abstract information about odors. This is not a criticism of such research, which is clearly shedding much light on how people actually talk about smells across the world's cultures. I simply wish to underscore the challenges faced in interpreting the cross-cultural data on odor terms. Cross-cultural research requires both experimental and ethnographic approaches whereby researchers spend significant time with the speakers of diverse languages to try to understand the nuances with which those speakers talk and think about odors and other sensations.[15]

Another methodological tack that can now be taken is the creation of large databases filled with transcriptions of conversations and stories from many languages, so that those databases can be analyzed computationally to better understand the language of smells. This approach has long been used to understand a host of phenomena in well-documented languages like English. Now the approach is being adopted in the description of lesser-known languages. For example, linguists used this method to help describe the olfactory terms in the Cha'palaa language of Ecuador. This language was found to have fifteen abstract odor terms, discovered simply when Cha'palaa speakers were asked to name odors. Many of the smell terms proved to be relatively common in speech. In the database linguists compiled of Cha'palaa speech, which consisted of hours of natural conversation, eight of the abstract terms were attested. These are presented in the table.

The eight abstract smell terms evident in recorded Cha'palaa conversations, with approximate English translations:

Cha'palaa Smell Term	Approximate Smell-Related Meaning
pudyu	stench, generally negative
andyu	fragrance; good food, generally positive
pindyu	sweet smell; perfume
pe'dyu	rotten smell
sendyu	fishy or metallic smell
jedyu	strong, acrid smell
jemeedyu	strong smell of alcohol
lushdyu	smell of freshly cut plants or plant seeds

The Cha'palaa study's finding is particularly noteworthy, as it demonstrates that speakers of some languages do not simply have many abstract smell terms at their disposal, but that they actually use those smell words commonly in conversation. Recall that in English there are smell terms like "petrichor" that are very rare in actual conversation. The authors of the study contrasted the frequency of smell terms in Cha'palaa with their frequency in two other languages: English and Imbabura Quechua. The latter language was selected because it is spoken in the same geographic region as Cha'palaa, with similar environmental conditions. The conclusion of their study was simple: "Speakers of Cha'palaa have more complex linguistic resources dedicated to talking about olfaction than speakers of Imbabura Quechua and English, and they also talk about smell more often than speakers of those languages."[16]

As researchers investigate the odor words of the world's languages, they are finding that some of our assumptions about how people talk about and think about smells may be biased by our understanding of a relatively narrow cross section of the world's cultures. Odors are not as ineffable as we once thought; they can be named with abstract terms. This abstract odor naming is not restricted to languages in one world region. But just how widespread is it? Just how much do humans vary in their sense of smell? We still have much to learn about how humans smell, and about how smells are encoded in the world's languages.

Conclusion: The Senses

Based on the previous two sections of this chapter, we can see that the careful study of linguistic diversity is changing our understanding of how humans talk and think about colors and odors, and to a lesser extent is even influencing our understanding of how people see and smell.

Researchers still debate how much the linguistic differences in basic terms for hues and smells impact how people think about colors and smells even when they are not talking. I have tried to steer clear of most of these debates here, though some of the work discussed does suggest that linguistic differences influence how people think about colors and smells even when they are not talking. What I have emphasized is that it is now clear that languages categorize visual and olfactory sensations in remarkably distinct ways.

In the years to come we should get a richer sense of how the world's languages refer to a wider array of visual stimuli, olfactory stimuli, and stimuli detected by our other senses. Much of the information related to other senses has remained anecdotal. Perhaps the clearest example of field-changing work is a study by a large team of researchers, also led by Majid, working on about two dozen languages worldwide. This study, published in the *Proceedings of the National Academy of Sciences,* helped to elucidate not just how languages refer to colors and smells, but also how they refer to other very basic sensory stimuli: sounds, shapes, tactile feelings, and tastes. The researchers systematically examined how speakers of these unrelated languages, spoken in diverse world regions, refer to stimuli across sensory domains. For each uniform set of stimuli, they tested speakers of those languages to see how consistent they were at choosing basic terms for the stimuli. So, for example, all the study's participants were asked to label the same bitter taste. Then Majid and colleagues quantified the degree of consistency of the responses, both within and across languages. Did every speaker of a given language use the same term to describe it? Or was there a range of responses? By examining the degree of consistency of speakers' labels across a variety of types of stimuli, the researchers were able to get some idea of how precisely and abstractly certain stimuli are encoded in the world's languages. They found, for example, that colors do tend to be more abstractly and precisely encoded when contrasted to smells, and they are labeled relatively predictably across most languages. Yet there are exceptions to these tendencies. For example, in the Umpila language of northern Australia, smells seem to be more precisely encoded than colors. That is, speakers of the language consistently label odors with the same predictable terms but are relatively unpredictable in how they label hues.

Perhaps the most intriguing result of this multiyear, multiauthor study related not to odors but to tastes. Tastes, it turns out, are very predictably and consistently coded in the many diverse languages of the sample. In fact, there is no evidence suggesting that colors are more codable than tastes, contrary to a common assumption based on a few WEIRD languages. This assumption is understandable. How many abstract tastes can you name? I suspect that the list is much shorter than the list of eleven basic color words in English. Beyond salty, sweet, bitter, and sour, most people do not use abstract English taste terms very consistently. Even those terms are vague, but it turns out many languages have a richer and less vague set of abstract taste words.

Another interesting finding obtained through the study related to how languages describe auditory stimuli. Subjects were presented with various types of sounds, including loud and soft sounds, as well as high-pitched and low-pitched sounds. They were asked to describe the sounds with basic words from their languages. Some expectations regarding how people refer to such auditory stimuli were violated by the experimental results, however. In the words of the authors, "It is oft-stated that all languages use a high-low metaphor to describe variation in pitch, and this ubiquity of linguistic encoding reflects the fine-tuning of ear anatomy . . . In our sample of diverse languages, however, the most prevalent way to talk about variation in pitch was through the equivalent of a big-small metaphor instead, followed by high-low and thin-thick."[17] In my experience as a professor, many college students do not realize that referring to sounds as being "high" or "low" is based on a particular metaphor, much like the way we depict time, with the future ahead of us. Somehow a high-pitched sound seems objectively higher along some real-world dimension, but of course this is not the case. High-pitched sounds simply have greater frequencies, measured in terms of cycles per second (Hertz). It makes sense that more languages refer to high-pitched sounds as being "small-pitched" since small things in nature, like mice or insects, tend to make sounds that have greater frequencies. In contrast, big things like elephants and lions tend to make sounds with reduced frequencies.

In short, languages vary tremendously with respect to how they encode and describe basic stimuli experienced through the senses. The exploration of linguistic diversity helps us better understand how we as a species talk and think about the stimuli encountered in our physical environments. In the next chapter, we will see that new types of studies centered on linguistic diversity are shedding light on other aspects of our relationship with the world around us.

5

Desert Ice

ALL HUMANS LIVE at the bottom of the same ocean of air. But we live in different seas, with distinct characteristics: different air densities, different temperatures, different humidity levels, and so on. These distinctions affect much of our lives, from the clothes we wear to the weather we talk and think about. Some environmental effects on how we talk are agreed upon by scholars, but other proposed effects are more controversial. The connections between environment and language discussed in this chapter, whether controversial or not, underscore the extent to which human speech and associated thought can be environmentally adaptive. The mere existence of such linguistic adaptation should not be surprising given how incredibly adaptive our species is, not only at the genetic level but also at the behavioral and cultural levels.

As a background to help contextualize the discussion of how our communication systems adapt to environmental factors, let us consider just some of the nonlinguistic ways in which we are adaptive.

In Amazonia, perspiration often covers one's body like a literal wetsuit, and it feels stifling throughout much of the day. Reprieve from the humidity in this particular "sea" of air, which already tests the surrounding air's capacity to carry water molecules, is elusive since much of the perspiration saturating your skin does not evaporate. On many occasions I have heard tourists of European descent complain about their discomfort, questioning aloud how they can sweat so much. In the region in which I was raised, soccer is prevalent along the riverbanks of the Amazon's many tributaries, much as it is in the more populated parts of Brazil. More than once I have played soccer with both indigenous and *branco* (white) players on a riverbank field. Usually the contrast between the sweating of the two populations was pronounced; those of us of European descent were, on average, comparably and predictably drenched in sweat. Our perceived extent of perspiration is as maladaptive as it is frustrating. What is the point of your body trying to cool itself off through the evaporation of sweat if the sweat does not actually evaporate from the skin? The sweat does evaporate, of course, just more slowly than one would like. In the drier air of many parts of the world, particularly in the higher latitudes far from the equator, sweating heavily is a more effective cooling strategy since the liquid on your skin evaporates more quickly.

People native to Amazonia and the jungles of other places like Africa and Southeast Asia perspire too, of course. In fact it is unclear how well population-level differences in sweat glands explain such anecdotally observed differences on the soccer field, particularly since the amount someone sweats is determined by all sorts of genetic and nongenetic factors, including fitness level, drug usage, disease, and the like. Yet people in jungle regions appear to perspire a bit less on average. In one study examining the sweating of Koreans and Africans, it was observed that Africans from the tropics generally had lower sweat gland density and sweat gland output than Koreans, even when exposed to the same temperatures.[1]

People from the tropics also tend to have much less body hair than Europeans, perhaps in part since body hair inhibits heat radiation away from the body while we do things like walk and run. After all, humans lose most of their excess heat through radiation, not sweating. People with genes that were selected for in northern latitudes tend to exhibit a few physiological characteristics that make them better adapted for the regions in which their ancestors lived. These characteristics relate not just to perspiration and hair but, interrelatedly, to body size. It has long been observed that people from cold regions are typically heavier than those in warm regions. This principle, known as Bergmann's rule, actually holds across a variety of species. While there is debate over the extent to which heat differences explain this "rule," it is easy to see why some consider extremities in climate to be a likely candidate for explaining such physical adaptations. Larger bodies were perhaps more likely to survive and reproduce in places like Northern Europe that have frigid winters. A larger frame reduces the ratio of the skin's surface area to the body's volume, meaning heat is better preserved. Big, stocky bodies make much less sense in the warm jungles of New Guinea, the Indian subcontinent, equatorial Africa, or Amazonia; thinner bodies will eliminate heat more efficiently. As a result, those with thinner frames may be slightly more likely to reproduce in hot places. Over many cycles of reproduction, such likelihoods result in clear cross-region tendencies in body types. There have been times when I was in an indigenous village and felt like some sort of giant, even though my height is average in a city in North America or Europe. Many Amazonian men are only about five feet tall (1.52 meters), thin and wiry in build, so I am disproportionate in their midst. I have felt outsized in other parts of the world as well, Cambodia for instance, but it is no coincidence that every time I felt much larger than the average man around me, I was in a tropical locale.[2]

Other environmental adaptations are evident when surveying the world's populations. People of Northern Eurasian heritage tend to have certain features, including light skin (and associated light-colored blue and green eyes), that may help them process vitamin D more efficiently in the higher, darker latitudes where the sun's ultraviolet radiation is less prevalent. In contrast, the darker skin colors of most of the world's populations allow them to maintain folate levels that are critical for metabolism, while also allowing them to synthesize vitamin D effectively given the sun-rich environments in which they live. I should stress that, despite such extensive physical adaptations to the world's varying environments, humans exhibit little genetic diversity when compared to other mammals and primates. Our closest relatives, chimpanzees, exhibit more genetic diversity than we do despite being confined to Africa in their noncaptive environments. A primatologist colleague of mine at the University of Miami remarked to me once that more genetic variation can be observed across just two small populations of chimps than we observe across all human populations. Yet humans were the species that was able to conquer all the world's major environments. We did not develop the ability to live in such diverse environments primarily through biological adaptations, as other animal types have done. Consider the *Felidae* family of mammals: cats have adapted to most of the world's nonmarine ecologies, but they have done so through speciation and over a much longer time span. In contrast, humans are a single species that behaviorally and culturally have adapted to myriad environments. We are adapted for adaptation. As anthropologists are fond of pointing out, cultural pressures, not environmental ones, are now the main drivers of our genetic adaptation. To cite one of many examples, men that are adept at using a bow and arrow may be more likely to pass on their genes in many cultures, and the use of a bow and arrow is obviously more important in some cultures than others.[3]

Our cultures continuously adapt to different environments at rates that our genes cannot, offering individual humans key advantages that have been acquired over centuries or millennia of living in particular environments. Intriguingly, individuals are often unaware of the motivation for these cultural adaptations, as the adaptations are selected for gradually, over centuries in some cases. Cultural adaptations are selected even if the members of the cultures in question are not aware of why their behavior is adaptive. Consider again the case of vitamin D, which is also associated with a particular behavior: eating cod. The Scandinavians' habitual ingestion of cod fish and the oil in its liver helps to explain how they maintained such strong body types over centuries in the high latitudes in which they live, latitudes that receive much less sunlight than equatorial regions. UV rays are critical to the production of vitamin D, which is in turn critical to the body's production of calcium. Without sufficient quantities of that vitamin, children can develop rickets and older adults can develop osteomalacia. In short, people without enough vitamin D are more likely to develop weak and deformed bones. While lighter skin helps people process vitamin D more effectively in high latitudes, it does not make populations immune from rickets and osteomalacia. Cod oil is rich in vitamin D. The fact that Scandinavians have eaten it for many centuries, though many outsiders have considered it repulsive, helps to explain the Vikings' success in sailing to and conquering new lands. Although the Vikings had no knowledge of the causal chain linking vitamin D to fewer cases of rickets, their consumption of cod oil was "selected for" with time as their cultures' successes and likelihood of survival and reproduction benefited from that consumption. The connection between cod oil and vitamin D, like the connection between sunlight and the production of vitamin D, was not made scientifically until the twentieth century. By that time, cultural evolution had been offering indirect evidence of the connection for centuries.[4]

Here is another fascinating example of nonconscious cultural evolution: Many groups today eat manioc after subjecting it to a lengthy preparation process that helps to reduce levels of hydrocyanic acid in the tuber that can otherwise lead to severe illness. The process involves multiple steps over numerous days, as evident in cultures throughout Amazonia. Members of these cultures are often at a loss to explain why the steps are required. This manner of preparation has evolved over countless generations, and no doubt many unfortunate people prepared manioc incorrectly along the way, suffering the effects. The preparation techniques that survived were the ones that enabled manioc eaters to consume the food without suffering those ill effects, even if they did not know why. These and other examples of nonconscious cultural adaptation have been documented extensively in the last few decades. Harvard anthropologist Joe Henrich has brought attention to many of them in his work, which includes an influential book on cultural evolution, *The Secret of Our Success*.[5]

I offer this background on cultural evolution because I have wondered for some time how much the cultural and behavioral adaptation of humans extends to their communication systems. Linguists have not conducted substantive research on this question until fairly recently.

Earlier in the book we saw some indirect ways that environmental factors can potentially affect language. Recall the temporal gestures of the Nheengatú, discussed in Chapter 1, whose language requires speakers to point to the sky when describing the time at which an event occurred.

Would such a gestural requirement evolve in a region in high latitudes with frequently cloudy weather? This seems unlikely. Languages in equatorial, sunny places do not generally require that speakers point to the sun to mark the time of a described event, yet people would need to be in places where time is tied to a year-round predictable path of the sun across the daytime sky for languages to come to rely on such gestures. Such indirect adaptation is hard to debate, but do languages adapt in more direct ways to external environmental pressures?

Words Adapt

In the Introduction I mentioned the famous (perhaps infamous) observation that the Inuit have many basic words for snow. While their number of words for snow has been exaggerated and distorted in the zeitgeist, the larger point that this observation underscores, namely that the words of languages adapt to environmental factors, seems commonsensical. Yet common sense does not replace research and can mislead us in serious ways. Consider again the example of words for snow. What predictions might common sense truly make here? If a group of people lives in a very snowy locale, perhaps snow becomes such a pervasive facet of the environmental background that it is less salient, and maybe even less worth thinking and talking about, and therefore less likely to be encoded with many words. Or perhaps the pervasiveness of snow implies that people are likely to think and talk about it a lot, and as a result they need to make fine-grained distinctions that ultimately result in many words for the phenomenon. This latter prediction is the one associated with the words-for-snow trope. These divergent predictions made by "common sense" have been stressed in work on this topic by cognitive scientist Terry Regier.[6]

Regier and his colleagues decided to tackle this topic not with intuition but with big data and computational methods. They took to Twitter, analyzing tweets in diverse languages spoken in both warm and cold regions. They found that people in cold places tend to talk much more about snow and ice than speakers of the same language residing in warmer places, at least judging from their tweets. This suggests that snow and ice are not simply boring background phenomena that are unworthy of thought or conversation, but rather that they are frequently highlighted in speech in cold places. The researchers then addressed another related question: Do languages in warmer places tend to make distinctions between "snow" and "ice," or do they tend to conflate these words for crystalline water? This is the natural counterpart to the question made famous by the work of Boas and others. Regier's team addressed the issue with a direct approach: they examined words for snow and ice in about two hundred languages representing many diverse language families and geographic regions. They observed that most languages have distinct words for ice and snow, as in English. In about one-sixth of the languages surveyed, however, no such distinction was made. These languages were spoken only in warm geographic regions. To rule out the possibility of coincidence, the researchers looked at nearly one thousand other word types to test whether the warm-weather languages just happened to make less fine-grained distinctions for a variety of phenomena, including air and wind. The team of researchers observed that while many languages do not have separate basic words for air and wind, such languages are spoken in both warm and colder regions. Out of all the word pairs they examined, the ice / snow pair was clearly an outlier. Ice and snow are distinguished lexically throughout much of the world but are collapsed into a single word category in languages in warm regions only.

Two key points from the study are relevant to contextualizing other recent work on how we talk in and think about our surrounding environments. First, intuition and our traditional assumptions can get in the way of fully understanding the environmental effects on language. Second, the environment appears to affect a language's words for snow / ice in somewhat unpredictable ways. Whereas languages that do not distinguish words for ice and snow are found almost exclusively in warm regions, plenty of languages in warm regions do in fact have separate words for ice and snow. Many languages had to be examined for the relevant pattern to surface, and care had to be taken to make sure the uncovered pattern was not due to shared inheritance between a few languages of the same family, or due to patterns in borrowing in a few regions. For instance, given the contemporary worldwide influence of English, the distinction it makes between snow and ice could have been adopted by many languages.

In Chapter 4, we saw how words for colors and for smells may be adaptive in subtle ways. It appears that industrialization has yielded more brightly colored focal objects that people think and talk about often, and that this pressure has impacted the basic color terms in the world's languages. Analogously, words for odors may be affected by interactions between lifestyles and the environment. The effects of environment and culture on words for odors and colors may be indirect when compared to the effects of environmental factors on words for ice / snow. Yet they, too, are only evident upon careful inspection of data from many diverse languages, indicating the necessity of such a large-scale approach that is not overly reliant on the languages of WEIRD people.

Here is another subtle and more indirect effect of the environment on words and the meanings they transmit. In a study based on data from about five thousand dialects, I found that words for "one" and "two" tend to be shorter in the languages of industrialized societies than in those of hunter-gatherer and foraging societies. Words generally become shorter the more frequently used they are. (This point was popularized in academic circles almost a hundred years ago by the Harvard linguist George Zipf, a point we will return to in Chapter 6.) Given this finding, I suggested that the phenomenon of shorter number words was due to their greater frequency in speech in larger, industrialized populations. It is somewhat surprising that cultural factors affect the frequency and shape of number words as basic as "one" and "two." Less surprising is the now well-established finding that large agricultural and industrialized societies are more likely to have more number words than small, isolated populations of hunter-gatherers. Such industrialized societies rely much more extensively on elaborate numerical concepts, which are fairly recent innovations in human history. Since it has been claimed that some environments are more conducive to the spread of agriculture, one could interpret this finding—that "one" and "two" are particularly common words in large agricultural societies—as a very indirect result of probabilistic environmental pressures. This theme of subtle probabilistic effects of environmental factors on language, including cultural factors that are associated with particular environments, is receiving growing attention by numerous scholars.[7]

Let us consider one other potential effect of the environment on words and the thoughts they convey: languages in warm places are less likely to have distinct words for "arm" and "hand," a finding supported by the work of a linguist named Cecil Brown. Before getting to the supposed motivation for this association, let us take a look at the correlational support offered in its favor. Brown examined 617 languages to test whether they had distinct basic terms for "hand" and "arm." Obviously English does, so it was categorized as a "differentiating" language since it distinguishes these seemingly separable body parts. It turns out that many languages do not make this distinction with basic word choices. In fact, 228 of the languages Brown surveyed do not separate "hand" from "arm," and the wrist is not a key separator of basic words in these languages. For instance, in the Lonwolwol language of the linguistically rich island nation of Vanuatu, the word for "hand" is *va,* and the word for "arm" is also *va.* In the Gur language of Burkina Faso, the word for "hand" is *nu,* and the word for "arm" is also *nu.*[8]

How might this difference across languages relate to the environment? When Brown examined the locations of the 389 languages of the differentiating kind, it became clear that they are spoken all around the globe. In contrast, the languages of the 228 nondifferentiating languages are located primarily in equatorial or near-equatorial regions. In other words, this is similar to the global association noted by Regier and colleagues with respect to words for "ice" and "snow." The pattern uncovered by Brown is less stark geographically, but similar. Here is Brown's counterintuitive guess as to why the pattern exists: "The presence of tailored clothing covering the arms greatly increases the distinctiveness of arm parts and renders more likely their labeling by separate terms. In addition, ancillary apparel such as gloves and mittens also increases the salience of arm parts. Since nonequatorial zones where cold weather is frequent are usually associated with the presence of tailored clothing and other arm gear, languages spoken in these areas are significantly more inclined to lexically distinguish 'hand' and 'arm' than those spoken in equatorial zones." While this explanation remains a hypothesis only, the arm-labeling finding suggests another way in which environmental factors might come to influence the kinds of words used in a given language. Once again we are talking about a probabilistic environmental effect, and there are exceptions to Brown's hypothesis in his sample set of 617 languages. On balance, though, the crosslinguistic data are supportive of his hypothesis.

Via an innovative experimental method, researchers have shown that some words for spatial language are also adaptive. As we saw in Chapter 2, people in many cultures refer to the space around themselves differently from the egocentric approach that is the default in English. Rather than referring to items as being to the "left" or "right" of their own body or the person with whom they are speaking, speakers of many other languages are more likely to refer to cardinal directions established geocentrically. As I noted, some of the environmental features referred to in these geocentric systems are specific to a culture's ecology, for instance the ubiquitous references to "uphill" and "downhill" terms in some of the languages of the highlands of Central America and New Guinea. Nevertheless, many languages in mountainous regions do not use geocentric terms as their default spatial reference tools. We cannot predict with much accuracy the kind of spatial terms a given culture will use just because of the environment in which it developed, particularly since all cultures are made up of people with the same basic bodies that can be used as points of reference when talking about the location of things. This leaves us simply with some relatively weak evidence suggesting that the environments in which languages reside help influence the strategies of spatial thought used by their speakers.

Recently, though, a team led by Jonas Nölle, a language researcher at the University of Glasgow, has developed a new and promising experimental approach to this topic. One might assume that exploring this issue experimentally would require the logistical work of taking speakers to diverse landscapes far from their homes. Nölle instead decided to pursue the issue with technology that has been around for some time but has only recently been refined sufficiently to allow for such an experimental use: virtual reality. He and his team designed a virtual environment that could be explored simultaneously by two experiment participants. The individuals could communicate with each other while simultaneously immersed in the virtual environment. There, they played a game in which one participant had to tell the other how to find certain items, called *orbs*. One of the participants was a *seeker*, meaning they had to collect the orbs. The challenge was that they could only see an orb when it was within five virtual meters of themselves. Anything outside that range was invisible to them, but it was not invisible to the other participant, the *director*. The director had to tell the seeker where to go to find the orb in the virtual environment, much as, say, a retail store employee might give directions to a customer looking for a product in a store. Because the participants were immersed in a virtual environment, Nölle and his team could switch that environment between two environments they had designed. One of them was a virtual forest, with many trees in a flat place. The other was a slope, which resembled a real-world hillside or mountainside. All the participants spoke English, a language in which egocentric directions like "left" and "right" are common. For example, in the case of an English-speaking store employee giving directions to a customer, we would expect them to say something like, "Head straight down that aisle, then make a left, and the item will be on your right." Critically, though, English allows for other sorts of directions that are not egocentric, evident in words like "north" and "south" or like "uphill" and "across." In many languages (including Tzeltal, as previously discussed), such terms are regularly used for giving directions, even when the directions do not involve literal hills and slopes. The question is whether environment type systematically impacts the spatial terms used by English speakers. If it does, such evidence for a systematic effect in one language would offer support for the idea that the way spatial-cognition strategies evolve is, at least in part, influenced by the environments in which the language develops.[9]

Nölle's team found that, regardless of environment, English speakers tended to use the common default strategy of employing egocentric spatial terms like left and right. This was true across the twenty-one pairs of people that were tested. Directors typically told seekers to do things like turn right, head straight, turn left, and so on. Nevertheless, in many cases the directors and seekers used geocentric terms. They almost never used geocentric terms in the forest environment, but they did use them a sizable percentage of the time in the hill-like environment. In short, English speakers' spatial strategies, and the terms they use in association with those strategies, are apparently dictated in part by the physical environs in which they are communicating.

Let us imagine that one group of English speakers became shipwrecked on a flat island and lived there for centuries, while at the same time another group became stranded on a mountainous island, and that each group lived on its respective island for centuries. Their vocabularies would likely change in different ways over that time. One of the differences we might predict, especially in light of the results from Nölle's team, is that those people on the mountainous island would come to rely more heavily on terms like "uphill" and "downhill," while on the flat island such terms would probably fall out of use. After all, the people on the mountainous island would often need to think and talk about such concepts, while those concepts would be immaterial in a flat place. The differences in spatial language that emerged across the two groups would likely be apparent to anyone who eventually had the opportunity to communicate with both populations. All of this may seem a bit obvious, so it is worth taking the mental exercise a step further. Suppose that both populations, speakers of these two new English-derivative dialects, eventually migrated to other lands. The dialects might still carry with them distinct default spatial reference systems, but the origins of those distinct systems might now be unclear. With time, the dialects' default spatial terms might change again, but for some time the terms would likely be influenced by the two distinct island environments on which the groups had been shipwrecked. Framed differently, while distinct environments influence how spatial terms are used and therefore how languages evolve along this parameter, that influence is not necessarily reflected in contemporary data for any individual language. Any global associations between environmental factors and language, for instance between mountainous terrain and certain default spatial terms like "uphill," might have plenty of exceptions. This latter point holds across any possible associations between environment and language.

Sound Systems Adapt—But How Much?

Words are created via sounds resulting from distinct sequences of movements in our vocal tract. As we learn to speak a language, we must focus on what we are doing with our vocal tracts while our brains simultaneously distinguish the sounds emanating from the mouths of others. This exercise can be cognitively intense at times, particularly since humans use a dizzying array of sound types. You have perhaps considered how distinctive the sounds in some languages seem. Maybe the click sounds common to Sub-Saharan Africa sound exotic, or the nasal vowels of French, or the tones of Mandarin—to which we will turn shortly. Yet the range of sounds in the world's languages is even more expansive than most people realize. A new database of linguistic sounds gives us some sense of the range. Largely the work of Steven Moran, like me an anthropology professor at the University of Miami, the database contains over three thousand sounds that have been documented in the world's languages. A few sounds are quite common across languages, for instance the nasal sound at the beginning of "milk." This consonant is used in over 90 percent of languages. However, many sound types occur in only a small fraction of the world's languages. The sound at the end of "bath," which is made by putting the tip of the tongue between the front teeth, is a rarity from a global perspective. It is uncoincidentally hard to learn for speakers of many languages, while the [m] sound is comparably easy to learn.[10]

The most critical component of the vocal tract is the larynx, which houses the vocal cords. The vocal cords are basically thin flaps of skin that are less than an inch long and whose primary function, critical to the survival of the many species that have them, is to keep stuff out of the lungs and the trachea. The vocal cords also make a lot of noise when they vibrate together, which they do if they are held close together while air rushes past them. That loud vibration is what makes speech audible, though what the vibration sounds like depends on many factors, including how people manipulate their tongue. Humans have exapted the vocal cords and other parts of the vocal tract that have more primal breathing and / or digestive functions in order to create speech.

The vibrating vocal cords are affected by many factors, some of which are imperceptible yet still have a pervasive effect on speech. Consider these two similar-sounding words: "gore" and "core," as in "There was a lot of gore in that horror film" and "The core of the earth is hot." If we use the international phonetic alphabet (IPA) to transcribe each individual sound produced when the two words are spoken, the words are transcribed roughly as [goʷɹ] ("gore") and [koʷɹ] ("core"). As we see in their IPA transcriptions, the words' first sounds are [g] and [k], respectively. These two sounds are called velar stops in linguistics. That means they are made by raising the back of the tongue so that it touches the velum or soft palate at the back of the roof of the mouth. The sounds are largely similar, with the exception of one key point: the [g] sound requires that you vibrate your vocal cords while you raise your tongue to touch your velum, while the [k] sound does not. This is what makes the two sounds so perceptually distinct, allowing us to convey distinct thoughts like "gore" and "core." Both of these sounds are easy to make: kids tend to acquire them early in life, and they are common in many of the world's languages. Yet they are not equally common, likely because one of the sounds is a little easier to make than the other. Can you guess which one? The answer is [k], the first sound in "core." The reason is simply that it is a bit unnatural to vibrate your vocal cords, as you are required to do when making the [g] sound, when the back of your tongue closes off your airway by touching the top of the back of your mouth. This is due to basic aerodynamics: in order to vibrate your vocal cords, you need to have plenty of air rushing out of your lungs and through the larynx, where the vocal cords sit. When I teach phonetics courses, I often have students say the [s] and [z] sounds loudly, alternating between them. If you do the same while simultaneously touching your larynx (the bump on your throat), you will be able to feel in a tactile way the vibration of your vocal cords turning off and on. How rapidly the vocal cords vibrate depends on a host of factors, including their size. My own vocal cords tend to vibrate an average of 110–120 times per second (110–120 Hz) during normal speech, though this frequency varies a lot. When asking a question in English, one's vocal cords vibrate much faster toward the end of a sentence; this is referred to metaphorically as a rising pitch even though nothing is technically going up. For vocal cord vibration to be maintained in a sound like [z], the air has to keep rushing past the vocal cords. In a sound like [z], your mouth is not completely closed, so the airflow can easily be maintained. The airflow required for vocal cord vibration is most easily maintained for vowel sounds, since the mouth remains mostly open during the articulation of vowels. In the case of a sound like [g], however, keeping one's vocal cords vibrating is a trickier matter. As the air passes through the larynx and reaches the space behind the place of contact between your tongue and roof of your mouth, it has nowhere to escape. This buildup of air pressure means that it quickly becomes harder to get air to flow past the vocal cords and make them flap in the wind, so to speak. For this reason, [g] sounds tend to be shorter than [k] sounds, since the latter do not require vibrating vocal cords.

Linguists have long been aware of these factors, but they have also debated whether the factors actually have a sizable effect on the world's languages. In one survey of 567 languages, the linguist Ian Maddieson found that the [g] sound is a bit less likely than sounds like [k] to be used as a "phoneme" in the world's languages. A phoneme is a sound that is used to turn one word into another one with a completely different meaning. For example, if I swap out the first [k] sound of [koʷɹ], "core," with [g] to make [goʷɹ], "gore," the word's meaning totally changes. Listeners do not just hear a mispronunciation, as they might if I swapped the [k] sound out with many of the other sounds that exist in the world's languages. Because of the existence of word pairs that differ in terms of only the sounds [k] and [g], we know that these two sounds are phonemes in English. The thoughts conveyed to a listener can vary dramatically depending on which of these sounds is produced. In Maddieson's study, he observed that the [k] sound is more likely to be a phoneme than the [g] sound across the nearly 600 languages surveyed. However, this tendency was very minor, so it remained unclear whether the aerodynamic factor described above had any substantive effect on how common these sorts of sounds are in speech.[11]

Just because a sound like [g] exists as a phoneme in a given language does not mean it is as common in that language as a sound like [k]. In a study published in the journal *Language* in 2018, I examined the frequency of all the sounds in the transcriptions of basic words for about half the world's languages. What I found is that [g] is used much less often than [k] across the world, even in languages that contain both sounds. The results of the study suggest that the subtle differences in the effort required for the vocal cords to be vibrated, even for sounds like [g] and [k] that are common across languages, actually have a pretty pervasive effect on the rate at which languages use the relevant sounds. It is not surprising that languages gravitate somewhat toward easier-to-articulate sounds. What is surprising is that even very subtle, almost imperceptible, differences in the ease with which two sounds are made can affect the use of sounds in pronounced ways. I doubt you have ever thought, for example, "'Gore' sure is a tricky word to say"—or "goo" or "gap" or countless other words with the [g] sound. Languages adapt and, with time, come to rely to a greater extent on sounds that are just a tiny bit easier to make. Environmental factors also have effects, albeit perhaps indirect, on the sounds we use in speech.[12]

One indirect effect of environmental factors on the sounds used in speech, which is now well supported, is that languages spoken by agriculturalists are more likely to contain certain sound types. Given that large-scale agriculture was apparently more likely to evolve in certain geographic regions, this suggests that languages in some environments were somewhat more likely to eventually come to rely on the sounds in question because of where those languages were spoken over long periods. The claim that some regions in the world are more likely to produce large-scale agriculture has been made elsewhere and is based on a number of observations. For instance, some key crops and domesticated animals that facilitate large-scale agriculture happen to be native to certain parts of the world and grow more easily in particular climates. It is not a complete geographic coincidence that the agricultural revolution took hold first in the Fertile Crescent (as opposed to, say, the Sahara) and spread to other regions of similar latitude and climates. Of course, many crops are found in diverse global regions, but large-scale agriculture was by most accounts more likely to develop in certain regions prior to being transmitted across cultures. Further, that cross-cultural transmission was impacted in some instances by geographic factors. The increased reliance on agriculture in certain environmental contexts is due, for instance, to the ideal growing conditions of crops like wheat and barley, and the animals initially required to grow them at large scales. Some of these conditions were met in the Fertile Crescent, for instance, which even many millennia ago possessed the relevant growing conditions and domesticable animals. To be clear, the relationship between geographic factors and agriculture is hardly a simple and deterministic one. Many cultures live in regions where agriculture would be possible but maintain other subsistence strategies. Conversely, many cultures have developed agricultural practices in regions that do not seem particularly conducive to such practices, particularly after borrowing agricultural practices following cross-cultural contact with agriculturalists.[13]

The hypothesis that geographic factors impact the likelihood that a culture relies on agriculture is nevertheless more intuitive than the other key claim I just made, that languages spoken by agriculturalists are more likely to contain certain sound types. How could the latter point be possible? And what kinds of sounds are we talking about? To answer these questions, we need to first take a look at the hypothesis offered by the linguist Charles Hockett in a paper from 1985. The paper's key claim was that agriculturalists appear to rely more on "labiodental" consonants like the first sounds in "fast" and "vape." Labiodental sounds are made when the bottom lip touches, or almost touches, the top incisors. (Hence the name: labio + dental.) If you say "fast," for example, you can feel a rush of air move past your bottom lip and your top teeth as you produce the first sound in the word. To understand why sounds like this might be more common in agricultural populations, another key piece of background information is required. As people age, their diet impacts how their teeth develop. People with softer diets often develop two characteristic dental features: overbite and overjet. The term "overbite" refers to the fact that the top incisors tend to overlap with the bottom incisors in resting position, with the lowest point of the top teeth being lower than the highest point of the bottom teeth. The term "overjet" refers to the fact that the top teeth tend to rest a bit farther forward of the bottom teeth. Overbite / overjet has become common throughout many of the world's cultures. In fact, people without this sort of bite often are given orthodontic treatment to develop it. In the United States, adults have an average overbite and overjet of about three millimeters each as adults. In these average mouths, the top teeth rest naturally directly above the bottom lip, not directly above the bottom teeth. As a result, when making a labiodental sound like the first sound in "fast," the bottom lip barely has to travel during articulation.[14]

Interestingly, the overbite / overjet bite type many of us now have is far from average in a historical sense. For the vast majority of our roughly two-hundred-thousand-year history as a species, the bite type that has been more common among adults is a so-called edge-to-edge bite type. In this bite type, the top incisors rest against the bottom incisors, so that the surface of the front teeth is flat when the mouth is closed. There is no pronounced overlap between the teeth. The reason this bite type is more natural among adults in a historical sense is that agricultural diets are a fairly new phenomenon. Until the last few thousand years, people's diets were not centered around soft foods like rice, bread, and the like. Furthermore, in pre-Neolithic times people did not typically use utensils to make pieces of food smaller. Instead, their daily eating routine involved a lot more grinding and cutting with the teeth. This more intense wear yielded an edge-to-edge bite during adolescence. The edge-to-edge bite type is apparent in the teeth of humans in the archeological record, but it is also often evident in contemporary populations that maintain subsistence norms that are more characteristic of the vast majority of human history: hunter-gatherers. Impressionistically, I can say that most hunter-gatherers I have encountered have edge-to-edge bites. The pattern is definitely more common among Amazonians than among, say, Americans. Nonanecdotal findings collected in some populations also support such impressionistic assessments.[15]

Given the preceding factors and given that humans have a tendency to make sounds that require less effort, assuming the sounds can still effectively tease apart word meanings, we can now see the motivation for Hockett's hypothesis. If it takes less effort for cultures with soft diets to make labiodental sounds, then these sounds should generally be more common in such cultures. Conversely, labiodental sounds should be less common in cultures with harder diets and that do not use utensils. Hockett's hypothesis was largely ignored until the publication of an extensive study in *Science* in 2019. The authors of the paper, led by Dámian Blasi and Steven Moran, used a host of methods to test Hockett's claim. They found that the languages of hunter-gatherers are much less likely to have labiodental phonemes than the languages of agriculturalists. They observed this pattern with a sample of about two thousand languages, while controlling for the fact that many languages inherit sounds from the same ancestral languages or borrow sounds from nearby languages. A researcher on the team, Scott Moisik, also conducted elaborate 3D biomechanical modeling and was able to demonstrate that labiodental sounds do in fact require much less energy to produce for speakers with overbite / overjet. Basically, the lip muscles have less work to do when producing an [f] or a [v] sound if the bottom lip is resting right under the top teeth. Another interesting piece of evidence they offered was historical: in Europe, labiodental sounds have become more and more prevalent over the last few thousand years alongside the advent and spread of agriculture and softer diets.[16]

In another study, cognitive scientist Sihan Chen and I examined data from about three thousand languages and found that labiodental consonants are indeed very rarely used in the languages of hunter-gatherers when compared to the languages of other populations. We also decided to test Hockett's hypothesis in a more direct way. We examined videos of speakers who spoke the same language, English, but who varied according to their bite type. After all, some English speakers do have edge-to-edge bites like those common in hunter-gatherer populations. What we found was clear evidence for the pattern within the same language: English speakers with overbites produced labiodentals at about the rate we would expect—pretty frequently, in fact, given the many words like "fast" and "for" that are expected to have labiodentals. Yet English speakers with edge-to-edge bites used labiodental sounds at a rate closer to that typical of hunter-gatherers. Many of the supposed labiodental sounds in words like "for" were pronounced more like "por," with the bottom lip coming close to or even making contact with the top lip instead of the top teeth. The speakers we looked at were celebrities, which meant our findings could easily be replicated by other interested parties. Here is one bit of trivia from the data we analyzed: the singer Freddie Mercury, who had the most pronounced overbite of the speakers we examined, also produced more labiodentals than anyone we studied. Put simply, many of the [p] and [b] sounds in his interviews were pronounced more like [f] and [v]. In short, numerous types of data now exist to suggest that Hockett was right: softer diets, a somewhat recent innovation, have come to affect how some sounds are used to transmit meaning. These types of data encompass historical evidence from several regions, biomechanical modeling findings, and the frequency of labiodental sounds across many languages and individuals.[17]

The relationship between bite type and labiodental consonants ultimately hints at a relationship between the environments in which people live and some of the sounds they use to distinguish their thoughts when communicating. It is an indirect and probabilistic relationship, to be sure, not a deterministic one. Yet there is a plausible chain of connection between the environment and the use of a particular type of consonant. Some parts of Europe, for instance, favored certain kinds of agriculture that led to softer diets when contrasted to those of hunter-gatherers. Softness of diet leads to the commonality of overjet and overbite among most adults, and this common bite type means that certain sounds, like [f] and [v], are just a bit easier to make for adults with softer diets than for hunter-gatherers. To me, this indirect environmental connection is the most interesting facet of Hockett's hypothesis and the various findings now supporting it. They hint at the sometimes nearly imperceptible relationship between humans, their languages, and their environments.

If the environment influences linguistic sounds in very indirect ways, via subsistence strategies and their effects on bite types, could it do so in more direct ways? Are speakers of some languages more likely to use a given type of sound than speakers of other languages because of external factors like temperature and humidity that can impact the actual operation of the vocal tract? At first this may seem an outlandish suggestion, but we have already seen that even common sounds like [g] and [k] are affected by very subtle aerodynamic factors operating on the vocal cords, factors that make [g] slightly less common. Relatedly, studies in laryngology have demonstrated effects of dry air on the operation of the vocal cords. The studies were undertaken with an array of methods, offering evidence for two key relevant findings. First, when the vocal cords are a bit drier, more perceived effort is sometimes required for them to vibrate as the viscous layer covering them dries. Second, dry air can reduce the precision with which the vocal cords vibrate. For example, if someone's vocal cords are dried out artificially, they will have a bit more trouble producing precise pitches or frequencies. This is a well-known fact for professional singers, some of whom use humidifiers in their rooms prior to performances. When a human breathes dry air in through their nose, the nasal cavity generally humidifies the incoming air so that by the time it reaches the vocal cords it is not dry. Yet many people breathe through their mouths regularly during the day and while sleeping. Also, when exercising or needing greater oxygen intake for other reasons, people breathe through their mouths. Additionally, people with nasal blockages due to illness inhale cold, dry air through their mouths. In short, despite the great job the human body does of humidifying the air we breathe in, dry air often makes its way to the vocal cords. Furthermore, the nose does not always humidify air completely in very dry environments.[18]

I wondered whether the effect of dry air on the vocal cords has any impact on the sounds used in languages. One hypothesis I developed, based on the demonstrable effects of ambient air on the vocal cords, relates to tones. Tones are variations in pitch, or the frequency at which the vocal cords vibrate, variations that change the meaning of one word into another. In English we do not use pitch to distinguish words, however, as is done in tonal languages like Mandarin. Mandarin has four basic tones used to distinguish meanings. Some tonal languages have only two or three tones; others have many more than Mandarin. In languages with complex systems of tones, many kinds of precise variations in pitch are required for each word. For example, the following four words in Mandarin all consist of the / ma / syllable: "horse," "to scold," "hemp," and "mother." The difference between these words is not in the consonant and vowel used but in the frequency at which the vocal cords vibrate during the production of the consonant and vowel. In the word for "mother," the / ma / syllable is produced with vocal cords that are vibrating relatively fast throughout. In the word for "horse," on the other hand, the / ma / syllable is produced with vocal cords that are initially vibrating quickly, then slow down, then speed up again. The actual frequencies of vocal cord vibration depend on many factors, including whether the speaker is male or female, the tones of surrounding syllables, and so forth. Still, to be intelligible in a tonal language, one must produce specific pitch patterns associated with individual words.

Given such factors, I speculated that languages spoken over centuries (and even millennia) in very dry regions might be less likely to use complex tonality. Whereas many factors are involved in how languages become tonal, there is much we do not know about those factors. So the way to start to test the hypothesis was by simply looking at the world's languages that have complex tonality. Are they less likely to occur in dry regions? The answer is yes. Languages with complex tonality have not developed in very dry regions, as far as we can tell, even after controlling for a variety of confounding factors like the fact that most languages, regardless of tonality, are spoken in humid and equatorial regions. With two colleagues, I demonstrated this point in a 2015 study in the *Proceedings of the National Academy of Sciences.* The study instigated much debate, and many linguists were not convinced that dry air impacts whether languages develop complex tonality, stressing for example that languages without complex tone also use pitch in intricate ways. For instance, as I noted before, in English we increase the frequency of vocal cord vibration when asking questions. Still, such uses of pitch typically require less precision over short durations than the uses of pitch required to contrast the meaning of / ma / in four different ways. While the topic remains controversial, some linguists now consider it possible that ambient air impacts how languages have evolved. Assuming for the moment that this hypothesis is on the right track, the spoken sounds we must learn to discriminate vary in part because of the environmental conditions in which our linguistic ancestors lived. English speakers, for instance, notoriously struggle with learning complex tones and even struggle with perceptually discriminating them because they need not cognitively group pitch in such ways to speak English. It may be that environmental factors have helped to foster such disparities in categorization, over the long-term.[19]

While we are all familiar with the adage that "correlation is not causation," correlations often gesture in the direction of causal connections that can be supported through other methods, though sometimes those connections are indirect. (For instance, ice cream sales and drownings correlate through an indirect relationship motivating the increase in both: higher temperatures.) More exploration of this topic is required via novel approaches. The innovative methods adapted by Nölle and others, in the exploration of the role environment plays on language and thought, is encouraging in that it suggests a new generation of researchers may explore such topics in ingenious ways. In contrast to just a decade ago, some language researchers now believe that such exploration is warranted.[20]

Conclusion: Ecology and Evolution

As I noted earlier in the chapter, adaptation to extensive ecological variation is arguably humanity's greatest trick. We are the only species found in every major habitat on the world's surface. Our adaptation extends to our genes, as evidenced by sweating profiles, skin color, and body size differences across populations. Much more critically, it extends to our behaviors in conscious and nonconscious ways, as evidenced by the Norwegians' appreciation of cod fish oil and the ability of Amazonians to remove poison from manioc, among countless other examples. Given the pervasiveness of human adaptation, it would perhaps be more surprising to find that languages do not adapt to ecological factors.

What is clear is that languages are adaptive in many ways. Some of the adaptation is obvious, for instance the fact that words for snow vary across languages, in both obvious and fine-grained ways. Some of it is much less obvious, for instance the use of spatial terminology that is affected by the physical environment in which languages evolve. Some of it is clearly evident only from large-scale quantitative tests, which have just recently come into vogue in language research. While I have focused here on large-scale quantitative tests related to the physical environment, other large-scale tests have suggested how languages' grammars adapt to external social, as opposed to physical, pressures. Some of the social influences on grammars will be discussed in Chapter 6.

With luck, time will tell us the precise extent to which languages, like other aspects of human behavior, are adaptive. As noted, the study of cultural evolution is demonstrating the subtle ways in which human behavior and thought are adaptive and therefore vary across environments. Many adaptive tools and behaviors were not developed intentionally, but rather were selected for with time as they proved more successful. Think of it this way. For any given ecological challenge, individuals within and across cultures are bound to generate all sorts of behaviors to try to address the challenge. Some of these behaviors are seemingly random, much like random mutations in genetic replication. In the case of manioc processing, for example, it is quite possible that the first folks to soak the plant, or to squeeze out its juice prior to cooking it, were considered strange for that behavior. Or perhaps they did so accidentally, much like those who first fermented alcoholic drinks. Yet some of the behaviors proved more successful at treating the plant's toxicity than others. With time, the successful variations would naturally have been selected for by people longing to eat manioc, much as genes can be selected for depending on environmental factors. The selection of some behaviors out of a pool of random behavioral variants is essential to the evolution of cultures as they adapt to particular niches and challenges. Critically, the selection happens regardless of whether people realize why their behavior is evolving in the way that it is. What I have suggested in this chapter and in other work, like some other contemporary researchers, is that language is another aspect of human behavior in which we can see adaptive processes at work. Some features in languages can be selected for in a probabilistic and gradual manner, like other aspects of human behavior, because those features are slightly better adapted to certain environments. Successful adaptation could be due to distinct but related pressures. For example, some types of sounds may require less effort to produce in some environments, and some word types make communication a bit more efficient in certain environments.

Critically, we are only becoming aware of the potential extent of linguistic adaptation as we study data from thousands of diverse languages. Although linguists still disagree about the extent of environmental adaptation evident in languages, a growing number believe that we must begin to more seriously consider environmental factors if we are to more fully understand language and associated cognitive processes. In a paper on the topic, a team led by linguist Christian Bentz drew the same conclusion when discussing how language change should be modeled. "Language diversity cannot be understood without modelling the pressures that physical, ecological and social factors exert on language users in different environments across the globe," they concluded.[21] Given that such factors were never really included in traditional models of language, one wonders how much our understanding of language will change in the coming years as researchers begin to more seriously consider how languages adapt to their social and physical environments. In Chapter 6 we examine some discoveries demonstrating how distinctive social environments, including the face-to-face environment in which conversation typically occurs, can help to shape language. As we will see, these discoveries help to reveal how people think as they talk.

6

Seeing Speech

THE WIDESPREAD INTRODUCTION of face masks during the COVID pandemic, for all its benefits to public health, did make communication a bit more difficult in some contexts. During a portion of the pandemic, I taught college students while both they and I wore face masks. This was tricky at times, despite the high-quality microphone I used and the high-fidelity speaker systems in the classroom. It was so tricky because, well, we could not see each other's mouths as we spoke to each other. During the pandemic many people became acutely aware that we are all lip-readers. Maybe we do not lip-read as well as people who have practiced it extensively, but we all do it throughout the day.

When we are in noisy environments, we pay particularly close attention to the lips of the people with whom we are conversing. Often the visual information we gather is critical to understanding a word. In a crowded restaurant, maybe you do not hear whether your dining companion said "father" or "bother" because someone knocked over a glass at a nearby table. In most cases the context in a sentence allows us to easily decipher which of two similar-sounding words was uttered, but certainly not in all cases. In some instances speakers' lip and visible tongue movements are particularly critical. Even if you have not taken a course in phonetics, you have a lifetime of experience with face-to-face interactions. You know, for instance, that in the first sound of "father," the bottom lip touches the top incisors, while in the first sound of "bother" the bottom lip touches the top lip. The first sound in "father" is a labiodental consonant, as discussed in Chapter 5, while the first in "bother" is a bilabial consonant. The associations between the movements you see on people's mouths and the sound waves you hear while you see those movements are critical to speech perception. Obviously one cannot draw such associations when conversing over the phone or with a person who is wearing a face mask, which can make speech comprehension feel a bit more onerous—unless, for example, you are blind and quite used to communicating without visual assistance. Face-to-face interactions continue to be the default form of communication across the world's cultures and were the default before *Homo sapiens* ever left Africa. As a result, speech perception benefits from the key kinds of stimuli we obtain during face-to-face interactions: sounds emanating from people's mouths and visual information emanating from their bodies—primarily their mouths but not entirely, as we will see a bit later.

The Face-to-Face Environment

The conversational benefit of information written on people's mouths is perhaps best underscored by something known as the McGurk effect, first uncovered by researchers in the 1970s. In the last few decades the effect has been observed in all sorts of experimental conditions, and it is easy to replicate even in a classroom context. In my courses I sometimes play an audio clip of someone saying "ba" repeatedly. At the same time, I show students a video of the same person repeating what appears to be "ga." Since the audio clips and the video clips are synced perfectly, students hear "ba" exactly when the person on the screen appears to say "ga." As the students watch and listen, I ask them to write down the syllable that they are hearing. You might guess that students write "ba," or perhaps complain that what they are hearing does not match the video. Yet that is not what happens. They write down the syllables without complaint, but what they write down is not "ba." Most often they write "da." I then ask them to close their eyes and listen to the same audio file as it repeats over and over. As they do so, a wave of smiles or looks of surprise works its way through the class. They immediately recognize that they have been hearing "ba" the whole time, but have been deceived by their eyes. They are then asked to open and close their eyes as the audio file repeats itself. They find that they hear "ba" when their eyes are closed and "da" (or something like that) when their eyes are open. Remarkably, even if you are well aware of what is happening, the visual stimuli continue to play tricks on what you think you are hearing. I have been aware of the McGurk effect for many years, but I am no less susceptible to it. When I open and close my eyes during the exercise, the audio file seems to change from "da" to "ba" as I do so, over and over. On an intellectual level I know that only "ba" is being played, but this makes no difference to my hearing. Our speech perception does not merely consist of sound frequencies hitting our tympanic membranes (eardrums) and then being transmitted, via the cochlea and a series of nerves, to the brain. Speech perception is a holistic process that integrates visual and auditory information in the cerebral cortex. This is true across cultures and has apparently characterized speech perception since humans lived only in Africa. Face-to-face interaction is the default form of language, after all, so it makes sense that humans would be visually attuned to the faces of others. However, as we saw in the last chapter, languages vary in terms of how much they rely on some sound types made with the lips, implying that speakers of some languages may need to pay a bit more attention to the mouths of others.[1]

We are also attuned to the hands and arms of those with whom we are speaking. As already discussed, much work has shown that manual gestures are more critical to speech than we once realized. In extreme cases like Nheengatú temporal gestures, discussed in Chapter 1, one could argue that knowledge of certain gestures is required to speak a language in a "grammatically correct" manner. More widely, gestures can reflect underlying cognitive processes that occur while someone is speaking, for instance when an English speaker gestures behind themselves while talking about the past. Gestures are also used to emphasize verbal cues during speech. We often use larger manual gestures when speaking loudly, and some particularly exaggerated gestures can correspond to points of emphasis during spoken sentences. This coordinated use of gestures and vocal emphasis cues listeners, drawing their attention to key points in the verbal stream. In the face-to-face environment, people have learned to pay attention not only to the acoustic stream emanating from others' mouths, but also to the closely associated manual stream of gestures emanating from their hands. This aspect of communication, the paying attention to speakers' manual gestures while simultaneously reading their faces, results in a newly discovered kind of manual interference in speech perception. Coined the "manual McGurk effect," the phenomenon was uncovered via a series of experiments published in 2021. Below I will discuss one of these experiments, which tested how the perception of manual gestures influences the auditory perception of word-level stress. First, though, some relevant background on word-level stress is necessary. While the experiment in question was conducted with speakers of Dutch, I will use English to illustrate the phenomenon since it has the same relevant characteristics of word-level stress.[2]

One of the key components of stressed syllables in English words is that their pitch is higher. "Pitch" refers to the frequency at which the vocal cords vibrate during the production of a sound. (Technically, "pitch" refers to the perception of that frequency, but the word is commonly used to refer to the actual frequency of vibration of a speaker's vocal cords.) As noted in the discussion of tone in Chapter 5, many languages use precise pitch patterns to disentangle the meanings of words. Although languages like English and Dutch do not do this, they do use pitch for many other, arguably less complex, purposes. These purposes include word-level stress: stressed syllables tend to have slightly higher pitch. Relatedly, stressed syllables tend to be louder. "Loudness" also technically refers to a perceptual quality, one that in speech is determined largely by the amplitude of someone else's voice. When speakers' vocal cords hit each other with more energy, traveling a greater distance from each other during each vibration, the amplitude of their voices is increased and they sound louder. This increased loudness is used to, among other things, emphasize particular syllables in speech. In addition to their increased loudness and pitch, a stressed syllable in a word is typically longer compared to unstressed syllables. While there are other aspects of word-level stress in English (for instance, unstressed vowels are often reduced to a vowel that sounds like "uh"), these three features—increased pitch, loudness, and duration—are critical. This is also true in many other languages, including Dutch. The features are so critical to word-level stress that they can actually be used to distinguish words in some cases. In fact, in English these acoustic cues are used to disentangle many pairs of nouns and verbs that are written the same way. For instance, if you say "CON-vert" you are using a noun, referring to someone who has been converted. In contrast, if you say "con-VERT" you are referring to the action of converting someone. A "PER-mit" is issued to someone to allow them to do something, but you "per-MIT" someone to do something. If you say "OB-ject" you are referring to a noun, a thing. But if you say "ob-JECT" you are using a verb to refer to an expression of opposition. Not all the meaning associations between such verbs and nouns are so transparent. Still, English contains well over one hundred words that change meaning depending on where the stress is placed, including "record," "abstract," "defect," "update," and so on.

What does all this have to do with manual interference in auditory perception? Well, one way in which gestures are integrated with the phonetic articulation of language is through their coordination with stress. If you watch someone give a public lecture, you will often observe that they gesture more notably when they are emphasizing particular points or words. In fact, the gestural motions often include downward hand movements that coincide with stress in words and syllables. One experimental study conducted in 2007 found that people produce "beat gestures," as well as eyebrow movements and head nods, in association with words that are emphasized more than surrounding words. The study even found that when listeners heard two words and were asked to rate how acoustically "prominent" each was, they were biased by visual information. When they observed someone making a manual gesture or an eyebrow movement on only one of the words, they were more likely to perceive that word as having greater acoustic prominence. The gestures they observed impacted how their brains processed the sounds they heard.[3]

Newer experimental evidence suggests that the perception of manual gestures influences how people perceive auditory stimuli in more subtle ways also. Twenty-six speakers of Dutch were asked to listen to made-up Dutch-sounding words. The words had two syllables each, for instance *bagpif*. The first vowel was presented in such a way that emphasis was ambiguous, sometimes sounding more like a typical stressed "a" vowel in Dutch and at other times sounding unstressed. The unstressed variety of this vowel in Dutch has a slightly different quality than the stressed variety and is also shorter, much like in English. The made-up words varied along a continuum, so that some words were particularly ambiguous—that is, they were not clearly stressed or unstressed. The Dutch participants watched and listened to a video of someone producing the made-up words. Critically, the person speaking was also gesturing up and down with his right hand. While the participants were not asked to focus on the speaker's gestures, those gestures clearly affected what they heard. As noted above, speakers often produce manual downbeat gestures in which the hand moves down when they are accentuating something. This association between downbeats and emphasis appeared to affect what the Dutch participants were actually hearing. When the downbeat occurred on the first syllable of a made-up word like *bagpif*, the ambiguous vowel in that syllable was actually perceived in ways that were more consistent with a typical stressed syllable. When speakers were asked to select whether they had heard *bagpif* or *baagpif*, the second version having a long first vowel (consistent with typical Dutch stress), they reported hearing *baagpif* more often when they had witnessed a downward gesture on the first syllable. In other words, their visual perception affected their auditory perception as their brains integrated the two streams of information. This is a similar phenomenon to the McGurk effect, but in this case the visual stimuli that affected the auditory perception originated not in a speaker's mouth but in their hands. For this reason the authors of the study coined the term "manual McGurk effect" to refer to the phenomenon.

Note that we would not expect this cognitive phenomenon to surface for speakers of all languages in the same way it surfaces for Dutch speakers, since many languages do not have the same types of word-level stress patterns.

The McGurk effect and the newly uncovered manual McGurk effect demonstrate that the perception of speech is affected in subtle ways by the face-to-face environment that has been the basic form of human communication for dozens of millennia, shaping how we produce speech. It also shapes how we listen. We are active listeners, offering not just vocalizations but also gestures to let speakers know that we are paying attention to them and that we agree, or perhaps do not, with the sentiments they are expressing. The gestures may be facial, as we nod our heads or move our eyebrows in accordance with what we are hearing. These observations may seem commonsensical, but if you ever decide to omit such gestures or vocalizations during conversation you will be instantly reminded of just how critical they are. The person with whom you are conversing will be quickly dismayed by your lack of such responses.

It is not just perceptual and cognitive factors that are shaped by these face-to-face pressures. Speech production has also evolved to address such pressures. Face-to-face talking is the default form of communication across the world's cultures, but as language researchers like Nick Enfield have argued over the last decade, linguists themselves have often lost sight of the fact that language is shaped by the pressures of face-to-face talking. Enfield's research on landscape terms was discussed in Chapter 2. He has stressed in other work that planning and articulating phrases takes place primarily as we listen to others and (typically) as we pay attention to their faces. This is because, in addition to being face-to-face in nature, talking is organized into turn-taking. As we listen to someone talk, we are often thinking about what we will say in our next turn. While there is some cross-cultural variation in how face-to-face turn-taking works, turn-based conversation between two individuals nevertheless appears to be the default worldwide. Intriguingly, worldwide tendencies in this turn-taking have only recently been discovered, tendencies that reflect common ways in which humans plan and articulate their sentences. I would like to focus on one of these tendencies, one that is clear across cultures.[4]

First, though, answer this question. How much time do you let pass after someone else's turn in a conversation before you start talking? Or, conversely, how much time do the people you speak to typically let pass before they start talking after you have stopped? Most people are well aware that it becomes socially unacceptable to leave someone "hanging" by failing to participate in a conversation, by remaining silent after another person has stopped talking. In fact, it does not take long at all before this gap of silence can come across as rude and lead to miscommunication that requires social repair of some kind. In 1989 sociologist Gail Jefferson noted that few English speakers allow more than one second of silence before taking their turn in a conversation after the person to whom they are speaking goes silent. If a silence of greater than one second creeps its way into a conversation, it is often an indicator that the conversation is not going well or that one or both participants are ready to be done with it. Jefferson's analysis was based on thousands of conversations, and the pattern was very robust. It has also been observed in much subsequent research.[5]

Yet one second is not some magic number, and the truth is that we rarely let gaps between turns take that long in a conversation. In many cases there is even overlap between turns: we start talking before another person has stopped talking as we perceive cues that their turn is coming to an end. Linguists Stephen Levinson and Francisco Torreira conducted a study of over twenty thousand transitions between speakers conversing in English. The length of the transitions—the gaps between turns in conversations—varied from about negative one second to about one second. (Transitions of less than zero seconds represent cases of speaker overlap or interruption.) The vast majority of transitions, however, lasted somewhere in the neighborhood of 200 milliseconds. In other words, in English conversations people tend to take only about one-fifth of a second to start talking after another has stopped. A fair amount of psycholinguistic research suggests that people take longer than one-fifth of a second to plan a phrase or sentence. This means that face-to-face conversation is such a well-oiled machine that speakers can anticipate the end of another speaker's turn and begin planning their own next phrase before the other person's turn has ended.[6]

This pattern is not unique to English, either. Separate studies on German and Dutch have also observed that most transitions between turns in conversation last somewhere around 200 milliseconds. These are closely related languages, but studies with unrelated languages have uncovered similar though not identical results. In a 2009 study on ten languages representing a few unrelated families, English was found to have a fairly typical mean transition time. For that study, researchers focused not on all transitions between speakers, but on the transitions between yes / no questions and the responses to those questions. The average duration of a transition between such questions and their responses in English was found to be 236 milliseconds. The shortest average transition observed was in Japanese, at only 7 milliseconds. The longest observed, at 469 milliseconds, was for Danish. Japanese and Danish appear to reside at extreme ends of the continuum of conversation transitions. (The delay between yes / no questions and their responses depends in part on the nature of the response: "yes" answers tend to arrive much quicker in English, "no" answers take about twice as much time to arrive, and other responses like "I don't know" take even longer.)[7]

Much of the research I have covered in this book points to the ways in which languages vary more than we once thought. There are no language universals agreed on by linguists, as stressed in the Introduction to this book. There is also no widely agreed-on evidence that languages take the structure they take because of a specific language gene or set of language genes. Speech is startlingly diverse in ways we have missed or glossed over in much research on language, partially because of an intense focus on such a small subset of languages. Yet as the present discussion underscores, we have also missed or glossed over some interesting ways in which languages are similar. It is just that the kinds of similarity we have failed to appreciate are of a very different sort from the kinds of similarity we have aimed to find in linguistics. Many linguists have spent untold hours looking for universal patterns in the grammars of the world's languages, with little success. While such commonalities may not have been uncovered, at least not to the satisfaction of some linguists, there are other clear commonalities that we have overlooked. These include patterns in turn-taking in face-to-face conversations. Perhaps we have taken this face-to-face environment for granted, overlooking all the interesting ways in which it helps to shape communication. The face-to-face environment puts limitations on the kinds of turns that people can take while communicating and even places some limits on the duration of the transitions between those turns. Languages follow the same general pattern: people take turns talking, and they only stop for extremely brief periods between turns. All populations share the same cerebral hardware that allows us to process what we are hearing while planning what we want to say next. In the light of that similarity, though, it is worth stressing that there are apparently differences across cultures in terms of how people plan their next phrase while simultaneously listening to others. For example, Japanese speakers and Danish speakers vary along this dimension, at least judging from the time they take between turns.

Why is it that seemingly basic aspects of speech, like the visual attention paid to gestures or the way people process turn-taking, are only now being illuminated? In my view, we are only now exploring in earnest certain basic facts about language because our enterprise has long been too focused on two-dimensional representations of speech. Writing is an incredibly powerful tool, obviously, and allows us to do things like phonetically transcribe preliterate languages. This transcription has enabled linguists to document languages even in the absence of audio recordings or video recordings. This is great in many respects, but writing came to be seen by some as an almost perfect distillation of communication. This overreliance and overemphasis on the written form arguably yielded an undue focus on certain exotic features of language—say, grammatical characteristics like the passive voice (which is not actually that common in conversations)—while simultaneously deemphasizing some very basic and pervasive features of language, for instance the fact that it is governed by face-to-face turn-taking and produced with elaborate manual and facial gestures. Only now, as many linguistic analyses are based on video and audio data (and often on quantitative analyses of them), not just written data, are we growing to appreciate what we have missed. And there are other sorts of data we have only now begun considering. As one of many examples, my own current research, conducted with collaborators at the University of California San Diego, examines how the sounds of speech emit aerosol particles that can carry airborne pathogens. This is hardly an avenue of research that follows from an exclusive focus on the written word.

As noted in the following section, the social context in which communication happens is a powerful shaper not just of phenomena like turn-taking and the visual perception of gestures that helps our brains process speech. In addition to the basic face-to-face environment, the more specific cultural context in which a language is spoken can, it turns out, impact speech in interesting ways.[8]

Specific Sociocultural Environments Can Impact Grammar

While there are clear commonalities in how speakers construct conversations through turn-taking, there are clear differences as well. Japanese speakers take less time to reply to questions than Danish speakers do, for instance. This is an interesting fact and likely reflects some differences between Japanese and Danish cultures. A Japanese child adopted by Danish parents would of course learn to speak Danish, and their postquestion delays would be similar to those of other Danish speakers. I am simply highlighting the obvious: there is no genetic motivation for such a behavioral difference across populations, so it must be cultural.

Beyond the minor cultural effects on how turn-taking in conversations work, bearing in mind the general patterns that exist worldwide in such turn-taking, other cultural effects on language also exist. There are obvious cultural effects on words—for example, Karitiâna has no native word for sandwich or burrito since the Karitiâna do not traditionally eat such items. What about cultural effects on grammar, the structure of a language, as opposed to its words? In fact, evidence increasingly shows that cultural-specific social categories can impact a key part of grammar: its morphemes. Morphemes are units that have distinguishable meanings, like word roots and suffixes. For instance, in our discussion of references to time in Chapter 1, I noted how languages vary with respect to the kinds of suffixes they use to denote when a particular event happened in relation to the time at which someone is speaking.

Such temporal morphemes are commonly referred to as tense markers. Yet there is an impressive array of morpheme types in the world's languages, most of which you have probably never heard about.

Many volumes have been written on the topic of morphology, the study of morphemes, with all sorts of interesting morpheme types presented from around the world. Let me offer you two types you might not be familiar with, both of which come from Karitiâna. One of them is part of a broad category of morphemes that linguists refer to as evidentials. Evidentials are morphemes, usually suffixes or prefixes, that reveal how the speaker came across the information they are talking about. Evidentials often refer to whether the speaker directly observed an event they are describing (in which case their evidence is strong) or whether they only heard about the event (in which case their evidence is weaker):

(1) *a takatat-saryt*
"You went, I heard."

In this sentence we see that there is a -*saryt* suffix that can be attached to verbs in Karitiâna, in this case the verb *takatat* ("went / go"). If a speaker adds this suffix to the verb, it means they heard that a given event happened but did not actually witness it. Their evidence is indirect and based on hearsay. Another suffix in the language is used when a speaker only thinks that something happened; in other words, their evidence is based on introspection. This all may seem a bit unusual, but consider how often in English we preface our own sentences with caveats like "I think that" or "I heard that." These expressions are ubiquitous in English and clearly serve a similar function to the required evidential suffixes of Karitiâna.

Another morpheme type that exists in many languages is referred to as a "desiderative" marker, which denotes that a speaker desires that a given event take place. In Karitiâna the desiderative morpheme is also a suffix attached to verbs, as in the next example:

(2) *yn itat-awak*
"I want to go."

The *-awak* suffix in this case lets the listener know that the speaker wants to leave or go somewhere. Such desiderative markers do not exist in English, but here again we use common expressions for the same purpose. We often preface verbs like "go" with "I want to," for example. We will come back to the case of "I want to" in just a bit. Although morphemes like evidentials and desideratives and many other types are absent in English, they are fairly common in the world's languages. Similar functional and communicative pressures, common to most or perhaps all cultures, motivate their existence across so many languages. Yet morphemes vary widely in terms of how common they are, hinting that communicative needs can vary in culture-specific ways that help to shape grammar. In fact, some morpheme types only exist in a single language and are due to specific communicative pressures in particular contexts. For instance, linguist Nick Evans has described types of suffixes in some Australian languages that refer to the unique characteristics of the kinship systems of the cultures that speak those languages. In discussing such phenomena, Evans offers the following insights: "A complex of invisible hand processes . . . lead to the emergence of structured systems that reflect culturally salient categories, connections, and oppositions. The result of these processes is a series of linguistic structures that, although common in the Australian culture area, are unknown anywhere else in the world."[9] What are these processes governed by "invisible hands"? Well, the simplest way to think of it is that culturally salient phenomena are referred to frequently via words in conversations, and this conversational frequency and associated predictability leads to those words becoming part of the grammar of a language. To understand how that happens, we need a brief diversion into another major finding from language research: with time, highly predictable words are shortened and may turn into prefixes and suffixes.

Back in the 1930s, Harvard linguist and statistician George Zipf made a series of groundbreaking observations on language. Most famously, perhaps, he noticed that some words are exceedingly frequent in language, an order of magnitude more frequent than most words. This pattern is quite regular and is referred to as "Zipf's law." Basically, it suggests that in a given language, the most frequent word is about twice as frequent as the second most frequent word. It is about three times as common as the third most frequent word, about four times as common as the fourth most frequent word, and so on. This is oversimplifying the observation a bit, but overall the generalization holds quite neatly across all the languages and data sets that have been examined. Besides word frequency, Zipf's law also describes the distribution of many other phenomena in the world around us. It also describes individual sounds. In one of my own studies, I observed that if we look at a set of common words for any language, we will observe that one sound in the language will occur much more frequently than other sounds, often about twice as often as the second most common sound. For example, in many languages the [m] sound is much more common than any other sound in everyday words. Zipf offered another key insight relevant to our current discussion: the most frequent words tend to be short ones like "the" and "of." In Zipf's words, "The magnitude of words tends, on the whole, to stand in an inverse (not necessarily proportionate) relationship to the number of occurrences."[10] The less frequent the word, the greater its length in terms of number of sounds. Very common words tend to be very short.

What is impressive about Zipf's observations is just how well they hold across different languages and data sets; they have been replicated time and again in the decades since he published his ideas. Extensive debate continues, however, as to why the observations hold so neatly. With respect to the fact that frequent words tend to be "phonetically reduced" or shortened over time, research now offers strong evidence that this happens because highly frequent words are quite predictable. Essentially, when we say very common words, our listeners can predict what word is coming out of our mouths early in the word. This means that we are biased to shorten words since much of the phonetic effort they require is a bit unnecessary. After all, one of the key biases that shapes words and languages more generally is the principle of less effort: all things being equal, we would rather expend less effort to get our thoughts across.

Work by University of California Berkeley cognitive scientist Steven Piantadosi and colleagues suggests that a word's overall predictability is a better indicator of its likelihood of being shorter than its frequency alone. In other words, the predictability of a word is not just a function of how common it is. While highly common words tend to be a bit predictable, determining how predictable they are depends on the context. For example, if I say, "She stepped onto the," you know that certain words are likely to occur next. I might say, "She stepped onto the train," or "bus," or "platform," or "stage." But I probably will not say, "She stepped onto the building." (Even though I could, perhaps in a narrative about a Lilliputian woman.) Even though "building" is a common word, it is much less predictable in this context. In this sentence, anyhow, a word like "bus" contributes less information than an unexpected word like "building." As we hear a sequence like "stepped onto the," our brains are already expecting a word like "bus," or a few other alternatives, to occur next. Intriguingly, if you study all the contexts in which a given word like "bus" occurs, by looking at millions of words in sentences people have actually said, you can see how informative that word is.

Words that more commonly occur in highly predictable contexts are less informative, on average, when compared to words that do not occur in such predictable contexts. Words that are on average less predictable are generally more informative. For instance, if a word like "bus" tends to occur very commonly and predictably at the end of only a few phrases (e.g., "stepped onto the"), it will be less informative than some words of equal overall frequency in the language. In many common idioms the last word is entirely predictable. If I say, "That's it, that's the last _____," you know that the next word I say is likely to be "straw." While "straw" occurs in other contexts too, its extreme predictability in this idiom means that it is not a particularly informative word in this context. It is not telling the listener anything that they would be unlikely to guess before it was said.[11]

In the study of Piantadosi and colleagues, involving the analysis of the co-occurrence of words in massive data sets in ten languages, it was observed that the mean informativity of a given word is a very clear predictor of how long that word is. Words that are relatively predictable across all the contexts in which they occur tend to be shorter than less predictable and more informative words. This does not mean that Zipf was wrong, since highly frequent words are generally more predictable. If two words have the same overall frequency in a given data set, the word that tends to occur in more predictable contexts will be shorter, since it has less informativity. The less informative word will be shorter because speakers can communicate their intended meaning to listeners even if they say the word quickly or shorten it. To take this to the extreme, imagine if "straw" only ever occurred in the expression "that's the last straw," and conversely "that's the last" was only ever used before "straw." In this made-up scenario, there would be no point in ever saying "straw": once a person said "that's the last," "straw" would be superfluous. Obviously in actual speech words are not so uninformative. Words do vary, however, in terms of how unpredictable and informative they are.

As noted previously, suffixes and prefixes are morphemes that were once separate words. This is part of a phenomenon called "grammaticalization," which linguists like Joan Bybee have shed light on in the last few decades. Basically, as words get used in very predictable contexts, they become shorter due to their lower informativity. Sometimes those shorter words also become obligatory. In these cases it is as though the words get reduced phonetically because of their regular occurrence and predictability across multiple similar contexts, but it is also weird if speakers leave them out completely. Suffixes and prefixes are essentially shortened and obligatory forms of what were once separate words that occurred in a very predictable place. While in most cases the actual words that led to a given suffix or prefix are lost to time, in other cases we can see a transition in process, as words turn into morphemes. To take one of many examples, in English we often say, "I want to" or "I am going to" before a verb: "I want to eat," "I am going to eat," and the like. We say this so often, in fact, that words like "going to" are becoming shorter because of their intense predictability. If you transcribe actual English conversations, you will find that people hardly ever say "I want to" or "I am going to." Instead what you hear is "I wanna" and "I'mana." In fact, if English were an undocumented indigenous language, a linguist might initially conclude that "wanna" and "mana" are prefixes attached to the following verb. While not all phonetically reduced words become suffixes or prefixes, suffixes and prefixes come from words that were very frequent and predictable in particular contexts before or after certain words of a particular category (verbs in the case of "wanna" and "mana"). As these words are reduced with time, they are gradually grammaticalizing into suffixes and prefixes.[12]

You might be wondering how all this relates to social and cultural factors impacting grammar, since I have stated that Zipf's observations hold across every language so far tested. Yet thinking back now to the cases of exotic morphemes in some languages, for instance those Nick Evans has described in Australian languages, the reason that such kinship-based morphemes exist should now be a bit clearer. These morphemes were not invented or accepted by a committee at some point in time. Instead, speakers of these languages thought and spoke about the relevant kinship concepts so often that certain words became very frequent and predictable in particular contexts. They became phonetically reduced to the point that they were no longer separate words, but suffixes. In this way the morphemes in a grammar can be shaped by communicative forces that are unique to particular cultures, just as they can be shaped by communicative forces that are common to many of the world's cultures. The latter is true of tense suffixes, or the evidential suffix found in Karitiâna and many other languages, or countless other examples of common suffixes and prefixes.

An increasingly common adage among contemporary linguists is "Grammar is shaped by usage." There are variants to this adage, such as "Words that get used together are fused together." The new work of computational researchers like Piantadosi and others helps us to understand the cognitive motivations for the shortening and fusing of words, while the ethnographically informed work of fieldworkers like Nick Evans helps us to understand the sorts of culturally specific forces that come to shape grammatical phenomena like exotic-seeming suffixes. Relatedly, other ethnographically informed field research has demonstrated that certain languages are *unlikely* to contain particular grammatical phenomena because of cultural factors. For instance, Daniel Everett (my father) has documented a series of features that are lacking in the grammar of Pirahã, an Amazonian language that has all sorts of uncommon features. In a 2005 paper, he synthesized many of the inter-esting features he had observed in the previous decades during which he had studied the language, including a complete lack of precise number words and singular or plural suffixes. (Numerous scholars ver-ified this through basic arithmetic experiments.) The crucial point here is that the Pirahã people show no interest in number words and explicitly avoid them due to their status as foreign words. Unlike most cultures, the Pirahã did not adopt number words when they came into contact with them. Given that their culture has traditionally prohibited the use of outside numbers, it is perhaps less surprising that it also lacks plural or singular suffixes. If you never talk about a concept, there will be no exceedingly common and predictable word denoting that concept, and no way for a morpheme to develop out of that word.[13]

Given that communicative needs are similar across cultures but also vary in culturally specific ways, all this research suggests that we cannot understand languages and their grammars completely if we do not ex-plore the distinct cultures in which those grammars are used and in which they develop. A given culture may require speakers to talk about some concepts frequently, but not necessarily concepts that are common in other cultures. This is a key finding from field research in linguistics over the last few decades, contravening the once-popular suggestion that grammars are shaped primarily by universal factors. Other kinds of social variation, beyond culturally specific factors like the criticality of certain kin relationships in some Australian groups, may also affect grammars in ways we are only now coming to see. For example, research by psychologists Gary Lupyan and Rick Dale suggests that languages spoken by small populations tend to develop more complex morpho-logical systems, systems that include things like elaborate prefixes and suffixes, when compared to the languages of larger populations. This pattern only became evident once they surveyed the suffixes and prefixes of about two thousand languages, and the implications of the pattern they uncovered are debated. One interpretation of the pattern is that, since widely spoken languages tend to have many second-language speakers who learn the relevant languages as adults, the languages evolve to accommodate the cognitive needs of adult learners. Since adults learn second languages less efficiently than children learning their native language, it makes sense that languages with so many nonnative speakers would eventually develop less complex prefixing and suffixing. Experimental work also demonstrates that when people are asked to make up languages, larger groups of experimental participants end up developing languages that have less exotic suffixes and prefixes. Like Lupyan and Dale's research, such experimental work suggests that languages evolve in ways that are sensitive to the number of speakers who are using them. Just as they may gradually adapt to physical environments in subtle ways over the long term, as suggested in Chapter 5, languages can also adapt to social environments in subtle ways. Yet they also adapt in culturally specific ways, as certain words and the concepts they convey become highly frequent in some populations to the point that in some cases they end up turning into suffixes or prefixes.[14]

Conclusion: The Natural Habitat of Language

You might excuse linguists for missing the sort of pattern uncovered in Lupyan and Dale's work, prior to the availability of large data sets such as those on which they relied. Yet it is perhaps surprising that the study of language has missed until relatively recently some of the other phenomena discussed in this chapter. Why are many linguists just now realizing the extent to which grammars are shaped by communicative pressures associated with the face-to-face environment, or by factors that vary more markedly across cultures? One part of the explanation, noted above, is that we have often been fixated on two-dimensional representations of speech. Another part is likely that, during much of the twentieth century in particular, language researchers were focused primarily on studying things like grammatical patterns in idealized and written sentences, and often in Indo-European languages or the languages of other WEIRD populations. With notable exceptions, such as studies of sociolinguistic patterns, mainly in neighborhoods in the United States, we were not sufficiently focused on the actual sociocultural environments in which conversation is produced. Until we began equally weighting data from truly distinct cultures, cultures that can differ markedly in terms of their reliance on particular concepts, we were prone to missing some key observations about speech. To quote Nick Enfield, because of this focus on nonnaturalistic data divorced from conversations in diverse cultural environments, "even the most accomplished linguists have little to say about how language is used in its natural habitat."[15] Today, more and more linguists are focusing on the natural habitat of language in cultures around the globe.

7

The Nasal Start to "Nose"

SOMEONE ONCE POINTED out to stand-up comic Jim Gaffigan, after he had made a joke about the obesity of whales, that whales were not actually fat but were simply covered in blubber. In retelling this story of being corrected, Gaffigan finds humor in the person's interpretation of whales' nonfatness. In his words: "Blubber? That's like the opposite of muscle. It goes, like, muscular, toned, flabby, and then like a mile away is blubber. If fat made a noise it would be blubber." In this last instance of "blubber," Gaffigan draws out the first syllable, so it sounds more like "bluhh-ber." His audience laughs, the notion that the word "blubber" sounds fat clearly resonating with them.

How can a word sound like fat, which is noiseless? It is a lot easier to understand how a word can sound like a particular noise someone wants to convey symbolically. In childhood we are taught about onomatopoeia, when words vaguely resemble the noises they represent. "Roar," "bark," "splash," and other examples are often used to drive home the point in elementary school. Supposedly these words sound like real-world auditory stimuli. If they did so very well, we might expect that more languages would have these very same words, or words close to them, since the sounds of lions roaring, or dogs barking, or things splashing do not differ depending on the language one speaks. Yet onomatopoeic words vary substantially across and even within languages. And a given instance of onomatopoeia can represent many distinct sounds. The "banging" on a drum and the "banging" of one's head against a wall sound similar, perhaps, but certainly not identical. Still, most or all spoken languages seem to have onomatopoeic words of some kind, and the variation in such terms does not change the fact that words like "bark" emulate a noise or category of noises in nature in a way that most words do not. People understand that the sounds produced when someone says "splash" resemble at least a little the sounds of, for example, a child splashing water around in a pool. (This resemblance likely relates to the very high aperiodic frequencies created in both instances, but we will sct that discussion aside.)

This reasoning does not really apply to blubber, though, since fat is not a sound. Is there still some way in which the word "blubber" directly resembles fat? Some might argue that hitting a fatty surface makes a noise that resembles the sounds of "blubber," but this seems debatable. Furthermore, other words are similar phonetically to "blubber" in a key way while also denoting concepts that are at least tangentially related to fat. These include "blimp," "blob," and "bloat." What is going on here? There seems to be a way in which the *bl-* sequence at the beginning of these words, the sequence that Gaffigan stretched out verbally, refers to round or oval things. Yet *bl-* is not a prefix with a clear meaning, and you cannot attach it to any noun of your choice in order to signify roundness or ovality or fatness. What is *bl-*, then? It is what linguists call a phonestheme, a sequence of sounds that quasi-systematically encodes a loose meaning. Phonesthemes are interesting because, like cases of onomatopoeia, they represent instances in which meaning is connected to particular sounds in ways that are not completely arbitrary. They are an example of sound-meaning systematicity, though they are not iconic in the same way that onomatopoeia is, since the sounds of a sequence like *bl-* do not mimic some sound in the real world.

One of the key tenets of modern linguistics is that language is overwhelmingly arbitrary. By "arbitrary," I mean there is no natural or inherent connection between the sounds in words and the meaning of those words. For that reason, a word for the same thing or concept can sound very different across the world's languages. It does not matter what sounds a population uses to convey a meaning. Influential linguists have long proposed that the arbitrariness of words is one of the crucial elements of speech. These linguists were well aware of onomatopoeia; they simply believed that arbitrariness is at the core of speech while iconic elements like onomatopoeia are at the periphery. After all, onomatopoeia is arguably a bit idiosyncratic and incidental to language, seemingly not critical to its functioning or even to its development in the minds of children. Phonesthemes, which have been the subject of an increasing number of studies, fall less neatly into this perspective centered around arbitrariness, pointing instead to sound-meaning associations that are not totally arbitrary. In the case of phonesthemes like *bl-*, there is even a sort of mapping between meaning and sounds that has a tenuous basis in some physical connection. Phonesthemes, whether evocative of sounds or not, are more pervasive in speech than we once realized, and more systematic than onomatopoeia.[1]

Linguist Benjamin Bergen has drawn attention to many of the phonesthemes that exist in English. These include, *bl-*, just mentioned, but also sequences like *sn-*, *wh-*, *tr-*, *sw-*, *spr-*, and *gl-*. Let us look at these in turn. *Sn-* is used in words that are associated with the mouth or the nose, words like "snicker," "snore," "snot," and "snout." Perhaps not coincidentally, these words involve a nasal sound, made by allowing frequencies to resonate in the nasal cavity, not just the mouth. We will come back to that connection below. *Wh-*, meanwhile, is used in words referring to specific kinds of sounds, words like "whisper," "whine," "whirr," and "wheeze." *Tr-* is associated with loud or deliberate kinds of walking, for instance, "tread," "tromp," "trudge," and "trot." *Sw-* connotes actions with arcing movements via words like "swing," "sweep," "swoop," and "swipe." *Spr-* is used in words denoting actions in which there is movement away from a center, words like "spread," "spray," "sprawl," and "sprout." And in the last example considered here, *gl-* is found in a series of words related to light or vision. These include "glisten," "gleam," "glow," "glaze," and "glimmer." Phonesthemes are clearly not a rarity in English speech.

One of the interesting things about phonesthemes besides their surprising commonality is that they are not cases in which speech simply mimics sounds in nature. In the case of *gl-*, for example, the sound sequence calls to mind something visual, and it does so across sensory modalities: something audible is representing something visible. Increasingly, language researchers are realizing that such cross-modal correspondences abound in the world's spoken languages. Many words or word fragments are nonarbitrarily associated with physical qualities. Note that I say "spoken languages" and not "languages." In the case of signed and written languages, words often directly represent concepts in iconic ways, for instance when a gesture directly resembles an action or object. This fact has long been recognized, and in fact people sometimes overestimate how much signed languages are iconic. In many cases the symbols used in signed languages are pretty arbitrary too. If that were not the case, people who do not speak signed languages would be able to understand a fair amount of signed language conversations, but that is plainly not the case.

Language researchers have become more aware of the pervasive role of iconicity in linguistic thought, and more broadly the associations between certain sounds and certain meanings, through some new methods. These methods have been used to explore phenomena like phonesthemes and what linguists call "ideophones." Ideophones are words that are directly evocative of particular physical sensations. These include auditory sensations, as in the case of onomatopoeia, but also nonauditory stimuli like particular colors or movements. For instance, many ideophones include instances of reduplication, in which a word or syllable is repeated to represent an action occurring repeatedly. For example, in the Kisi language of Sierra Leone, *hábá* means "wobbly," but *hábá-hábá-hábá* means something like "prolonged wobbling." Unlike phonesthemes, ideophones serve as words by themselves. While linguists have long recognized the existence of phonesthemes and ideophones, we are only now beginning to appreciate how much of a role they play in speech in some of the world's languages.[2]

Ideophones, it turns out, can represent all sorts of sensory concepts, with varying degrees of abstraction that are somehow still tied to a physical characteristic of some kind. Some ideophones are borrowed across languages precisely because there is seemingly a natural fit between the word and the meaning perceived by speakers of different languages. Consider for example the name for the playing style of the Futbol Club Barcelona under the reign of manager Pep Guardiola, a style that was critical to the team's success for many years. The style involved, among other factors, the midfield players utilizing intricate combinations of passes as they changed positions with quick steps over short spaces. The approach could be mesmerizingly effective at times, able to cut up defenses that often seemed helpless. The name for the style, now famous among football fans worldwide, is "tiki-taka." For those of us who first heard the term from Spanish commentators during Barcelona matches, it immediately felt like a natural descriptor for what we were seeing. While there was no word for the style in English, it only took hearing "tiki-taka" once to intuit what the Spanish commentator meant. The term, however, is not Spanish in origin but was first utilized by a speaker of Basque, the non-Indo-European language spoken in the Bilbao region of Spain. In Basque, "tiki-taka" means to take light, quick steps, and there does seem to be a resemblance between the word and the sound that a series of such steps might make. Perhaps for that reason "tiki-taka" was adopted by Spanish speakers. I have heard it used frequently by English- and Portuguese-speaking football commentators and know it is used in many other languages. (In English I have even recently heard it used in basketball contexts, suggesting a greater semantic extension of the term.)

Now "tiki-taka" is a word at the core of the soccer fan's vocabulary. Whereas linguists have studied ideophones since at least the nineteenth century, and discussions have transpired about the arbitrariness or nonarbitrariness of the sounds of words since at least the time of Plato, twentieth-century inquiries into speech largely minimized the role that ideophones and other nonarbitrary correspondences between sounds and meanings play in creating words. Some of the most influential linguists of the twentieth century downplayed that role by suggesting that language was fundamentally arbitrary, that words generally have no natural connection to the meaning they represent. Perhaps this is because those linguists, like so many other prominent linguists and social scientists, were biased by a reliance on data from WEIRD populations. When we look at languages spoken by folks in non-WEIRD populations, the supposedly peripheral nature of iconic speech becomes more contestable. Many African languages have extensive sets of ideophones. This point has been noted by field linguists since the nineteenth century, but only relatively recently have attempts been made to fully understand such ideophones from a comparative, crosslinguistic perspective.[3]

In a 1930 book on Ewe, a West African language with a rich set of ideophones, the German linguist and missionary Diedrich Westermann noted, "The language is extremely rich in means of translating an impression into sound. This wealth arises from an almost irrepressible desire to mimic and to describe by one or more sounds everything heard or seen, or any impression however received. These expressions we call picture words."[4] These "picture words" would now be called ideophones. In follow-up work on Ewe ideophones many years later, linguist Felix Ameka noted that ideophones are pervasive in Ewe and also very much integrated into the grammar of the language. Some ideophones can serve as interjections in Ewe, as they often do in other languages, which can give the impression that they serve a very restricted grammatical function. As Ameka notes, though, in Ewe certain other ideophones serve as nouns, some as adjectives, others as verbs, and still others as adverbs. They function at the core of Ewe grammar and are very frequent in speech.

Nor is Ewe is alone in that respect. Languages with extensive sets of ideophones have been documented in regions including West Africa, Southeast Asia, and South America. Perhaps the most extreme case that has been documented is the Gbeya language, an African language with thousands of ideophones. Extensive research on this language was conducted in the mid-twentieth century by a linguist named William Samarin, whose work on ideophones eventually came to influence some of the scholars whose current research on ideophones is at the vanguard of the work that now questions the extent of arbitrariness in speech. (These scholars include the aforementioned Bergen as well as Mark Dingemanse, a linguist at Radboud University.) Samarin published extensively on the many ideophones in Gbeya, showing how they were far from trivial or peripheral elements in the language.[5]

In the next two sections we will look at research demonstrating how iconic language elements like ideophones, along with other nonarbitrary meaning-sound pairings, are more critical to speech than had been previously assumed. While they are critical to speech, however, the use of such elements clearly varies across populations. All people may use iconic relationships between sounds and concepts as they communicate, but speakers of languages like Gbeya appear to do so more frequently than, for instance, English speakers. Before turning to the newfound criticality of iconicity to speech, let me offer some brief comments on the factors that allow for such nonarbitrary combinations in speech, beyond the obvious fact that people can use the sounds of speech to mimic sounds in nature. These comments are distilled from the work of others. One factor relates to embodied cognition, the notion that many of the ways we think about things are shaped by how we experience the world through our bodies. For example, the fact that the *sn-* phonestheme occurs in references to nose-related things like "snouts" and "sneezing" may not be coincidental, since *sn-* requires a nasal sound. When we say *sn-*, it feels like our nose is involved. This is not a coincidence: we have a proprioceptive connection to our nose during the articulation of *sn-*. Here is another type of physical connection between the sound in a word and what the word denotes: When we say "teeny weeny" to describe something very small, we are making our oral cavity as small as possible by raising our tongue to the front of our mouth. We are technically using a "high front" vowel, transcribed as [i] phonetically.

In contrast, if we say something is "huge" we are using a vowel that requires a much more expansive oral cavity. In both cases there is a direct parallel between the size of what is being represented and the size of the mouth opening used to represent it. Along the same lines, when we say "teeny weeny" we may increase our pitch to emphasize how tiny something is. The higher pitch allows for another direct connection with nature, since tiny things and animals like mice tend to make high-pitched sounds. Conversely, if we say something is "huge" we may lower our pitch, drawing on the association between large things and lower pitches. These sorts of words do not represent instances of direct mimicry of noises in our environments, but they nevertheless appeal to physical connections made between our bodies and the universe around us. They are, in a broad sense, cases of embodied cognition. In the realm of the iconic use of words, embodied phenomena abound. To cite just one more intuitive example, consider that if you say something took a long time, you might lengthen the word "long," as in, "She took a looooong time." In such an instance, the duration of the word can represent the duration of a completely unrelated event.[6]

New Evidence That Words Aren't So Arbitrary After All

In 2016 a large research team led by Damián Blasi produced perhaps the most interesting study to date on the frequent role that systematic sound-meaning associations play in speech. The study examined data from 4,298 different languages (about two-thirds of the world's total), representing 359 different lineages. A lineage is a group of related languages or a single language that has no existing related languages. The latter is typically called a language "isolate." Each isolate is the sole remaining language from a family whose other members are no longer spoken. Blasi and colleagues looked at word lists for each of the languages, lists that contained transcriptions of forty to one hundred basic concepts. The words in the lists are generally common and are relatively unlikely to be borrowed across languages. This means that the words are typically ancient, in the sense that they have been inherited across many generations of speakers of the same language. The words denote basic pronouns like "I," "we," and "you," but they also denote a range of concepts for body parts, environmental features like "moon" and "sun," and a host of action types. Since each language's word list represents roughly the same set of concepts, Blasi and company were interested in whether some concepts tend to get encoded with the same sounds across all the world's languages.[7]

In the study, the researchers offered evidence for a host of previously undetected correspondences between meanings and sounds, correspondences that surfaced across the bulk of the languages tested. As Blasi and colleagues were well aware, it is difficult to demonstrate that such correspondences are meaningful and not due to chance. For example, let us say that in a large number of languages the word for "sun" has an [n] sound in it. Is this a meaningful correspondence or is it just coincidence? As we saw in Chapter 5 when discussing other research (including my own) that looks at data from thousands of languages, there are many confounding variables that need to be controlled. For instance, in this made-up case, the [n] sound is one of the most frequent consonants in the world's languages. In order to demonstrate that [n] is actually associated with "sun" in a nontrivial way, we would need to show not just that [n] is very common in words signifying the concept "sun" but also that it is more common in words for "sun" than it is in other words. Another key variable that needs to be controlled for is language relatedness. Let us say that [n] is particularly common in words for the concept "sun," but that this commonality is primarily due to the fact that a few very large language families like Indo- European have many languages with a *sun*-[n] correspondence. In this case the commonality of the sound-meaning pairing would simply be due to the relatedness of certain languages whose ancestral tongue happened to have a word for "sun" with an [n] nasal sound. Another critical variable to be controlled for is language contact. Even though the words that Blasi and colleagues tested are words for common concepts that are only borrowed relatively rarely, they can still be borrowed. So we could find that an inordinate number of languages have the *sun*-[n] association just because they borrowed the word "sun" from English or other languages with the correspondence.

Blasi and colleagues examined the data while using a variety of statistical methods to make sure than any sound-meaning associations they uncovered were not coincidentally due to factors like those just mentioned. What they found surprised many linguists, including me. While there is no systematic association between the word for "sun" and any sound, a number of systematic correspondences did surface. Some of them have no clear motivation. For instance, the word for "star" is particularly likely to include a [z] sound, though clearly this association does not hold in English. Yet some of the associations uncovered have plausible explanations. The word for "small" in the world's languages is particularly likely to use a high-front vowel [i], as in the case of "teeny weeny" discussed above. This association has been speculated about for some time given the factors I mentioned earlier, and it had been observed anecdotally in a small set of languages. Other previously suggested associations were also supported in the results. The word for "breast" often involves the [m] sound, which is a sound that babies frequently make while suckling. The study also uncovered associations that had not previously been suggested, including the intriguing fact that the word for "tongue" across the world's languages is inordinately likely to require the [l] sound. This sound is technically called a lateral sound because it involves bunching the tongue up at its sides. One possibility is that bunching the tongue makes it a bit more perceptually salient, so there is a proprioceptive connection between "tongue" and the [l] sound. Other sound-meaning pairings can be explained with greater confidence. Perhaps most tellingly, the word for "nose" often involves a nasal [n] sound across the world's languages, as it does in English. There is a clearer motivation in this case. When we produce an [n] sound the vibrations made by our vocal cords resonate in the nasal cavity, so [n] probably feels like a natural way to draw attention to the nose. This *nose*-[n] parallel is a nonarbitrary sound-meaning association that has distinguishable physical motivations.

The results produced by Blasi and colleagues point to systematic sound-meaning pairings that exist even in basic words. These are not just examples of onomatopoeic words that some might claim are peripheral to the core of language. Instead, the associations uncovered in the study highlight correspondences between sounds and words that are frequent within and across the world's languages. These correspondences are central to how humans encode some very basic concepts. They would never have been uncovered without a careful examination of the languages of many non-WEIRD populations and would have been undecipherable without a heavy reliance on computational and quantitative methods. In this sense, the study was similar to some of the other studies I have discussed. The researchers used large amounts of data from diverse populations to call into question a standard assumption in linguistics, when that assumption had been based for decades largely on inspections of only a subset of the world's languages, mainly those of WEIRD populations.

A couple of years before this influential study was published, another study received significant attention worldwide because it claimed that a particular kind of word is not arbitrary in form. In this case, the suggestion was not that a given sound in that word commonly occurred across the world's languages, but that the *entire word* was very similar across languages. The word was, simply enough, "huh." (Initially, "huh" might not even seem like a word, a point I will return to below.) Consider the function of the word. It is said in response to a statement that is either unclear or confusing. The confusion could arise from a lack of clarity in the audio signal, perhaps due to background noise. Or it could simply arise from the fact that the person saying the word does not agree with the person who has just made a statement. If someone told me, "Salah is a better player than Neymar," I might reply, "Huh?" even if I heard them clearly. As linguists put it, "huh" is an example of an interjection used to repair the conversation, to keep it on track. When the word is uttered in response to a speaker, the speaker is expected to repeat what they have just said: "I said Salah is a better player than Neymar." Or perhaps they catch a mistake and realize that they produced a meaningless or otherwise problematic sentence, correcting it appropriately.[8]

In the attention-garnering study under question, Mark Dingemanse and colleagues in the Netherlands described how this short repair word was not merely common in every language they tested; it took basically the same form. Consider the form of "huh" in English, phonetically. It is transcribed as [hã]. The [h] symbol means that it begins with a glottal fricative, which is basically the sound of air rushing past nonvibrating vocal cords. The [ã] symbol represents a sound in which the vocal cords vibrate while the mouth is pretty open and the tongue is placed low and fairly centrally in the mouth, all while the soft palate is lowered to allow vibrations to resonate in the nasal cavity. Finally, the word is usually produced with a rising intonation, as though the person producing the word is asking a question. Now consider the word used for the same repair function in Lao, a completely unrelated language: [hã]. In Lao the intonation also rises during the word, even though Lao is a tonal language. Of course, such a similarity could be coincidental, and it is possible that two languages just happen to have the same word for "huh."

The possibility of coincidence vanished when Dingemanse and colleagues examined phonetic transcriptions of repair words across thirty-one languages from distinct language families and global regions. In all the languages there were obvious similarities. They then focused on ten of the languages, all unrelated to each other, that had much richer acoustic data available. They discovered a series of robust commonalities in the acoustic data. Across all the languages tested, the researchers found that the word for "huh" was, without exception, monosyllabic. This was true even in languages that tend to prefer polysyllabic words. In all of them, the one vowel in the word was a low central vowel, and this vowel was never followed by a consonant. In many languages the vowel was not preceded by a consonant either, but if it was, that consonant was always [h] or a similar one. Finally, in all these unrelated languages the word was produced with a rising intonation. In short, the function of initiating repair in a conversation is signified with the same basic form across the world's languages.

One might argue that [hã] and its similar forms are not actually words but just instinctual grunts or some other primal element of communication akin to what other animals are capable of producing. Unlike grunts or cries, though, [hã] and its variants are learned at the same age as other words. Also, other primates do not produce a sound similar to [hã], suggesting that it is not some innate biological reaction. Furthermore, it is not produced in an involuntary fashion like grunts or cries. In short, [hã] is a learned word, one that serves a particular function in discourse but that has evolved to have a similar form across the world's languages. It is a word that involves minimal effort, hence the use of a basic open-mouth configuration and only one vowel, to demonstrate a lack of understanding and the need for a conversation repair. The typically rising pitch associated with the word drives home its function, as rising pitch is often, though not universally, associated with questioning. Although "huh" may not be a prototypical word, it is still a word. In fact, it is an important word because it is required to make conversations flow, as its universality reflects. The form that this critical word takes is similar across the world's languages, further calling into question the notion that nonarbitrary correspondences between form and meaning only exist at the periphery of speech. One might suggest that "huh" is at the periphery of speech, but given how critical it has been shown to be for conversation repair across so many languages, this position is increasingly difficult to support. It is a universal word that is central to speech, conveying a common thought in a predictable phonetic package.

The two studies discussed above are fairly new and offer novel insights into the systematic association between some sounds and some word types. Other relevant research on sound-meaning associations is much older but has been refined in interesting ways in the last few years. This is true with respect to a line of work that began quite a long time ago. In a book written almost one century ago, it was demonstrated that English speakers were more likely to label a spiky shape bearing sharp angles with the made-up word *takete* when given the choice between that word and *maluma*. On the other hand, they preferred naming a rounded shape *maluma*. The *takete* image looked a bit like a quickly drawn star, while the *maluma* image looked like two overlapping ovals. This basic finding has since been replicated with speakers of a number of languages. An oft-cited study from about twenty years ago helped to reinvigorate research on this topic. It demonstrated that people are more likely to label a two-dimensional shape with many sharp angles as *kiki*, while they are more likely to label a shape with rounded edges as *bouba*.

This study has been cited so often, in fact, that the effect it describes is now referred to simply as the *bouba-kiki* effect. Across a number of cultures it has been demonstrated that *bouba,* or words that sound like it, is a more natural label for rounded shapes, and *kiki,* or words that sound like it, serves as a better label of sharply angled shapes. I am guessing your own intuition matches this assessment.[9]

Debate persists as to why *bouba* might naturally associate with round shapes and *kiki* with sharply angled ones, with a variety of theories proposed. There are a few plausible reasons. A 2020 study, conducted by psychologist Arash Aryani and colleagues, offered perhaps the best insight to date. It suggests that the *bouba-kiki* effect might be motivated by the fact that some words like *kiki* elicit similar emotions as those elicited by particular shapes, in this case shapes with sharp angles. How, you might ask, can either a series of sounds or a representation of shapes elicit emotions? Well it turns out that some sounds that are found in *kiki* and *kiki*-like words, particularly [k], [t], and certain short vowels, arouse stronger emotions than many other sounds. Essentially, a series of short sounds are judged as being more abrupt, somehow connoting an abrupt shift in emotions. If you say a word like *kiki* aloud, you can perceive its staccato feel. The vocal cords stop during the production of the two [k] sounds and vibrate during the [i] sounds. If you are a native speaker of English, you may aspirate the [k] sounds, producing a puff of air alongside each [k]. There is a stop-start quality to the word, as it represents two distinct bursts of the same syllable. This abrupt stopping and starting may naturally arouse a feeling of abrupt change. In *bouba,* meanwhile, there is no aspiration, the vowels tend to be produced for a greater duration, and the vocal cords vibrate throughout the word. The word thus has a "smoother" pronunciation characterized by a less abrupt or stop-start phonetic sequence. Perhaps this contributes to less emotional arousal, less feeling of abrupt change.

Even given the rapid changes associated with a staccato-sounding word like *kiki,* this does not immediately explain the association with an image like a quickly drawn star or some other shape with multiple acute angles. Conversely, the less abrupt nature of a word like *bouba* does not explain the association with more rounded shapes. Yet research demonstrates that people have negative associations with objects containing sharp angles. Sharp angles are generally more dangerous than rounded edges in the real world, so there is a plausible motivation for this association. Additionally, sharp-angled edges are found on things that are more likely to break and snap when contrasted to objects with rounded edges. Breaking and snapping sounds are more similar to *kiki* than *bouba;* this fact, too, could create an association between the words and the images. Conversely, round things and drawings depicting them have been shown to create feelings of calmness, potentially motivating the association between rounded shapes and words like *bouba* that are less staccato and less abrupt sounding. Finally, it is worth noting that the pronunciation of *bouba* requires the use of the lips to a greater extent than *kiki,* given that *bouba* contains two bilabial [b] sounds and a vowel in the first syllable that requires a speaker to round his or her lips. This lip roundedness may also play some role in the association between *bouba* and round things.

While these cross-sensory associations between words and shapes are intuitive, the experimental support for them is only now surfacing. To test the theory that *bouba* and *kiki* words are associated with distinct kinds of arousal that are matched by the arousal created by certain visual stimuli, Aryani and colleagues developed a few tests. In one, they simply asked participants to rate a series of *kiki*-like and *bouba*-like words on a scale from "very calming" to "very exciting." Participants were also asked to rate a series of images of shapes on the same scale. The images and words used were taken from previous studies of the *bouba-kiki* effect. The twenty-four participants in the experiment consistently rated the *kiki* words and sharp-edged shapes as more exciting, the *bouba* words and rounded shapes as more calming. In another experiment, Aryani and colleagues created a series of 168 new words that had never been used in research on this topic. These words, which sounded similar to *bouba* or *kiki,* were presented to participants as audio files. Participants were simultaneously presented with images of rounded or sharp-angled shapes and asked which shapes best matched the sounds. Shapes with sharp angles were much more likely to be selected when participants heard the new words with "more exciting" acoustic characteristics, while rounder objects were more likely to be selected when the participants heard "less exciting" new words. In short, the results of this work suggest that there is underlying similarity between certain sounds and certain visual representations of shapes, since some sounds and shapes elicit similar feelings of arousal or excitement. This parallel arousal appears to motivate, at least in part, the *bouba-kiki* effect. But it does not mean that other factors, for example the rounded-lip configuration of sounds like the first vowel in *bouba,* are not also relevant.[10]

The studies discussed above all represent important new advances in our understanding of nonarbitrary associations between some verbal symbols, whether sounds or entire words, and some specific meanings. The English use of an [n] sound in the word "nose" is apparently not a coincidence. The English use of [hã] as a word to initiate repair in a conversation is not coincidental either. These associations are indicators of more pervasive sound-meaning parallels across the world's languages. Similarly, the robust nature of the *bouba-kiki* effect, and its apparent origins in the inherent arousal associated with certain sound sequences, points to fundamental associations across our senses, associations that exist in diverse cultures. Such cross-cultural parallels underscore previously unnoticed ways in which the words of speech are not entirely arbitrary. To be clear, the bulk of spoken words do appear to be arbitrary in form, as some influential linguists have long maintained. But we can now acknowledge that the linkage between words' meanings and sounds is much less arbitrary than we once thought.

Nonarbitrary associations are so pervasive, in fact, that they can be used to generate new words. Experimental work has demonstrated that people are capable of discriminating the meanings of made-up words based on the sounds used in those words, when they are given choices. For example, in one study researchers asked participants to play a back-and-forth charade-like game in which they were asked to use made-up words to convey meanings in thirty pairs of antonyms like "bad" and "good" or "fast" and "slow." In roughly two-thirds of the cases, the made-up words exhibited clear tendencies when each word was contrasted with its antonym. For instance, the made-up words that people produced to refer to "quiet" tended to have a higher pitch and lower volume than the made-up words for "loud." The words for "fast" tended to have higher-pitch sounds that were repeated when contrasted to the words for "slow." At least for some meanings, then, people can create new words that convey a given meaning more naturally than the content of their antonyms. Listeners who have no awareness of the new made-up words are able to pick out the meanings of those words when given limited choices. This suggests that the tendencies in the sounds used in the made-up words allow listeners to more naturally make sense of the new words.[11]

One of the most interesting studies to date on this topic was carried out by cognitive scientists Marcus Perlman and Gary Lupyan, who adopted an innovative approach to examine how people can create new words with iconic sounds that naturally represent meanings, while also examining how naive listeners interpret those meanings. Perlman and Lupyan created a contest in which eleven teams of participants were tasked with creating made-up words for thirty different meanings. The words were subsequently presented to others to test whether they understood them. The team that created the made-up words that were most easily interpreted won $1,000. This ensured that the teams were actually well motivated to create iconic, decipherable words. The thirty different meanings were divided into three categories: actions, nouns, and properties. Actions included concepts like "sleeping," "eating," and "cutting." The nouns to be represented included "tiger," "snake," and "fire." The properties included more abstract notions like "many," "good," and "this." After the teams created new words, those words were presented to over seven hundred people to test how comprehensible the words were. The listeners had to guess the meaning of a made-up word, given a restricted set of choices. They were also asked to rank how much the made-up words "sounded like" their meaning.[12]

So how did the teams do? Quite well, actually. When the listeners were asked to choose which of the meanings matched a made-up word, they did so at much higher rates than chance. When given a choice between ten meanings from the same semantic category, they selected the correct meaning almost 40 percent of the time, nearly four times the 10 percent rate that random choosing would yield when there are ten possible answers. When given a choice between ten meanings taken from all three categories, the listeners selected the correct meaning at a rate of about 36 percent, once again much higher than the 10 percent predicted by random choice. For the made-up words created by the most successful word-creating teams, the success rate was significantly higher. One team even managed to create made-up words for actions that were interpreted correctly nearly 75 percent of the time overall.

You might wonder how the teams successfully created new iconic words. Here are a couple of interesting examples. One team, when creating a made-up word for "cook," included the following sequence of sounds in the word: [bl bl bl bl] The reasoning was that this sounded like the bubbles of boiling water, a noise associated with cooking. Some teams used words with a falling pitch to represent "bad" and a more optimistic, rising pitch for "good." A variety of strategies were used to create associations between new words and their meanings, demonstrating how creative people can be when they are incentivized to generate new words that others can intuitively comprehend. To be clear, it is not as though iconicity is some magic tool for word generation; the meanings varied substantially in terms of how easy they were to represent. For example, the made-up words for some actions, notably "sleep" and "eat," were generally much more comprehensible than the words for "gather." Still, it was clear from this study that speakers can be surprisingly adept at inventing words whose sounds naturally convey their meanings.

One could argue that, while such results are intriguing, they do not offer evidence that languages actually rely much on iconic words. To a skeptic, perhaps people are good at using iconicity when they need to convey thoughts under unnatural circumstances, just as someone playing charades may be good at using new gestures to represent some concept to their teammate. The superficial scarcity of iconic and other nonarbitrary words may give the impression that systematic sound-meaning associations are not crucial to speech, but this impression ignores the fact that words are constantly changing and becoming more arbitrary. As noted in Chapter 6, for example, more common and predictable words are frequently shortened or changed in other ways to require less effort. The point is that the current form of a word does not necessarily indicate whether it was once iconic. Many words that once reflected natural sound-meaning parallels may no longer do so. In the same vein, the meanings of words can change with time, further complicating the detection of such patterns. It is in some ways surprising that many words, like ideophones, continue to exhibit such clear non-arbitrary correspondences between sound and meaning.

Iconicity Helps Kids Learn

Studies like Perlman and Lupyan's demonstrate that people can create made-up words that allow others to fairly naturally comprehend their meanings, showing that iconicity can play a key role in facilitating comprehension. Such findings might lead us to ask whether iconicity helps kids comprehend new words as they learn language. Indeed, an enduring mystery in the language sciences is how kids acquire language given the complexity of the task. Among other things, when kids learn to speak they learn how to make specific sounds and how to string those sounds together into words. They also need to learn how to string words together into sentences, a notoriously complex task that we will discuss a bit in Chapter 8. Perhaps most critically of all, kids must learn the meaning of the new words they hear all around them during the first years of life. This is also an exceedingly complex task. Even adults learning a second language struggle to remember the meaning of words, though they have a much better understanding of what sorts of concepts might be labeled by the words they hear in a foreign language. Children, on the other hand, must make sense of words without any prior experience with the meanings those words might label. While there is much developmental psychologists still do not know about how kids learn words, they have learned much in the past few decades. One of the key findings on this topic, now observed in a few studies, is that iconicity actually plays a crucial role in supporting kids' word learning.

Lynn Perry (incidentally, a colleague of mine at the University of Miami) is a developmental psychologist who has conducted a few of the key studies in this field. In the last few years she and her collaborators have published a series of studies on the amount of iconicity in children's speech. These studies suggest that iconic words are not peripheral to speech but are instead crucial to kids' language acquisition. Here I will focus on some of Perry's work that I believe to be particularly revealing regarding the role that nonarbitrary words play in scaffolding the learning of words and associated concepts. In one study, Perry and colleagues conducted a series of tasks with English and Spanish speakers. Among other things, the participants had to rate the iconicity of six hundred words in each of their languages. Each of the English words was a translation of a Spanish word, and vice versa. All of the words were taken from sets of words that are known to be learned relatively early by English- and Spanish-speaking children. The iconicity ratings generated by English and Spanish speakers differed for the word pairs. Sometimes the English speakers rated a given word to be very iconic while Spanish speakers rated its Spanish translation as less iconic. Conversely, sometimes the Spanish speakers rated a particular word as very iconic but its English translation was ranked as less iconic by English speakers. Perry and colleagues also had access to the typical age at which each word is learned. After all, even basic words are not acquired at the same age. For instance, 93 percent of children in the United States know the word "mommy" by the age of sixteen months, whereas only 52 percent know the word for "book" at that age, and only about 38 percent know the word for "cookie." When Perry and colleagues contrasted the iconicity ratings of the six hundred words with the age at which the words are learned, they found a robust association: more iconic words tend to be learned earlier. Since the iconicity ratings varied across languages, Perry and her team were able to discern that words ranked high in iconicity in English are more likely to be acquired earlier by English-speaking children, while the Spanish equivalents of those words are less likely to be acquired as early by Spanish-speaking kids. The reverse pattern holds as well: Spanish words that are ranked as being very iconic are typically learned earlier by Spanish-speaking children than their equivalents are learned by English-speaking kids. In short, a word's iconicity seems to play a role in how it is acquired. Iconic words like "teeny" tend to be learned earlier than noniconic words.[13]

In another study, Perry and colleagues focused on a larger set of about twenty-one hundred English words. All the words in the study had "age of acquisition" estimates, meaning Perry and colleagues were able to provide a figure representing the approximate age at which the word is typically learned. For each of the words, they also obtained iconicity ratings from at least ten other English speakers. This simple approach allowed Perry's team to contrast the average iconicity rating of each of the words with the average age at which the word is learned. A regression between age and iconicity revealed a very clear and significant relationship—which means, simply, that children learn more iconic words earlier. This is a nice finding, particularly given that it is based on such a large sample of words. The result held even when the researchers excluded obvious instances of iconicity (like onomatopoeia), suggesting that the association between iconicity and age of acquisition is subtle but pervasive.[14]

Do young kids learn more iconic words earlier because they are easier to remember and learn? Or do they learn them earlier because the concepts toddlers need to talk about are more easily referred to with iconic words than other concepts? Or do they learn them earlier simply because adults choose to use iconic words with young children at a high rate? Bearing in mind that the pattern could be due to a few interrelated factors, Perry and colleagues' study did at least offer an affirmative answer to the last of these questions. Examining the words based on their frequency in adult speech, they found a striking pattern: adults tend to use highly iconic words with kids at a much greater rate than they use those words with other adults. Also, looking at the frequency of relevant words in the speech of children, they found that words high in iconicity tend to be frequent in the speech of young kids. As kids age, though, words that are low in iconicity become comparatively more common.

Such results suggest that, far from being a peripheral feature of speech, iconic words play a substantial role in language acquisition when contrasted to completely arbitrary words. Many critical issues are still to be explored before we can fully understand this role. For example, while we know that English-speaking parents use more iconic words with children, we do not know whether they do so to intentionally facilitate language learning. It is possible that, simply because kids tend to use such words, adults do so as well when speaking to kids. Or perhaps it is some combination of intention and coincidence. It seems plausible, though, that adults actively produce iconic words when speaking to children since such words seem to have natural associations with their meanings, allowing for kids to more quickly acquire them. As someone who has spent many hours talking to toddlers—including my own son, nephews, and nieces—I can say that this interpretation certainly matches my own intuition. What I find so interesting about the results of studies such as Perry's is not that adults use iconic words when speaking with kids, but that they do so in such a consistent and pervasive way. Furthermore, many of the iconic words they use with kids are not obviously iconic, so this pattern is not always easy to detect.

Conclusion: Nonarbitrary Foundations

Languages clearly encode many associations between sounds and meanings that somehow feel natural to members of diverse cultures. These nonarbitrary associations between sounds and meanings are not of a binary, either-or sort. It is not simply that some words are iconic and others are not. Some words, like "bang," may seem quite iconic, but other words, like "blubber," may only have a tinge of iconicity. Perhaps the fact that some iconic associations are so subtle has helped to motivate the trivialization of nonarbitrary words in speech. Similarly, the worldwide systematic correspondence between a sound like [n] and "nose" is subtle and difficult to detect without robust statistical analyses. In the light of such subtleties, it is understandable that some linguists have assumed that arbitrariness is a fundamental characteristic of human words. Another factor motivating this traditional assumption in linguistics is that most words do not exhibit nonarbitrary associations between sounds and meanings. As noted above, though, the contemporary absence of such an association between any given word and its meaning does not mean that such an association never existed in the word's history. It is also increasingly clear that many words, far more than we once thought, do exhibit such associations, which in turn play a key role guiding kids as they learn new words. We must now acknowledge that nonarbitrary associations between sounds and meanings are not peripheral to speech. Perhaps we would have reached this conclusion earlier if modern linguistic theories had been based on non-European languages. Many languages, like a few mentioned at the beginning of this chapter, have robust sets of ideophones and other obvious examples of iconicity, suggesting that while iconicity is important to speech, humans rely on this phenomenon to varying degrees. Japanese, for example, uses reduplication to refer to multiple entities. For instance, *goro* can refer to one object rolling, while *gorogoro* can refer to multiple objects rolling. Similarly, Japanese uses increased vowel duration in some cases to refer to increased duration of an action: *haQ* signifies a short breath, while *haaQ* refers to a long breath.

It is clear now that nonarbitrary words play quite a substantial role in speech, particularly in some cultures, allowing humans to more naturally learn and transmit key concepts. Many studies also show the pervasive role of iconicity in signed languages. Since this book is primarily about speech-related phenomena, I have not addressed them here. It is worth noting, though, that research on iconicity in signed languages highlights in even more glaring ways the role that iconicity can play in human communication. Research on signed languages has in fact helped to inspire some of the work discussed in this chapter. For example, prior to Perry's work on the usage of iconic spoken words with young kids, it was observed that the signs used with young deaf children tend to be more iconic than ones used among adults.[15]

Finally, it is also worth noting that the research discussed in this chapter is informing new ideas on how languages first evolved. The idea that iconicity played some role in the first human languages is not novel. It is easy to envision how a small hominid dwelling in East Africa during the Paleolithic might have made a sound to imitate a lion's roar in order to warn others of a nearby predator. Such suggestions are ancient. Given the widespread assumption in linguistics during the twentieth century that the sounds of words are fundamentally arbitrary, such suggestions seemed to offer little insight into how language evolved. If we have been drastically underestimating humans' capacity for creating nonarbitrary word-meaning associations, though, then we might also have underestimated the role that iconic associations played at the dawn of speech.

Japanese psychologist Mutsumi Imai, who has been at the forefront of demonstrations that sound symbolism is critical to children learning to speak, has made compelling suggestions that iconicity also played a critical role in the evolution of speech. She and others have pointed out that iconicity could have played a central role in the first languages, even more central than the role it plays in today's languages. As Imai and colleagues have noted, it is logical that as humans used a greater number of new words and realized they could make more fine-grained meaning contrasts than those allowed for by iconic representations, they would have innovated new words without relying on iconicity. Nonarbitrary word-meaning associations have their limits, after all. Under this account, even though humans eventually came to realize that all concepts could be denoted via arbitrary words, they still likely relied heavily on the use of nonarbitrary associations when generating the first words. Setting aside such reasonable speculations, what we can claim with confidence is that nonarbitrary associations between sounds and meanings are critical to how we encode concepts into words.[16]

8

Big into What?

WORDS ARE COMBINED into phrases and sentences in a dazzling array of patterns, collectively referred to as syntax. The complexity of syntax has long confounded researchers. Consider, for example, the previous sentence. There are all sorts of patterns in the order of the words of that sentence, patterns that are familiar to you and me and other speakers of English. Those patterns are critical to the transmission of meaning and to how we think as we create sentences. It was no coincidence that I put "complexity" after "the," or "syntax" after "of," or "researchers" after "confounded," to cite just three examples of many in that sentence alone. You and I know that "researchers" should follow the main verb of this particular sentence, in this case "confounded." If I put that word somewhere else it would change the sentence's meaning or make it confusing. And we know that articles like "the" should precede nouns, as should prepositions like "of." These and other patterns, sometimes referred to as "rules" as though they represented inviolable edicts voted on by a committee, help to give English sentences a predictable ordering of words. It is this predictable ordering that is usually referred to when linguists talk about a language's syntax.

Without syntax, it would seem, statements could not be understood, because they would be transferred from speaker to hearer in a jumbled mess of words. This is, it turns out, a bit of an oversimplification since a number of the world's languages do not have rule-governed word order to the extent that English does. Still, let us stick with the oversimplification for now, because it hints at something meaningful about speech. Many languages, like English, tend to put the subject in front of the verb, and the verb in front of the object, as in "The syntax confounded the researchers" or "Sergio kicked Neymar." In other languages another order may hold, for instance the object may precede the verb, as in "Sergio Neymar kicked." In fact, the latter sort of ordering seems to be more common than the former across the world's languages. Most languages have default word orders: Strong conventions determine how units of meaning are encoded sequentially, even iconic words like those discussed in Chapter 7, and these conventions help make language intelligible. Still, the conventions can be exceedingly complex and take kids and adult language learners years to learn. Here is an illustration of a particular word order that helps convey meaning in English:

(1) Sergio kicked Neymar and ran away.

This is a very straightforward sentence, but note that you must be familiar with a convention to understand who did the kicking (Sergio) and also who did the running away (again, Sergio). I do not need to say "Sergio kicked Neymar and Sergio ran away" for you to interpret the sentence. A word-order convention of English lets you know that, because Sergio came first in the sentence, he is also the (omitted) person who did the running away. This convention does not exist in all languages. In some Amazonian languages, the equivalent sentence would mean that Neymar, the one being kicked, ran away. The point here is simply that there are countless "rules" about things like this in English syntax, and as English speakers we often fail to appreciate how many such conventions we must be aware of to convey our thoughts and comprehend those of others. Similarly, speakers of other languages must be familiar with an incredible array of distinct word-order conventions.

Syntactic conventions can be exceedingly complex, and any given language contains so many of them that linguists have long wondered how individuals can learn them. To many linguists in the twentieth century, learning language was largely about learning syntactic rules like those related to who did the second action in a sentence such as the one in example (1), rules that helped people produce and decipher sentences. Various theoretical models were put forth to offer frameworks for understanding how human syntax, with all its complexity, is even possible. Some of the models suggested that humans are genetically hard-wired to decipher syntactic patterns, predisposed to make sense out of the stream of words they begin hearing at birth. These models focused on the complex syntactic rules of languages, especially a few well-studied languages like English. They suggested that learning a language was primarily a process of learning two components of the language: its dictionary or, more technically, its lexicon (which consists of all the units like words, prefixes, and suffixes, and the meaning of all the units), and its grammar. The grammar consists of the rules that allow people to put the lexicon's units of meaning into predictable orders so as to construct even larger units of meaning. An increasing number of linguists now think this "dictionary and grammar" model of language was misguided. According to them there is no real distinction between words and sentences, as odd as that claim may seem, and no material distinction between a dictionary and grammar. We will return to this point toward the end of the chapter. The dictionary-and-grammar view of language benefited from the rise, beginning in the mid-twentieth century, of the theory spread by linguist Noam Chomsky. His theory became the dominant paradigm for the study of syntax during the latter part of the twentieth century and continues to influence scholars in some circles today.[1]

One of the key distinguishing features of human languages, according to the Chomskyan paradigm, is a syntactic feature known as recursion. Recursion refers to the use of a structure within another structure of that kind, for instance when you place one clause inside another. If you are not sure about what a clause is, perhaps this helps: A clause consists of a subject and a predicate. All sentences have at least one clause, but some sentences have two or more clauses. In the following sentence a clause is inserted into another clause to form a coherent thought.

(2) Neymar knows [that he is a great dribbler].

In this example, the bracketed clause serves as the object of the whole sentence. It is a clause serving a function within a larger clause. We can also embed clauses recursively in the middle of each other, as in the following example.

(3) Neymar, [who likes to beat defenders [who think they can stop him]], placed the ball in the bottom corner of the goal.

Chomsky and others suggested that the ability to recursively combine clauses like these is at the core of human speech, implying that it was a key characteristic shared by all human languages. Countless studies have been published on recursive phenomena like embedded clauses, as boring as that might sound. Most of the relevant studies were on English and other European languages, though many were also on unrelated languages. In the last fifteen years or so, however, some linguists have made prominent suggestions that recursion is not so fundamental to syntax, and language more broadly, since embedded clauses like those evident in the previous two examples seem to be lacking in some languages. In 2009, linguists Stephen Levinson and Nick Evans pointed out that, judging from the data, syntactic recursion is not actually found in all languages. Part of the evidence they relied on comes from the famous case of the Pirahã, an Amazonian language I have already discussed. My father published a series of papers around fifteen years ago that described the absence of evidence for recursion in Pirahã (among other things), contradicting the claims of Chomsky and others regarding the proposed universality of recursion in the world's languages. Instead, the language does not seem to allow for clauses to be placed inside each other but only placed next to each other. Recursive structures equivalent to "Sergio kicked the boy who ran" have yet to be documented in the language. Instead the Pirahã equivalent of this sentence would be something like "Sergio kicked the boy. The boy ran."[2]

To someone outside linguistics, this may not seem to be a particularly controversial claim—namely that a language in the Amazon places clauses next to each other instead of embedding one inside the other. To many linguists, however, it became a hot topic. Some expressed skepticism that such a language could exist. To others, like Levinson and Evans, it was not an implausible claim given the extreme diversity of the world's languages and given that claims of "linguistic universals" always seem to fall apart as the number of languages considered grows and grows. As it stands, no outsider has been able to show that Pirahã speakers use recursion of the kind predicted by Chomsky and colleagues. Some might counter that this is simply because only a handful of people have actually learned Pirahã, as it is exceedingly difficult for outsiders to learn, by all accounts, and so our data on the topic are limited. From this perspective, maybe we just have not come across recursion in the language yet despite the hundreds of hours of recordings. To date, anyhow, no clear evidence for recursion in Pirahã has been offered.[3]

The topic of recursion in Pirahã became popular both inside and outside academia, with articles published in venues as diverse as *Language* and the *New Yorker* on the topic. As linguist and syntactician Geoffrey Pullum has noted, part of what was lost in the discussion of Pirahã was the fact that it is not the only language that undermines the notion that recursion is a fundamental feature of syntax. In a 2020 article, Pullum surveyed a series of studies of non-WEIRD languages from the last few decades, all of which appear to lack recursion. Let us consider some of the examples discussed by Pullum.[4]

Pullum notes that Ken Hale, a linguist who studied Australian languages, observed back in the mid-1970s that clauses in the Warlpiri language are not embedded inside each other but rather just loosely adjoined. This appears to be the case in other Australian languages as well. Around the time that Hale was making his observations, a linguist named Des Derbyshire published a series of findings on the Amazonian language Hixkaryana. Derbyshire noted the absence of recursion in the language. Instead, he said, the syntax of the language relies on similar strategies as the syntax of Pirahã. Derbyshire, who had spent decades as a missionary working with and living among the Hixkaryana, found that Hixkaryana clauses are simply placed next to each other rather than inside each other.[5]

A much more widely spoken language in which recursion does not seem to be relied upon is conversational Indonesian, one of the languages with the most native speakers. Linguist Robert Englebretson made this point in a comprehensive grammar of Indonesian. Indonesian is not the last example that could be offered, but it illustrates the point that some non-Amazonian and non-Australian languages may not rely on recursion during conversation. It is very difficult to prove the complete absence or impossibility of recursion in a given language. What we can observe, however, is that there are multiple languages that have been documented in the last few decades for which we have no clear evidence of recursion. This should likely give us pause prior to considering recursion a key feature of syntax and, more broadly, to considering recursion critical to how we think in order to speak. Another factor that might give us pause is that recursively embedded clauses are relatively infrequent in speech, even in the many languages like English that allow them.[6]

All the discoveries of languages that lack recursion date to the latter part of the twentieth century but have received much more intense scrutiny in the first part of the twenty-first century in the wake of the findings from Pirahã and in the subsequent well-publicized debates on recursion. Note that none of the exceptional languages are Indo-European. This is not surprising in the sense that the languages of many regions are so distinct when compared to the languages of better-documented language families. Many of the languages indigenous to Amazonia are completely unrelated to each other, let alone those of other regions. The findings on languages with "unusual" syntax offer another case in which the extent of diversity of speech, like other facets of human behavior and thought, has been underestimated because of a research bias on people and languages in WEIRD populations. Even today, the vast majority of syntactic research is conducted on the languages of speakers of a handful of WEIRD languages. Like many claims about universals in human psychology that may be called into question by examining very distinct populations worldwide, claims about universals in syntax tend to face challenges once a truly representative sample of the world's languages is considered. Evans and Levinson suggest that all linguistic universals that have been proposed, including recursion, do not hold up to closer inspection. Conversely, many very complex phenomena that do not surface in WEIRD languages and which have never been proposed as universals are actually very common in many languages of regions like Amazonia. To scholars like Evans, Levinson, and many others like myself, the common perception of certain linguistic "universals" originated at least in part in the biased sample of languages that served as the basis for linguistic inquiry during much of the twentieth century. As that bias waned with the continued documentation of unrelated languages worldwide, the evidence for universals uncoincidentally began to wane as well.

How We Really Construct Sentences

Immediately after finishing my doctorate but prior to landing a job as a university professor, I had the privilege of teaching English for a semester at a community college on the border between California and Mexico. Every day my students drove from Mexicali, the city across the border in which they lived, to Southern California, where they worked and went to school. This proved to be a very rewarding experience since they were some of the most diligent students I have ever taught—and I have now been fortunate enough to teach students from many universities. The students were diligent because their continued employment depended, at least in part, on how well they learned English. One of the key classes they took was on English grammar. My original approach to teaching the course, born of naivete, was based on the dictionary-and-grammar model of language that I discussed in the last section. My aim was to focus on the basic syntax of English, showing them word-order patterns that they could learn alongside words that could then be inserted into the sentence types they had learned. It did not take long for me to realize my approach was all wrong. My students began pointing out how the phrases and sentences they were most concerned with learning did not mesh well with the version of English I was outlining on the board.

For instance, a student asked me what was meant by "He hit the books." Is the subject, "he," actually hitting books? No, I replied, that is just an idiom, a group of words whose meaning is not really decipherable from the individual words. Of course I knew that English had many such idioms, but until I actually tried to teach English to people who really needed to learn it, I had never appreciated just how ubiquitous idioms are in speech. The questions that follow the introduction of even one idiom like this seemed unending. What if, instead of "hitting the books," someone is "hitting the weight room"? "Hitting the X," a student indirectly pointed out, seems to mean something that is not predictable from the knowledge of just the words and the order they come in. Simply put, the dictionary-and-grammar model does not allow us to interpret a phrase like "hitting the books." When a student asked whether one could use the "hitting the" idiom with other nouns besides "books" or "weight room," it immediately became clear that one could. We can say, for instance, "My son is hitting the pizza pretty hard," and fluent speakers would understand that my son is eating a lot of pizza and probably enjoying it.

As I taught that course, so many of the students' questions related to idioms. "What does 'kick the bucket' mean?" Or "face the music"? Or, less specifically, "What does it mean to say that 'I am big into something'? Like, 'I'm big into sushi'?" Or "I'm big into churrasco"? (One of my students raved, accurately, about Brazilian churrasco.) For each idiom brought up by the students, I would stop and explain what it meant and how it could be applied. It was at this moment that students' interest grew. They would nod and mention how often they had been confused by that particular idiom. By the end of the semester the course had transformed into lectures that were largely dedicated to exploring English idioms and some of the metaphors on which the idioms rely. For instance, the expression "life is a journey" is an idiom, but it reflects a larger metaphor relied upon by English speakers, evident in other idioms such as "I went through a tough time" or "there are obstacles ahead." As noted in Chapter 1, languages use various metaphors to describe time in terms of space. Many of the idioms we use relate to pervasive metaphors in our language that help us cognitively process abstract phenomena like time. In part because of this pervasiveness of idioms and associated metaphors, my Spanish-speaking students thanked me repeatedly for this instruction because they said it was much more practical and useful in their daily lives when compared to the information offered in the English grammar textbook we were supposed to be using. As one student told me, it helped them better understand how English speakers really think. In retrospect this should not have come as any surprise to me as someone who had spent so much time studying linguistics. While I was of course familiar with idioms prior to the class, it was the first time I had been confronted with the extent to which idioms matter to those that really need to learn English as quickly as possible. That's because there are countless frequent idioms in English. You cannot speak English with any fluency if you are unfamiliar with the most frequent of them. Idioms are everywhere.

Perhaps more critically, though, it is sometimes difficult to discern when an expression stops being an idiom, a specific set of words, and when it becomes something more malleable, in which case other words can be inserted into the idiom. Like being "big into X"—is that an idiom even though the last word is completely interchangeable? Perhaps, depending on how one defines an idiom. What is clear is that phrases like "big into X" and "hitting the X" are what many linguists now call "constructions." A construction is simply a pairing of a form, typically a series of words or kinds of words, with a particular meaning. If that definition seems incredibly vague, hopefully this discussion will clarify why it needs to be so vague while also highlighting why constructions are now seen as critical to talking and thinking.

To the linguists who are proponents of the increasingly influential theory of "construction grammar," learning language is largely about learning all kinds of constructions. Some of the constructions are very specific, what we often refer to as idioms, but constructions vary tremendously with respect to how specific they are. To proponents of construction grammar, my initial difficulties in teaching English would have come as no surprise because the dictionary-and-grammar model of language is a poor model in the first place. That is because there is no clear distinction between the dictionary, the collection of words (and suffixes / prefixes) in a language, and grammar. Instead, there are only constructions. Princeton's Adele Goldberg, one of the founders of this new approach to studying language, considers constructions to include all pairings of form with meaning, including words, idioms, partially filled idioms like "big into X," and even patterns like the common subject-verb sequences of English that can be filled with countless potential words. According to this broad definition, when humans learn how to speak they are memorizing certain forms and how those forms match up with meanings they are trying to convey or aims they are trying to accomplish while speaking. Some of the forms are very specific, for instance the sequence of sounds in a given word like "car," but others are much more schematic, for instance the subject-verb-object sequence that speakers learn to memorize as an English transitive clause.[7]

To linguists like Goldberg, you are basically doing the same thing when you learn words and when you learn idioms like "kick the bucket" or "going great guns" or "give the devil his due." As we have seen, and certainly my students along the Mexican border underscored this point to me, you cannot decipher the meaning of idioms by breaking them up into their components and piecing those components' meanings together in predictable ways with grammar. Instead, we just learn what "going great guns" means as a unit, just like we learn a word like "car" or a combination of a word and a suffix like "cars." In the case of "cars," we are combining two constructions that we know. One is very specific, "car," and the other is more abstract, what we might write as "noun + s." We combine "car" with this latter more abstract construction we have memorized in order to create "cars." While idioms like "kick the bucket" are learned as a very specific form, other constructions are less specific in that they also allow us to swap in words in particular places or slots, like the "big into X" construction or the "noun + s" construction. Such constructions are much more malleable and adaptable. The most critical and fairly straightforward insight that Goldberg and other proponents of construction grammar have offered is that, once we recognize the existence of constructions that vary in abstractness and how "filled out" they are, we see that words and syntax can be characterized as different sides of the same coin (to use another idiom). The structural templates of clauses and sentences represent abstractions that must be learned and memorized just like words. It is no surprise that my students faced challenges learning idioms, because there is no way to learn idioms besides spending lots of time memorizing them. The truth seems to be, however, that we also must memorize partially filled out idioms like "big into X" or "hitting the X," and even more abstract constructions like subject-verb-object sequences, sequences that are not filled out with specific words at all. For these more abstract constructions, we simply know that certain word types occur in a particular sequence. From the perspective of construction grammar, then, the dictionary versus grammar distinction is problematic, as many language teachers have learned, because there is in fact no clear distinction between words and grammar.

To get a better sense of what constructions are and how they help explain away the need for a completely distinct syntax component of language, let us look at a few more examples. Consider first another case of a malleable idiom-like construction that can be used in many ways, but that is more complex than "big into X":

> (4) The more you think about it, the less you understand.

With some reflection, we can see that this idiom can be filled out in myriad ways. Example (4) is just one instance of an abstract construction that could be described schematically as follows:

> (5) The Xer the Yer.

Think of all the X's and Y's you can insert into this abstract construction:

> (6) The faster you run, the quicker you get to your destination.

Or something as simple as "the sunnier the better" when referring to vacation destinations. Here is another:

> (7) The more you get to know her, the more you like her.

And another:

> (8) The more she gets to know him, the more she regrets her decision to leave her last boyfriend.

It is not difficult to offer specific examples of this construction that are quite different in terms of their specific forms and meanings. The number of words vary and the precise meanings being conveyed vary. Yet we can also see that there is an underlying pattern forming the core of the construction. In all cases we are saying, "The Xer the Yer." If you are a fluent speaker of English you have likely used this construction on many occasions and certainly have heard it. If you put yourself in the position of my former Mexican students, however, you might see how difficult this construction would be to learn. Is it an idiom? No, not really. Does its meaning follow neatly from some basic syntactic rule that applies to all English sentences? Not really either. This construction type, like so many others, indicates that the line between idioms and syntax is somewhat artificial. There is a continuum from less abstract constructions to more abstract ones, and the "The Xer the Yer" is simply closer to the abstract end of that continuum than, say, "bite the bullet" or "break a leg." Different cultures accumulate many different constructions, which help to form what we call the grammars of the languages of those cultures. Like other aspects of cultural evolution, the constructions help to meet needs in specific sociocultural contexts. Learning other languages, particularly ones unrelated to our own, is difficult largely because it requires learning an incredible array of new construction types, from the specific to the abstract.

Some abstract constructions have no prespecified words at all. Let us consider a few clauses whose structure is defined not by any specific prefilled words but simply by the fact that they contain a subject and an object and an indirect object. Such clauses are traditionally referred to as ditransitive. The indirect object in the next three ditransitive clauses is the person who is being given / made / served something.

(9)   Jude gave her the guitar lesson.
(10) He made her the picture frame.
(11) The bartender served him a signature microbrew.

Underlying each of these very distinct sentences is the same ditransitive construction, consisting of this basic schema:

Subject—Verb—Indirect Object—Object

The preceding example sentences neatly match this abstract template. Some verbs are much more common in the template, particularly "give." Other verbs, like "serve," are also common in the construction because their meaning is consistent with the transfer of something from one person (or animal or object) to another. Certain other verbs also seem to match the notion of transfer, though perhaps not as clearly, for instance when we cook or prepare things for others:

(12) I grilled her the panini.
(13) Kim baked her nephew a batch of brownies.

Or when we transfer information to others:

(14) I wrote her the letter.
(15) She taught me the method that won the award.

In the last example the direct object is itself a construction with a verb, "the method that won the award." This construction is inserted inside the ditransitive construction. As we see in these examples, the ditransitive construction can take different forms depending on the words used, but there seems to be some common meaning of the transfer of something shared across all the examples of the construction. One of the key insights offered by Goldberg and others is that abstract constructions carry meaning even apart from the meaning of the individual words they contain.

In the case of the ditransitive construction, even if we slot new verbs into the construction, verbs that do not convey the notion of something being transferred from one individual to another, the resultant phrase can still be interpreted because of the inherent meaning of transfer conveyed by the ditransitive construction itself. Consider:

(16) The bartender froze me some Jell-O shots.
(17) She engineered me a solution.
(18) She designed me a website.

On their own, none of the verbs in these examples inherently involve the transfer of something from one person or entity to another. "Freeze," "engineer," and "design" are not technically ditransitive verbs, not according to traditional grammar textbooks anyhow. Yet English speakers use such phrases all the time, and those listening to them understand what they mean. If you slot such verbs into the ditransitive construction, the construction itself still allows listeners to understand that there was some transfer involved. One way to think of this is that there are prototypical ditransitive sentences involving verbs like "give" and "serve," and there are also less prototypical cases like those I just offered. In all the cases, though, the ditransitive construction itself conveys the notion of transfer.

In truth, the meaning of sentences comes partially from the words (which are themselves tiny constructions) they contain and partially from the meaning of the constructions into which the words are placed. The following examples with the verb "slice," including a few adapted from examples Goldberg has given, help to drive home the point:

(19) The chef sliced the sashimi. (transitive construction)
(20) The chef sliced the customer a piece of pie. (ditransitive construction)
(21) The pie was sliced by the chef. (passive construction)
(22) He sliced away his fears of using his expensive Kato knife. (away construction)
(23) The samurai sliced his way through the castle's defense. (way construction)[8]

In each of these sentences someone is depicted as cutting something, but the type of construction used adds an additional component to the sentence's meaning. The construction in (22), the so-called away construction, is interesting because it gets used with the specific word "away" but allows an array of verbs preceding that word. The last construction, the way construction, also requires a specific word, "way," but is preceded by a possessive noun. Here are more instances of this construction:

(24) De Bruyne sliced his way through the midfield.

(25) They made their way out of the club.

(26) He found his way out of the enemy's position.

The way construction illustrates once again how constructions can be very abstract and schematic while also requiring specific words in particular slots in their schemas. Of course, the construction types I just mentioned represent but a tiny fraction of those that exist in English.

If we consider English sentences like "The chef sliced the sashimi" to be instances of a basic transitive construction, we can interpret the basic word order of English to simply represent the way in which a particularly common construction works: a subject precedes a verb, which then precedes an object. The basic word orders in the world's languages, then, could be interpreted to reflect how basic transitive constructions are built in those languages. The transitive constructions across languages have similar functions since they are used to convey that one entity is acting on another. The meaning conveyed by the constructions themselves, of something acting on something else, appears to be similar. But the forms they take differ dramatically worldwide. We now know that some languages, for instance Hixkaryana, use a basic transitive construction in which the object precedes the verb and then the subject, so "The sashimi sliced the chef" would be, counterintuitively to speakers of most languages, a normal way to describe a chef cutting raw fish for dinner.

To a growing number of linguists, *all* syntax can be explained by the myriad constructions that exist in the world's languages. There really is no such thing as syntax or grammar that is inherently different from learning words. Constructions and words vary only in terms of how abstract they are. Under this interpretation, when kids and others learn a given language, they are learning and memorizing countless constructions of varying degrees of abstraction and complexity. They are learning things like the basic transitive construction, the way construction, or completely prefilled-out constructions, that is, idioms like "kick the bucket." Or they are learning the many constructions that exist only in a language like Karitiâna or Hixkaryana or Mandarin. Under this interpretation, one reason that I initially faced such challenges teaching Spanish speakers aspects of English syntax is that there is no objective way to draw the division between idioms and other phrases. Idioms are just particular kinds of constructions, and constructions are at the core of language.

Conclusion: Our Changing Understanding of Words and Sentences

There is an interesting parallel between idiomatic language and iconic language, which I discussed in Chapter 7. Until recently, iconic words were thought to occupy spaces outside the periphery of the core components of language. And until recently, idioms were thought of as exceptional and relatively uncommon phrases that lay outside the core of grammar. The perception of both iconic words and idioms is changing rapidly. We now see that iconic words and other systematic sound-meaning correspondences are pervasive in speech and critical for kids learning how to encode concepts into words as they speak. Furthermore, the distinction between iconic and arbitrary words is not always easy to draw. Similarly, idioms and partially filled-out constructions are now recognized as pervasive and critical to how we speak, and to how we think in order to speak. And the distinction between idioms and other types of phrases is also hard to draw. In fact, the distinction may be impossible to draw since there is no clear motivation for separating idioms from other constructions. While iconicity and idioms are now seen to be critical to speech, we have also seen that the extent of clear iconicity in languages varies. In languages with a large set of ideophones, iconicity seems to play a more central role as people talk and think. We have also seen that the kinds of idioms and, more broadly, constructions that languages use can vary. Idioms that seem natural to speakers of one language may have no counterpart in another. An idiom that may seem normal to you as an English speaker, for instance "life is a journey," may seem odd to someone else if their language lacks both the idiom and the underlying metaphor reflected in it.

In this chapter I have focused on two of the most critical developments that have shifted our understanding of how humans around the world make sentences out of words. We have seen that one of the foremost proposals on a "universal" feature in the world's grammars is not well supported since there is no evidence of recursion in some languages. We have also seen that syntax can be explained largely by the impressive capacity of humans to decipher and memorize constructions, and to modify constructions to fit their communicative needs. There are many theories of syntax, but regardless of which theory a linguist might subscribe to, it is clear that those theories have had to wrestle with an impressive amount of diversity as languages from places like Amazonia and Australia have become better documented over the last few decades, helping to demonstrate that phenomena like recursion are not ubiquitous after all.

Much of the work that has transformed our understanding of syntax is also based on well-documented languages like English. The recognition of the ubiquity of constructions in English, with varying degrees of abstraction, has helped to illuminate languages in new ways. Framed differently, the recognition and study of constructions has suggested that syntax might not really be a unique and distinguishable characteristic of any language, including English. To some linguists, the study of syntax now simply represents the study of certain kinds of constructions, since constructions include everything from words, to idioms, to idioms that are not completely filled out, to completely blank templates for forms like ditransitive clauses. This interpretation impacts how we construe many aspects of grammar and associated thought, including the proposed centrality of recursion to grammar. To a proponent of construction grammar, the fact that some Amazonian and Australian languages lack recursion suggests that those languages happen to lack clause-type constructions that include a slot in which another clause can be inserted. Perhaps this should not be too surprising since there are many construction types, like specific idioms, that are not found in all or even most languages. This fact helps explain why it is so difficult to learn new languages: language learning requires the memorization of all sorts of new construction types that vary in their levels of abstraction.

This latter point suggests that people, including children, do not really learn syntactic and grammatical rules as much as they memorize associations between meanings and linguistic forms, associations we call constructions. We recognize and learn patterns in the speech around us, deciphering and memorizing constructions along the way. Conveying meaning effectively requires us to access the various memorized constructions that might be used in a given moment to transmit our thoughts. This interpretation implies that learning languages is perhaps not as unique a skill set as was once believed, since recognizing and learning patterns is what humans do in many experiential and behavioral domains. One of the appealing things about the construction-based approach to the study of syntax, to many language researchers anyhow, is that it does not require a search for some specific part of the brain that allows for syntax, one that is encoded in our genes. Searches for a language gene (or genes) have been unsuccessful. For those who believe in construction grammar, such a search is unnecessary in the first place.[9]

Finally, it is worth again underscoring the incredible diversity, far greater than we once realized, of spoken languages. This diversity extends to the grammars of spoken languages since those languages contain a countless array of constructions. Some cultures speak languages that lack constructions in which one clause can be inserted inside another—that is, they lack recursion—as work among the Pirahã and Warlpiri and other cultures has now shown. But the world's cultures use languages that vary profoundly in other ways, as we have seen throughout this book. Languages vary in terms of how they encode spatial relationships, how they encode colors, how they require speakers to use their vocal apparatus to create meaning, and so on. As this chapter highlights, they also vary in terms of how they string words together. Each language provides a distinctive array of constructions people must learn in order to convey and decipher thoughts.

Conclusion

PEOPLE HAVE BEEN TRYING to make sense of languages and linguistic diversity for millennia. Consider the story of the Tower of Babel, written over two and a half thousand years ago. We are told in Genesis that humans were constructing the tower to try to reach heaven. Dismayed by their hubris, God cast them into a world of linguistic confusion by creating diverse and mutually unintelligible tongues. Given that this story associates linguistic diversity with punishment, it shows that people have long been frustrated by the existence of that diversity, or at least by the cross-cultural communication issues such diversity can create. The Babel story also underscores how it has long been recognized that the origin of languages and linguistic diversity requires an explanation. The Hebrews were not the only ancient peoples who wanted to understand why the world's languages, or more specifically the languages in their corner of the world, were so different from each other. In fact, there are interesting parallels between the story of Babel and older myths in places like Sumer and Assyria, suggesting that the Genesis story represents an adaptation of other stories shared by people who were close to the Hebrews in space and time. The Assyrians and Sumerians were no doubt not the first people to offer myths on the origins of languages. People have long been trying to wrap their heads around those origins, and orally transmitted mythological accounts of the birth of linguistic diversity likely predate these written accounts by many thousands of years. Such accounts are not unique to the Fertile Crescent. It is not hard to see why people everywhere have long been puzzled by the existence of so many languages and where language comes from in general. It is clear that humans are the only talking species and that talking distinguishes how we communicate but also how we think. Grappling with the origins of speech is just one way of grappling with who we are and how we came to be so distinct cognitively, as a species. Linguistic diversity has long muddied cross-cultural contact and trade, heightening the fear of foreigners. Grappling with that diversity is hardly a new struggle either.[1]

Unsurprisingly, then, scholarly inquiry into language and linguistic diversity is not new. Well over two millennia ago, the Indian scholar Pānini was offering profound insights into the grammar of Sanskrit, including descriptions of aspects of its sound system and grammar. Greek philosophers, including Socrates and Plato, were offering treatises on the nature of communication during the same era as Pānini. The complexity of language is underscored by the fact that despite its having been studied for millennia by bright minds like Pānini, Socrates, Darwin, and countless others, there is still much we do not know about human speech. As we have seen in this book, we are still discovering critical things about languages and how they reflect our diverse cognitive experiences. This book has focused on a variety of discoveries on language and associated thought, but I should stress that there are many other related discoveries that I did not include. As first noted in the Introduction, my aim was to survey topics that would be of interest to a wide variety of readers, though my own biases have certainly influenced the subjects chosen. Given that I am not an expert on signed languages, for instance, the topics I chose all relate to speech (including gestures made alongside speech) as opposed to signed languages. But many fascinating findings on signed languages have been published in the last few decades.[2]

The themes discussed in the book were selected in part because they underscore how language is connected, in ways we probably still do not fully appreciate, to human thought more broadly and to other aspects of the human experience. It is increasingly clear that we cannot understand language without understanding things like cognitive associations between some sounds and some meanings, or without understanding the sociocultural and physical environments in which languages evolve. In coming to better understand such topics, we have come to better appreciate how language both encodes and affects the human cognitive experience. The study of language has arguably been invigorated of late because so many scholars are placing more emphasis on its interconnectedness with supposedly nonlinguistic phenomena. Partially because of this emphasis, language research has become truly cross-disciplinary. The discoveries discussed in this book were made not just by linguists, but by psychologists, anthropologists, and other researchers who prefer none of those labels. They were made by researchers who are simply interested in what we can learn from studying the world's myriad tongues. Researchers who increasingly recognize that speech cannot be understood if we divorce it from other facets of the human experience.

Researchers who now take it for granted that, to truly understand speech and thought, we must focus on the languages of WEIRD and non-WEIRD people alike.

The State of Language Research

Language is perhaps the most distinctive feature of our species. Our understanding of that feature is changing and, in so doing, is giving us new insights into what it means to be human. I hope this book has offered some sense of those insights: how linguistic discoveries are changing our understanding of the ways people talk and think about basic phenomena like space and time; how they are revealing in new ways how people talk and think across the distinct environments in which languages are used; and finally how they are reshaping our understanding of how people think as they create words and sentences.

There are also recurrent methodological themes evident in the research surveyed. Perhaps the most obvious one is that studies are now based increasingly on data from lesser-known non-WEIRD languages. To be clear, I am not suggesting that this is a brand-new development. At least since the Sanskrit grammarian Pāṇini, people have been studying non-WEIRD languages, though it is worth noting that Sanskrit is also an Indo-European language. At the beginning of the twentieth century, anthropologists like Franz Boas recognized that linguists needed to study diverse languages in places like the Americas in order to truly understand how language works. In 1917 Boas founded the *International Journal of American Linguistics,* the oldest American linguistics journal, in order to promote the study of such languages. The journal continues to publish studies on indigenous languages, but now there are many other related journals doing similar work. Such journals have served as outlets for countless findings presented during the twentieth and twenty-first centuries. Those findings have grown significantly in the last few decades. Furthermore, the findings are now available online and often published alongside actual linguistic data. The data now available on indigenous languages far exceed what was available even ten years ago and are often only a few clicks away.

This brings us to a second methodological trend evident in contemporary research on linguistic diversity. It has become much more computational in nature, and not just because the results of studies can be placed online. Field linguists and others have laptops with processing power and access to storage that were unfathomable just decades ago. High-fidelity audio and video data are increasingly the norm, regardless of the language being studied. These data highlight how people talk, rather than how linguists think they talk. Where once only a few languages could be studied with computational methods that analyzed large bodies of linguistic data for patterns, now such methods can be applied to many unrelated languages. We can see in the data how people worldwide use idioms and other constructions, or how they actually use sounds to encode meaning, or how countless other facets of language work in an empirically sound and less speculative manner. Related to this, experimental methods have become more common in linguistics and associated disciplines, even among linguists who work in remote locales. These days, field researchers can take software for creating experiments into the field. In some cases they can even take portable devices that test brain activity during speech. This latter new development, not discussed in this book, hints at the novel findings to be uncovered in coming decades as the distinction between lab-based work on WEIRD languages and fieldwork on non-WEIRD languages crumbles.

Related to these trends is perhaps the most pervasive tendency in language research: the greater reliance on quantitative methods. Data analysis via coding languages like R and Python is becoming the norm, as is the increased statistical literacy of language researchers. Many contemporary scholars were trained in PhD programs that emphasized quantitative data analysis and statistical literacy, or they have learned skills along the way that allow them to tackle questions with quantitative methods. The data resulting from such methods are now often published alongside the papers based on those data. This data transparency allows other researchers to more easily seek to replicate the findings in a given study. This trend toward open and collaborative science, reliant on the sharing of code and quantitative methods, is of course not restricted to language research, but it is transforming language research. The trend is not without its detractors. Some linguists would argue that many contemporary researchers are privileging data and statistical literacy over the understanding of traditional methods in linguistics. In truth, all the methods are necessary, both traditional and modern, as evidenced by the fact that the findings surveyed in this book are the product of studies based on a variety of methods. Perhaps the biggest source of those findings remains studies using tried and true methods of linguistic fieldwork that simply cannot be replaced by newer approaches: learning and describing languages that have received little documentation. Every time a linguist describes a language whose properties were unknown beforehand, our understanding of language and thought shifts a little bit. Sometimes a lot.

Just as we need continued studies using traditional field methods and others using quantitative, experimental, and computational tools, we need studies that integrate such approaches. That integration is happening more as linguists learn new methods but also as they collaborate with researchers in other fields. In this book we have seen the extent of that collaboration. Linguists are collaborating with data scientists, with neurologists, with computer scientists, and even with medical researchers to uncover new findings about talking and interrelated forms of behavior. As a result, their findings are being published in general science journals with broad reach and impact, not only in linguistics journals. This publishing trend is evident in the references cited in this book. It is a trend that is leading, in turn, to even greater collaboration, as nonlinguists are now reading research on language and developing their own testable questions and hypotheses. It is exciting to think of where these new questions and hypotheses will take the study of language and linguistic diversity.

The Clock Is Ticking: The Ongoing Extinction of Languages

The focus on non-WEIRD languages evident in this book faces some clear challenges in the coming years. As noted in the Introduction, we are presently standing at the intersection of two metaphorical lines. One of the lines is trending upward, along the y axis. It represents the growth of data on the world's seven-thousand-plus languages, an upward trajectory that owes itself to the work of field linguists worldwide and to the new founts of big data that are revolutionizing our understanding of speech. The other line is trending downward precipitously. It represents the amount of actual linguistic diversity in the world, which is diminishing as many small languages fade into oblivion. The reasons for their disappearance are varied, though they typically relate to the greater socioeconomic usefulness of more widely spoken languages. Worldwide, children in small cultures are migrating to languages in which they need fluency in order to acquire jobs and to consume media—languages like English, Mandarin, and Spanish. The ongoing disappearance of languages casts an ominous shadow on the prospects of future discoveries that are truly based on representative samples of the world's languages, not merely on a biased subset.[3]

The recent growth of linguistic data, and the growing body of insights generated from those data, has been the focus of this book. Many of the findings this book has described could not even have been guessed at just a few decades ago. Seemingly every month a new study is published, often one based on a newly available database or findings from a lesser-known language, that alters somewhat our understanding of speech and, sometimes, how humans think as they speak. The trend will likely continue, though one wonders if it can continue at the current rate given the continuous disappearance of so many languages.

Despite such clear trends, it is difficult to predict where the next decades of language research will take us, particularly given how unpredictable many of the findings discussed in this book were when they were uncovered. Although it is difficult to make specific predictions regarding future discoveries about language, we can predict that those discoveries will continue to enrich our understanding of how we talk and think.

NOTES

ACKNOWLEDGMENTS

INDEX

NOTES

INTRODUCTION

1. Boas's work on words for "snow" in Inuit is presented in Franz Boas, "Introduction," in *The Handbook of North American Indians* (Washington, DC: Smithsonian Institution Bulletin, 1911), 25–26. The gradual exaggeration of Eskimo words for snow is described in Laura Martin, "'Eskimo Words for Snow': A Case Study in the Genesis and Decay of an Anthropological Example," *American Anthropologist* 88 (1986): 418–423, as well as in Geoffrey K. Pullum, *The Great Eskimo Vocabulary Hoax* (Chicago: University of Chicago Press, 1991). Note that I have oversimplified matters here a bit, as the words for snow in the language are not really constrained by these particular word roots entirely. These roots can also be modified by a series of affixes in Inuit, which gives the impression that there are so many words for snow. However, this is a bit like saying that English has many words for "running" because I can say "I ran," "I will run," "I was running," and so forth. Inuit does not have dozens of word roots for snow.

2. Perhaps the best source on the classification of the world's many languages and language families is David Eberhard, ed., *Ethnologue* (Dallas: SIL International, 2020).

3. Note that I say the universalist perspective is becoming less influential, judging from the most impactful research today. An examination of the studies on language in high-impact science or cognitive science journals reveals a paucity of studies in the universalist paradigm. Nevertheless, given the rate of change associated with tenured professorships, it is not surprising

that many linguistics departments still adhere to the universalist paradigm in one form or another. For the widely shared study on the overreliance on English, see Damián Blasi, Joseph Henrich, Evangelia Adamou, David Kemmerer, and Asifa Majid, "Over-reliance on English Hinders Cognitive Science," *Trends in Cognitive Sciences* 26 (2022): https://doi.org/10.1016/j.tics .2022.09.015.

4. For a discussion of universal grammar and the apparent lack of support for any meaningful linguistic universals, see Nicholas Evans and Stephen Levinson, "The Myth of Language Universals: Language Diversity and Its Importance for Cognitive Science," *Behavioral and Brain Sciences* 32 (2009): 429–492.

5. Joseph Henrich, Steven Heine, and Ara Norenzayan, "The Weirdest People in the World?," *Behavioral and Brain Sciences* 33 (2010): 61–135, 61.

6. Caleb Everett, *Numbers and the Making of Us* (Cambridge, MA: Harvard University Press, 2017).

7. My parents were missionaries in Amazonia, where my two sisters (to whom this book is dedicated) and I were raised. My father eventually left that discipline and became a professor and linguist; some of his work is mentioned in this book. For more on that story, see Daniel Everett, *Don't Sleep There Are Snakes* (New York: Vintage, 2008).

8. These figures on language "death" are taken from David Graddol, "The Future of Language," *Science* 303 (2004): 1329–1331. See also Eberhard, *Ethnologue*.

1 YOUR FUTURE IS BEHIND YOU

1. Many of the findings on Karitiâna are taken from my PhD dissertation: Caleb Everett, "Patterns in Karitiâna: Articulation, Perception and Grammar" (PhD diss., Rice University, 2007).

2. This Yucatec Maya example is taken from Jürgen Bohnemeyer, "Temporal Anaphora in a Tenseless Language," in *The Expression of Time,* ed. Wolfgang Klein and Ping Li (Berlin: Walter de Gruyter, 2009), 83–128. For a comprehensive discussion of tense and how it is expressed in the world's languages, see Bernard Comrie, *Tense* (Cambridge, UK: Cambridge University Press, 1985).

Many of the points in this discussion, particularly those related to Yagua, are based on Thomas Payne, *Describing Morphosyntax* (Cambridge, UK: Cambridge University Press, 1997). For an in-depth discussion of how languages encode time and how space plays such a large role in that encoding, see Vyvyan Evans, *Language and Time: A Cognitive Linguistics Approach* (Cambridge, UK: Cambridge University Press, 2013).

3. Benjamin Whorf, "An American Indian Model of the Universe," *ETC: A Review of General Semantics* 8 (1950): 27–33.

4. John Lucy, *Language Diversity and Thought: A Reformulation of the Linguistic Relativity Hypothesis* (Chicago: University of Chicago Press, 1992).

5. For more on the role of how writing systems affect mental representations of time, see Christian Dobel, Stefanie Enriquez-Geppert, Pienie Zwitserlood, and Jens Bölte, "Literacy Shapes Thought: The Case of Event Representation in Different Cultures," *Frontiers in Psychology* 5 (2014): 290.

6. The discussion of Kuuk Thaayorre is based primarily on Lera Boroditsky and Alice Gaby, "Remembrances of Times East: Absolute Spatial Representations of Time in an Australian Aboriginal Community," *Psychological Science* 21 (2010): 1635–1639. Lera Boroditsky's influential work on the effect of language on thought includes Lera Boroditsky, "Does Language Shape Thought? Mandarin and English Speakers' Conceptions of Time," *Cognitive Psychology* 4 (2001): 1–22, as well as "Metaphoric Structuring: Understanding Time through Spatial Metaphors," *Cognition* 75 (2000): 1–28.

7. The reference to -*kaw* and -*kuw* is taken from Alice Gaby, "The Thaayorre Think of Time like They Talk of Space," *Frontiers in Psychology* 3 (2012): 300.

8. The study of speakers' body sway, when thinking about past and future events, is presented in Lynden Miles, Sarah Stuart, and C. Neil Macrae, "Moving through Time," *Psychological Science* 21 (2010): 222–223. The follow-up work referred to here is John Stins, Laura Habets, Rowie Jongeling, and Rouwen Cañal-Bruland, "Being (Un)moved by Mental Time Travel," *Consciousness and Cognition* 42 (2016): 374–381.

9. This discussion of Aymara is based on Rafael E. Núñez and Eve Sweetser, "With the Future behind Them: Convergent Evidence from Aymara Language and Gesture in the Crosslinguistic Comparison of Spatial Construals

of Time," *Cognitive Science* 30 (2006): 401–450. The examples are taken from that same paper.

10. The claims on Lisu and Tibeto-Burman languages are taken from David Bradley, "Space in Lisu," *Himalayan Linguistics* 16 (2017): 1–22, 2.

11. The Yupno data on which this discussion is based are found in Rafael E. Núñez, Kensy Cooperrider, and Jürg Wassmann, "Contours of Time: Topographic Construals of Past, Present, and Future in the Yupno Valley of Papua New Guinea," *Cognition* 124 (2012): 25–35.

12. The Tzeltal data and discussion are based most heavily on Penelope Brown, "Time and Space in Tzeltal: Is the Future Uphill?," *Frontiers in Psychology* 3 (2012): https://doi.org/10.3389/fpsyg.2012.00212.

13. See Simeon Floyd, "Modally Hybrid Grammar: Celestial Pointing for Time-of-Day Reference in Nheengatú," *Language* 92 (2016): 32.

14. Tupi-Kawahíb temporal reference is described in Chris Sinha, Vera Da Silva Sinha, Jörg Zinken, and Wany Sampaio, "When Time Is Not Space: The Social and Linguistic Construction of Time Intervals and Temporal Event Relations in an Amazonian Culture," *Language and Cognition* 3 (2011): 137–169.

15. One relevant study on temporal reference in Yélî Dnye is presented in Stephen Levinson and Asifa Majid, "The Island of Time: Yélî Dnye, the Language of Rossel Island," *Frontiers in Psychology* 4 (2013): https://doi.org/10.3389/fpsyg .2013.00061. For a discussion of Mian, see Sebastian Fedden and Lera Boroditsky, "Spatialization of Time in Mian," *Frontiers in Psychology* 3 (2013): https://doi.org/10.3389/fpsyg.2012.00485. Note that in this discussion, I have also focused primarily on deictic temporal reference. In linguistics, "deictic" refers to words or other aspects of language whose meaning is contingent on the context in which they are produced. For example, if I say "you," the person that the particular "you" refers to depends entirely on when and where I am, so "you" is a deictic word. When it comes to time, the actual days referred to by words like "tomorrow" depend on when the word is uttered. "Tomorrow" is inherently deictic, as it is grounded in a particular moment. Similarly, the spatially based expressions we have examined are generally deictic. If I state, "My past is behind me," the central reference point is the present context, the moment in which the phrase is uttered. So this usage of

the past-is-behind metaphor is an example of what we call deictic time or deictic temporal reference. Tense is inherently deictic as well. Past, present, and future refer to different times depending on when those particular tenses are employed. Much of temporal reference is not deictic but sequential, however, as it is not anchored to the moment in which a given word or phrase is produced. Instead, the temporal referents of sequential time are grounded to each other. If I say, "Monday follows Sunday" or "February comes before March," the validity of the phrases holds regardless of when I say them. As these particular examples demonstrate, sequential time can also be construed in terms of space. We can talk about events "following" each other or coming "before" each other. However, we often map sequential time onto space in a way that is not grounded on our bodies, wherein the future is forward or behind us, but in a way that is grounded on some external framework. In many of the world's cultures, this is now done with symbolic practices such as calendrical notation of various kinds. Many people now map time onto calendars in a left-to-right, top-to-bottom fashion wherein earlier dates occur to the left of later dates, and also occur above later dates. This kind of two-dimensional sequential reference to time is learned from such an early age that it seems quite natural to us. As noted above, such references are based at least in part on the direction of the writing system used in a given culture. This kind of spatial representation of time is hardly natural to all people but rather the result of a series of practices that have evolved in only a fraction of the world's cultures. It just so happens that a large percentage of the world's people now speak those languages.

16. For an extensive discussion of the way variations in numbers across the world's languages impact speakers' thoughts and their lives more generally, see Caleb Everett, *Numbers and the Making of Us* (Cambridge, MA: Harvard University Press, 2017).

17. For more on the topic of linguistic reference to time, see Evans, *Language and Time*. For more on how humans think of time and those aspects of temporal progression that are biologically ingrained, see Alan Burdick, *Why Time Flies: A Mostly Scientific Investigation* (New York: Simon & Schuster, 2017).

18. The quote from Rafael E. Núñez is taken from Núñez, Cooperrider, and Wassmann, "Contours of Time," 34.

2 TURN TO YOUR WEST

1. Human spatial cognition and the linguistic encoding of space have been written upon extensively in a variety of works. As a starting point for further reading on this topic, see Stephen Levinson, *Space in Language and Cognition: Explorations in Cognitive Diversity* (Cambridge, UK: Cambridge University Press, 2003).

2. For more on Guugu Yimithirr spatial reference, see, for instance, John Haviland, "Anchoring, Iconicity, and Orientation in Guugu Yimithirr Pointing Gestures," *Journal of Linguistic Anthropology* 3 (1993): 3–45. The anecdote about Roger is taken from Levinson, *Space in Language and Cognition*, 4.

3. Penelope Brown and Stephen Levison, "'Uphill' and 'Downhill' in Tzeltal," *Journal of Linguistic Anthropology* 3 (1993): 46–74.

4. The three widely agreed on spatial frames of reference, all discussed in this chapter, are egocentric, geocentric, and object-centered. Some have suggested that there are more basic spatial frames of reference. See, e.g., Eve Danziger, "Deixis, Gesture and Cognition in Spatial Frame of Reference Typology," *Studies in Language* 34 (2010):167–185.

5. See, for example, the extensive discussion of this topic in Peggy Li and Lila Gleitman, "Turning the Tables: Language and Spatial Reasoning," *Cognition* 83 (2002): 265–294.

6. These experiments in Holland and Namibia are described in detail in Daniel Haun, Christian Rapold, Gabriele Janzen, and Stephen Levinson, "Plasticity of Human Spatial Cognition: Spatial Language and Cognition Covary across Cultures," *Cognition* 119 (2011): 70–80.

7. For more on the spatial representations of humans and other hominids, see Daniel Haun, Josep Call, Gabriele Janzen, and Stephen Levinson, "Evolutionary Psychology of Spatial Representations in the Hominidae," *Current Biology* 17 (2006): 1736–1740.

8. The finding that people use about sixteen thousand words per day is taken from Matthias Mehl, Simine Vazire, Nairán Ramírez-Esparza, Richard Slatcher, and James Pennebaker, "Are Women Really More Talkative than Men?," *Science* 317 (2007): 82.

9. For more on the ways that vocation and landscape interact in the Dhivehi language, as well as in Marshallese, see Bill Palmer, Jonathon Lum, Jonathan

Schlossberg, and Alice Gaby, "How Does the Environment Shape Spatial Language? Evidence for Sociotopography," *Linguistic Typology* 21 (2017): 457–491.

10. For more on the diversity of spatial language within communities, see Palmer et al., "How Does the Environment Shape Spatial Language?"

11. For a survey of interesting facts about the Pirahã language, see the work of my father: e.g., Daniel Everett, "Cultural Constraints on Grammar and Cognition in Pirahã: Another Look at the Design Features of Human Language," *Current Anthropology* 46 (2005): 621–646.

12. Enfield discusses Lao landscape terms at length in Nick Enfield, "Linguistic Categories and Their Utilities: The Case of Lao Landscape Terms," *Language Sciences* 30 (2008): 227–255. The excerpt I use here is taken from page 235.

13. The special issue of *Language Sciences* was edited by Niclas Burenhult. The quote is taken from Niclas Burenhult and Stephen Levinson, "Language and Landscape: A Cross-Linguistic Perspective," in "Language and Landscape: Geographical Ontology in Cross-linguistic Perspective," ed. Niclas Burenhult, special issue, *Language Sciences* 30 (2008): 135–150.

14. These examples are taken from the same issue of *Language Sciences* edited by Burenhult.

15. For further discussion of Yélî Dnye landscape terms, see Stephen Levinson, "Landscape, Seascape and the Ontology of Places on Rossel Island, Papua New Guinea," *Language Sciences* 30 (2008): 256–290.

16. For more on the Lokono language related to landscapes, see Konrad Rybka, "Between Objects and Places: The Expression of Landforms in Lokono (Arawakan)," *International Journal of American Linguistics* 81 (2015): 539–572.

3 WHO'S YOUR BROTHER?

1. The most definitive work on Karitiâna kinship terms is Rachel Landin, "Kinship and Naming among the Karitiâna of Northwestern Brazil" (master's thesis, University of Texas at Arlington, 1989). See also the dictionary written by David Landin, *Dicionário e Léxico Karitiâna / Português* (Brasília: Summer Institute of Linguistics, 1983). David Landin and Rachel Landin were missionary linguists who were the first to document the Karitiâna language in detail.

2. See Daniel Everett, "Cultural Constraints on Grammar and Cognition in Pirahã: Another Look at the Design Features of Human Language," *Current Anthropology* 46 (2005): 621–646.

3. This quote is taken from Carnegie Mellon University, "Relatively Speaking: Carnegie Mellon and UC Berkeley Researchers Identify Principles That Shape Kinship Categories across Languages," press release, May 24, 2012, www.cmu.edu/news/stories/archives/2012/may/may24_languagestudy .html. The study in question is Charles Kemp and Terry Regier, "Kinship Categories across Languages Reflect General Communicative Principles," *Science* 336 (2012): 1049–1054.

4. For one excellent book on grammatical gender, based on data from many languages, see Greville Corbett, *Gender* (Cambridge, UK: Cambridge University Press, 1991).

5. Dyirbal's system of grammatical gender inspired the famous book by George Lakoff, *Women, Fire, and Dangerous Things* (Chicago: University of Chicago Press, 1987). Dyirbal gender was described in R. M. W. Dixon, *The Dyirbal Language of North Queensland* (Cambridge, UK: Cambridge University Press, 1972).

6. Thomas Payne, *Describing Morphosyntax* (Cambridge, UK: Cambridge University Press, 1997), 109.

7. In my first book I surveyed some of this research on linguistic relativity. See Caleb Everett, *Linguistic Relativity: Evidence across Languages and Cognitive Domains* (Berlin: De Gruyter, 2013).

8. The Yagua examples are taken from Payne, *Describing Morphosyntax*, 108. For more on Yucatec Maya's noun classifiers, see John Lucy, *Grammatical Categories and Cognition* (Cambridge, UK: Cambridge University Press, 1996).

9. This discussion is based on John Lucy and Suzanne Gaskins, "Grammatical Categories and the Development of Classification Preferences: A Comparative Approach," in *Language Acquisition and Conceptual Development,* ed. Melissa Bowerman and Stephen Levinson (Cambridge, UK: Cambridge University Press, 2001). Quote taken from page 271.

10. For one engaging survey of the cultural and linguistic effects on thought, see Mutsumi Imai, Junko Kanero, and Takahiko Masuda, "The Relation

between Language, Culture and Thought," *Current Opinion in Psychology* 8 (2016): 70–77.

11. This discussion of Miraña noun classes is based in part on Frank Seifart and Collette Grinevald, "Noun Classes in African and Amazonian Languages: Towards a Comparison," *Linguistic Typology* 8 (2004): 243–285. See also Frank Seifart, "The Structure and Use of Shape-Based Noun Classes in Miraña (North West Amazon)" (PhD diss., Radboud University, 2005). Note that I have simplified the spelling of Miraña words in my examples.

12. Greville Corbett, "Number of Genders," in *World Atlas of Language Structures Online*, ed. Matthew Dryer and Martin Haspelmath (Leipzig: Max Planck Institute for Evolutionary Anthropology, 2013), https://wals.info/chapter/30.

13. David Gil, "Numeral Classifiers," in *The World Atlas of Language Structures Online*, https://wals.info/chapter/55.

4 THE SKY IS *GRUE*

1. Brent Berlin and Paul Kay, *Basic Color Terms: Their Universality and Evolution* (Berkeley: University of California Press, 1969).

2. Brent Berlin, Luisa Maffi, and Paul Kay, *The World Color Survey* (Stanford, CA: CSLI, 2009). For more on the fifteen color terms of Korean, see Debi Roberson, Hyensou Pak, and J. Richard Hanley, "Categorical Perception of Colour in the Left and Right Visual Field Is Verbally Mediated: Evidence from Korean," *Cognition* 107 (2008): 752–762.

3. Harold Conklin, "Hanunóo Color Categories," *Journal of Anthropological Research* 42 (1986 [1955]): 441–446. For Lucy's comments on the limitations of Berlin and Kay's approach, see John Lucy, "The Linguistics of 'Color,'" in *Color Categories in Thought and Language*, ed. C. L. Hardin and Luisa Maffi (Cambridge, UK: Cambridge University Press, 1997), 320–346. Another critique of this approach is found in Anna Wierzbicka, "There Are No 'Color Universals' but There Are Universals of Visual Semantics," *Anthropological Linguistics* 47 (2005): 217–244.

4. See Anna Wierzbicka, "The Meaning of Color Terms: Semantics, Culture and Cognition," *Cognitive Linguistics* 1 (1990): 99–150.

5. Edward Gibson, Richard Futrell, Julian Jara-Ettinger, Kyle Mahowald, Leon Bergen, Sivalogeswaran Ratnasingam, Mitchell Gibson, Steven T. Piantadosi, and Bevil R. Conway, "Color Naming across Languages Reflects Color Use," *Proceedings of the National Academy of Sciences of the United States of America* 114 (2017): 10785–10790.

6. Jules Davidoff, Ian Davies, and Debi Roberson, "Colour Categories in a Stone-Age Tribe," *Nature* 398 (1999): 203–204.

7. For one study on the color-discrimination effects associated with terms for blue, and for many references on that particular topic, see Fernando González-Perilli, Ignacio Rebollo, Alejandro Maiche, and Analía Arévalo, "Blues in Two Different Spanish-Speaking Populations," *Frontiers in Communication* (2017): https://doi.org/10.3389/fcomm.2017.00018. Note that the right visual field is perceived by both eyes, and the left visual field is perceived by both eyes as well. In essence, the right visual field is perceived by a left set of retinal fibers in both eyes, and the left visual field is perceived by a right set of retinal fibers in both eyes.

8. Lewis Forder and Gary Lupyan, "Hearing Words Changes Color Perception: Facilitation of Color Discrimination by Verbal and Visual Cues," *Journal of Experimental Psychology: General* 148 (2019): 1105–1123.

9. Henning's quote is taken from Hans Henning, *Der Geruch* (Leipzig: JA Barth, 1916), 16. This section of his work is also cited in Asifa Majid and Niclas Burenhult, "Odors Are Expressible in Language, as Long as You Speak the Right Language," *Cognition* 130 (2014): 266–270.

10. See also Niclas Burenhult and Asifa Majid, "Olfaction in Aslian Ideology and Language," *Senses and Society* 6 (2011): 19–29.

11. See as well Ewelina Wnuk and Asifa Majid, "Revisiting the Limits of Language: The Odor Lexicon of Maniq," *Cognition* 131 (2014): 125–138.

12. Asifa Majid and Nicole Kruspe, "Hunter-Gatherer Olfaction Is Special," *Current Biology* 28 (2018): 409–413, 412.

13. Carolyn O'Meara and Asifa Majid, "How Changing Lifestyles Impact Seri Smellscapes and Smell Language," *Anthropological Linguistics* 48 (2016): 107–131, 126.

14. For evidence of elaborate color terms in the absence of such pressures, see Ewelina Wnuk, Annemarie Verkerk, Stephen Levinson, and Asifa Majid,

"Color Technology Is Not Necessary for Rich and Efficient Color Language," *Cognition* 229 (2022): doi: 10.1016/j.cognition.2022.105223. Epub 2022 Sep 13. PMID: 36113197.

15. For more on Totonac-Tepehua olfactory terms, see "The Challenge of Olfactory Ideophones: Reconsidering Ineffability from the Totonac-Tepehua Perspective," *International Journal of American Linguistics* 85 (2019): 173–212.

16. The results from Cha'palaa, along with this quote, are taken from Simeon Floyd, Lia San Roque, and Asifa Majid, "Smell Is Coded in Grammar and Frequent in Discourse: Cha'palaa Olfactory Language in Cross-Linguistic Perspective," *Journal of Linguistic Anthropology* 28 (2018): 175–196, 189.

17. Asifa Majid, Seán Roberts, Ludy Cilissen, Karen Emmorey, Brenda Nicodemus, Lucinda O'Grady, Bencie Woll et al., "Differential Coding of Perception in the World's Languages," *Proceedings of the National Academy of Sciences of the United States of America* 115 (2018): 11369–11376, 11374.

5 DESERT ICE

1. JeongBeom Lee and YoungOh Shin, "Comparison of Density and Output of Sweat Gland in Tropical Africans and Temperate Koreans," *Autonomic Neuroscience* 205 (2017): 67–71.

2. Bergmann's rule, like the related Allen's rule, is actually quite old. It dates to Karl Bergmann, "Ueber die verhältnisse der wärmeökonomie der thiere zu ihrer grösse," *Gottinger Stud* 3 (1847): 595–708. Allen's rule was described first in Joel Asaph Allen, "The Influence of Physical Conditions in the Genesis of Species," *Radical Review* 1 (1877): 108–140. Note that Bergmann's rule may not be due to the conservation of heat in mammals, however. This point is disputed in, for instance, Kyle Ashton, Mark Tracy, and Ala de Queiroz, "Is Bergmann's Rule Valid for Mammals?," *American Naturalist* 156 (2000): 390–415. Other accounts suggest that resource scarcity in some environments may account for the distribution described by Bergmann's rule. Regardless, the effect remains an environmentally motivated one.

3. While there is general agreement that lighter skin developed over the last fifty thousand to seventy-five thousand years as *Homo sapiens* reached higher latitudes, there is disagreement as to how much of this lightening was due

to facilitating vitamin D processing. See Andrea Hanel and Carsten Carlberg, "Skin Colour and Vitamin D: An Update," *Experimental Dermatology* (2020): https://doi.org/10.1111/exd.14142.

4. For a contemporary discussion of vitamin D consumption and its role in preventing rickets and osteomalacia, see Jan Pedersen, "Vitamin D Requirement and Setting Recommendation Levels—Current Nordic View," *Nutrition Reviews* 66 (2008): S165–S169.

5. Joseph Henrich, *The Secret of Our Success: How Culture Is Driving Human Evolution* (Princeton, NJ: Princeton University Press, 2015).

6. See Terry Regier, Alexandra Carstensen, and Charles Kemp, "Languages Support Efficient Communication about the Environment: Words for Snow Revisited," *PLOS ONE* (2016): https://doi.org/10.1371/journal.pone.0151138.

7. Caleb Everett, "Is Native Quantitative Thought Linguistically Privileged? A Look at the Global Picture," *Cognitive Neuropsychology* (2019): https://doi.org/10.1080/02643294.2019.1668368. For one account suggesting that agriculture and industrialization were favored in certain environments, see Jared Diamond, *Guns, Germs, and Steel* (New York City: W. W. Norton, 1999).

8. Cecil H. Brown, "Hand and Arm," in *World Atlas of Language Structures Online,* ed. Matthew Dryer and Martin Haspelmath (Leipzig: Max Planck Institute for Evolutionary Anthropology, 2013), https://wals.info/feature/129A#2/14.9/153.5.

9. Jonas Nölle, Simon Kirby, Jennifer Culbertson, and Kenny Smith, "Does Environment Shape Spatial Language? A Virtual Reality Experiment," *Evolang Proceedings* 13 (2020): 321–323.

10. The database is called PHOIBLE. See Steven Moran and Daniel McCloy (eds.), PHOIBLE 2.0, 2019. Jena: Max Planck Institute for the Science of Human History, http://phoible.org.

11. Ian Maddieson, "Voicing and Gaps in Plosive Systems," in *World Atlas of Language Structures Online,* https://wals.info/chapter/5.

12. Caleb Everett, "The Global Dispreference for Posterior Voiced Obstruents: A Quantitative Assessment of Word List Data," *Language* 94 (2018): e311–e323.

13. For one recent study on the effect of environment and cultural transmission on the degree to which a culture relies on agriculture, see Bruno Vilela, Trevor Fristoe, Ty Tuff et al., "Cultural Transmission and Ecological Opportunity

Jointly Shaped Global Patterns of Reliance on Agriculture," *Evolutionary Human Sciences* 2 (2020): e53.

14. Charles Hockett, "Distinguished Lecture: F," *American Anthropologist* 87 (1985): 263–281. Hockett was not the only researcher in the 1980s to suggest indirect effects of the environment on the sounds used in language. See, for example, John G. Fought, Robert L. Munroe, Carmen Fought, and Erin Good, "Sonority and Climate in a World Sample of Languages: Findings and Prospects," *Cross-Cultural Research* 38 (2004): 27–51.

15. See, for instance, Renata Bastos, José Valladares-Neto, and David Normando, "Dentofacial Biometry as a Discriminant Factor in the Identification of Remote Amazon Indigenous Populations," *American Journal of Orthodontics* 157 (2020): 619–630.

16. Dámian Blasi, Steve Moran, Scott Moisik, Paul Widmer, Dan Dediu, and Balthasar Bickel, "Human Sound Systems Are Shaped by Post-Neolithic Changes in Bite Configuration," *Science* 363 (2019): eaav3218.

17. Caleb Everett and Sihan Chen, "Speech Adapts to Differences in Dentition within and across Populations," *Scientific Reports* 11 (2021): 1066.

18. For one of many studies on the effects of dry air on the vocal cords, see Elizabeth Erickson and Mahalakshmi Sivasankar, "Evidence for Adverse Phonatory Change Following an Inhaled Combination Treatment," *Journal of Speech, Language and Hearing Research* 53 (2010): 75–83. For a survey of the research on the effects of dry vocal cords on phonation, see Ciara Leydon, Mahalakshmi Sivasankar, Danielle Lodewyck Falciglia et al, "Vocal Fold Surface Hydration: A Review," *Journal of Voice* 23(2009): 658–665. Note that ambient air can impact the vocal tract in more substantive ways over large timescales. Very cold, dry air has led to changes in nasal cavities in some populations. Marlijn Noback, Katerina Harvati, and Fred Spoor, "Climate-Related Variation of the Human Nasal Cavity," *American Journal of Physical Anthropology* 145 (2011): 599–614.

19. Caleb Everett, Dámian Blasi, and Seán Roberts, "Climate, Vocal Folds, and Tonal Languages: Connecting the Physiological and Geographic Dots," *Proceedings of the National Academy of Sciences of the United States of America* 112 (2015): 1322–1327. Another relevant study of mine, on the use of vowels in dry environments, is Caleb Everett, "Languages in Drier Climates Use Fewer

Vowels," *Frontiers in Psychology* 8 (2017): https://doi.org/10.3389/fpsyg.2017
.01285. That study includes citations to some of the relevant studies in laryngology motivating this line of work. The first issue of the *Journal of Language Evolution,* published in 2016, includes some of the objections scholars have presented to a potential influence of aridity on languages, along with a reply by me and my colleagues. For more on this topic and how such environmental effects could take place via known sound-change mechanisms, see, for instance, Caleb Everett, "The Sounds of Prehistoric Speech," *Philosophical Transactions of the Royal Society* 376 (2021): 20200195. It should be noted that the findings on complex tonality have not replicated well with another tone database. See Seán Roberts, "Robust, Causal and Incremental Approaches to Investigating Linguistic Adaptation," *Frontiers in Psychology* 9 (2018): doi.org/10.3389/fpsyg.2018.00166. A third related hypothesis of mine related to a specific sort of sound called an ejective. See Caleb Everett, "Evidence for Direct Geographic Influences on Linguistic Sounds: The Case of Ejectives," *PLOS ONE* (2013): https://doi.org/10.1371.journal.pone.0065275.

20. Note that I say correlations *often* gesture at causal relationships, not that they always do. Some correlations are accidental, even ones between linguistic and nonlinguistic factors. See Seán Roberts and James Winters, "Linguistic Diversity and Traffic Accidents: Lessons from Statistical Studies of Cultural Traits," *PLOS ONE* 8 (2013): e70902. Nevertheless, even correlations without direct causal connections between two factors often point at indirect but nonaccidental relationships between those factors. For instance, in the case of linguistic diversity and traffic accidents, both these features associate with less economically developed regions for nonrandom reasons.

21. See Christian Bentz, Dan Dediu, Annemarie Verkerk, and Gerhard Jäger, "The Evolution of Language Families Is Shaped by the Environment beyond Neutral Drift," *Nature: Human Behaviour* 2 (2018): 816–821.

6   SEEING SPEECH

1. The McGurk effect was first described in Harry McGurk and John MacDonald, "Hearing Lips and Seeing Voices," *Nature* 264 (1976): 746–748, https://doi.org/10.1038/264746a0.

2. Hans Bosker and David Peeters, "Beat Gestures Influence Which Speech Sounds You Hear," *Proceedings of the Royal Society B* 288 (2021): 20202419, https://doi.org/10.1098/rspb.2020.2419.

3. Aslı Özyürek, Roel Willems, Sotaro Kita, and Peter Hagoort, "On-line Integration of Semantic Information from Speech and Gesture: Insights from Event-Related Brain Potentials," *Journal of Cognitive Neuroscience* 19 (2007): 605–616.

4. Enfield has written extensively on a variety of topics in linguistics. Some of the discussion in this section is based on work discussed in Nick Enfield, *How We Talk* (New York: Basic Books, 2017).

5. Gail Jefferson, "Preliminary Notes on a Possible Metric Which Provides for a 'Standard Maximum' Silence of Approximately One Second in Conversation," in *Conversation: An Interdisciplinary Perspective,* ed. Derek Roger and Peter Bull (Philadelphia: Multilingual Matters, 1989).

6. Stephen Levinson and Francisco Torreira, "Timing in Turn-Taking and Its Implications for Processing Models of Language," *Frontiers in Psychology* (2015): https://doi.org/10.3389/fpsyg.2015.00731.

7. Tanya Stivers, Nick Enfield, and Stephen Levinson, "Universals and Cultural Variation in Turn-Taking in Conversation," *Proceedings of the National Academy of Sciences of the United States of America* 106 (2009): 10587–10592.

8. As I say, I am not the only linguist to make this point. Consider the following observation made by Enfield: "Conversation is the medium in which language is most often used. When children learn their native language, they learn it in conversation. When a language is passed down through generations, it is passed down by means of conversation. Written language is many a researcher's first point of reference, but it should not be." Enfield, *How We Talk,* 3.

9. Nick Evans, "Context, Culture, and Structuration in the Languages of Australia," *Annual Review of Anthropology* 32 (2003): 13–40, 35.

10. George Zipf, *The Psycho-Biology of Language* (New York: Houghton-Mifflin, 1935, 25). See also George Zipf, *Human Behavior and the Principle of Least Effort* (Boston: Addison-Wesley, 1949). My study on sound frequencies is Caleb Everett, "The Similar Rates of Occurrence of Consonants in the World's Languages," *Language Sciences* 69 (2018): 125–135.

11. Steven Piantadosi, Harry Tily, and Edward Gibson, "Word Lengths Are Optimized for Efficient Communication," *Proceedings of the National Academy of Sciences of the United States of America* 108 (2011): 3526–3529.

12. Joan Bybee, *Language Change* (Cambridge, UK: Cambridge University Press, 2015).

13. Daniel Everett, "Cultural Constraints on Grammar and Cognition in Pirahã," *Current Anthropology* 46 (2005): 621–634.

14. Gary Lupyan and Rick Dale, "Language Structure Is Partly Determined by Social Structure," *PLOS ONE* (2010): https://doi.org/10.1371/journal.pone.0008559. For more research on the influence of population size on language, see Limor Raviv, Antje Meyer, and Shir Lev-Ari, "Larger Communities Create More Systematic Languages," *Proceedings of the Royal Society* B 286 (2019): https://doi.org/10.1098/rspb.2019.1262.

15. Enfield, *How We Talk*, 7.

7 THE NASAL START TO "NOSE"

1. For more on phonesthemes, see, for instance, Benjamin Bergen, "The Psychological Reality of Phonaesthemes," *Language* 80 (2004): 290–311.

2. George Childs, "The Phonology and Morphology of Kisi" (PhD diss., University of California, Berkeley, 1988).

3. In a book published posthumously in 1916, Swiss linguist Ferdinand de Saussure, to some the founder of modern linguistic inquiry, famously claimed that the relationship between a "signifier" and the "signified" was arbitrary. Charles Hockett, another influential linguist (whose hypothesis on labiodental sounds was discussed in Chapter 5), wrote in 1960 that arbitrariness was one of the key distinguishing features of human speech. That is, for the vast majority of words there is no inherent connection between the sounds of the word and the represented item or concept. While both Saussure and Hockett were no doubt correct that most of speech is arbitrary, and while they also recognized the existence of some iconic elements in speech, they appear to have underappreciated the role of those iconic elements. See Ferdinand de Saussure, *Course in General Linguistics* (New York: Philosophical Society, 1959 [1916]). For one of Hockett's discussions of the

key features of language, including arbitrariness, see Charles Hockett, "The Origin of Speech," *Scientific American* 203 (1960): 88–111.

4. Diedrich Westermann, *A Study of the Ewe Language* (Oxford, UK: Oxford University Press, 1930), 187. This passage is also quoted in Felix Ameka, "Ideophones and the Nature of the Adjective Word Class in Ewe," in *Ideophones,* ed. F. K. Erhard Voeltz and Christa Kilian-Hatz (Amsterdam: John Benjamins, 2001), 25–48.

5. See William Samarin, *The Gbeya Language: Grammar, Texts, and Vocabularies* (Los Angeles: University of California Press, 1966).

6. Other examples are harder to explain. Is there any actual association between *gl-* and light-related phenomena like glimmering and glowing? It may seem unlikely, but some research now suggests that this sort of correspondence may originate partially between cross-sensory associations that are actually natural to some individuals: those with synesthesia. Synesthetes experience strong associations between phenomena from distinct sensory modalities. For those with this neurological condition, a given linguistic element may naturally associate with some visual stimuli, and those stimuli may be involuntarily triggered by the linguistic element. For example, many synesthetes perceive particular letters or numbers as having inherent colors, so when they say the alphabet, their mind's-eye view of each letter is colored. Some researchers have suggested that synesthesia underlies certain forms of systematic sound-meaning correspondences, since synesthesia is a natural form of sensory correspondence. Recent work has gone so far as to suggest that synesthesia may have helped to facilitate the evolution of language since the condition made it natural for some members of our species, at the advent of speech, to understand sounds to represent unrelated phenomena. Such speculations are hard to prove, of course, but they appear less unreasonable as we begin to see how pervasive nonarbitrary components of speech can be. For one discussion of synesthesia and its possible link to the evolution of language, see Antonio Benítez-Burraco and Ljiljana Progovac, "Language Evolution: Examining the Link between Cross-Modality and Aggression through the Lens of Disorders," *Philosophical Transactions of the Royal Society B* 376(2021): https://doi.org/10.1098/rstb.2020.0188.

7. Damián Blasi, Sørren Wichmann, H. Hammarstrom, P. Stadler, and Morten Christiansen, "Sound-Meaning Association Biases Evidenced across Thousands of Languages," *Proceedings of the National Academy of Sciences of the United States of America* 113 (2016): 10818–10823. Given the traditional assumptions in linguistics dating to Saussure, Hockett, and others, we would not expect there to be consistent associations between certain meanings and particular sounds. While this may seem an odd thing to even test, it is worth keeping in mind that many of the traditional assumptions in linguistics did not benefit from the data now available from thousands of languages, data like those at the core of the study of Blasi and colleagues.

8. Mark Dingemanse, Francisco Torreira, and N. J. Enfield, "Is 'Huh' a Universal Word? Conversational Infrastructure and the Convergent Evolution of Linguistic Items," *PLOS ONE* (2013): https://doi.org/10.1371/journal.pone.0078273.

9. Wolfgang Köhler, *Gestalt Psychology* (New York: Liveright, 1947 [1929]). The oft-cited study from about twenty years ago is Vilayanur Ramachandran and Edward Michael Hubbard, "Synaesthesia–A Windows Into Perception, Thought and Language," *Journal of Consciousness Studies* 8 (2001): 3–34.

10. Arash Aryani, Erin Isbilen, and Morten Christiansen, "Affective Arousal Links Sound to Meaning," *Psychological Science* 31 (2020): 978–986.

11. Marcus Perlman, Rick Dale, and Gary Lupyan, "Iconicity Can Ground the Creation of Vocal Symbols," *Royal Society Open Science* (2015): https://doi.org/10.1098/rsos.150152.

12. Marcus Perlman and Gary Lupyan, "People Can Create Iconic Vocalizations to Communicate Various Meanings to Naïve Listeners," *Scientific Reports* 8 (2018): 2634.

13. Lynn Perry, Marcus Perlman, and Gary Lupyan, "Iconicity in English and Spanish and Its Relation to Lexical Category and Age of Acquisition," *PLOS ONE* 10 (2015): e0137147.

14. Lynn Perry, Marcus Perlman, Bodo Winter, Dominic Massaro, and Gary Lupyan, "Iconicity in the Speech of Children and Adults," *Developmental Science* 21 (2018): e12572.

15. In the words of a few scholars who recently cowrote a paper on the topic, "The notion that the form of a word bears an essentially arbitrary relation to its meaning is changing in status from a proposed design feature into an

empirical observation that accounts only partly for the attested form-meaning mappings in the languages of the world. As the language sciences leave behind oversimplifying dichotomies to develop more refined models of the manifold relations between form and meaning, our understanding of language and mind will be much the richer for it." Mark Dingemanse, Damián Blasi, Gary Lupyan, Morten Christiansen, and Padraic Monaghan, "Arbitrariness, Iconicity and Systematicity in Language," *Trends in Cognitive Sciences* 19 (2015): 603–615.

16. Mutsumi Imai and Sotaro Kita, "The Sound Symbolism Bootstrapping Hypothesis for Language Acquisition and Language Evolution," *Philosophical Transactions of the Royal Society B* 369 (2014): 20130298.

8 BIG INTO WHAT?

1. See, for instance, Noam Chomsky, *Aspects of the Theory of Syntax* (Cambridge, MA: MIT Press, 1965).

2. See Nicholas Evans and Stephen Levinson, "The Myth of Language Universals: Language Diversity and Its Importance for Cognitive Science," *Behavioral and Brain Sciences* 32 (2009): 429–492.

3. The emphasis on recursion as the key component of syntax is evident, for instance, in Marc Hauser, Noam Chomsky, and Tecumseh Fitch, "The Faculty of Language: What Is It, Who Has It, and How Did It Evolve?," *Science* 298 (2002): 1569–1579. For the original presentation of a lack of recursion in Pirahã, see Daniel Everett, "Cultural Constraints on Grammar and Cognition in Pirahã," *Current Anthropology* 46 (2005): 621–646. See also Daniel Everett, *Don't Sleep There Are Snakes: Life and Language in the Amazonian Jungle* (New York: Vintage, 2009).

4. Geoffrey Pullum, "Theorizing about the Syntax of Language: A Radical Alternative to Generative Formalisms," *Cadernos de Linguística* 1 (2020): 1–33.

5. Desmond Derbyshire, *Hixkaryana*, (Amsterdam: North-Holland, 1979).

6. Robert Englebretson, *The Problem of Complementation in Colloquial Indonesian Conversation* (Amsterdam: John Benjamins, 2003).

7. See Adele Goldberg, *Constructions: A Construction Grammar Approach to Argument Structure* (Chicago: University of Chicago Press, 1995). See also Adele

Goldberg, *Explain Me This: Creativity, Competition, and the Partial Productivity of Constructions* (Princeton, NJ: Princeton University Press, 2019), and Adele Goldberg, *Constructions at Work: The Nature of Generalization in Language* (Oxford, UK: Oxford University Press, 2006).

8. These construction types are discussed in Goldberg's work, for instance, Goldberg, *Constructions*. The literature on construction grammar is now rich, with literally thousands of references that are accumulating rapidly.

9. Note that I say syntax-specific parts of the brain, not language-specific. Some recent work suggests that similar parts of the brain are activated for linguistic activities in speakers of forty-five languages in twelve language families. See Saima Malik-Moraleda, Dima Ayyash, Jeanne Gallée, Josef Affourtit, Malte Hoffmann, Zachary Mineroff, Olessia Jouravlev, and Evelina Fedorenko, "An Investigation across 45 Languages and 12 Language Families Reveals a Universal Language Network," *Nature Neuroscience* 25 (2022): 1014–1019. Given that language processing and the creation of constructions rely on specific kinds of pattern recognition and pattern creation, not to mention other skills that overlap across cultures, some degree of cortical specificity vis-à-vis linguistic behavior is perhaps unsurprising.

CONCLUSION

1. The story of the Tower of Babel is found in Genesis 11:1–9. For a discussion of the clear parallels between this story and other, earlier stories, see Petros Koutoupis, *Biblical Origins: An Adopted Legacy* (College Station, TX: Virtualbookworm.com Publishing, 2008).

2. For a discussion of Pānini and his works, see George Cardona, *Pānini: His Work and Its Traditions* (Berlin: De Gruyter Mouton, 2019).

3. For one of many studies on the disappearance of languages spoken by few speakers, see David Graddol, "The Future of Language," *Science* 303 (2004): 1329–1331.

ACKNOWLEDGMENTS

Jude and Jamie fill my life with happiness. It is a joy to share a pictur-esque home with them and Jasmine (a Samoyed who sat by my side as I wrote some of these pages). Thanks to Jude for making me laugh by offering unsolicited critiques of the chapter titles, sometimes while he played Frusciante riffs from across the room. I am the luckiest father. I am also immensely grateful to my extended family and for all that we share: Keren, Dan, Linda, Jim, Chris, Shan, Kris, Craig, BJ, Christopher, and my insanely cool nephews and nieces. Much love to all of them and my friends in the United States, Brazil, and elsewhere. My parents are loving people who placed me on a path to a wonderful life. This book is dedicated to my sisters, Shannon and Kristine, who have been con-stant sources of friendship and support since our days living a semi-nomadic existence together.

The University of Miami has been my academic home for fifteen years. I consider it an immense privilege to work on such a scenic campus, in a vibrant city, and with such fantastic colleagues. I cannot name them all here; that would be tedious, and any list would inevitably exclude someone. I have exceptional colleagues and collaborators at other institutions as well, and it would also be too tedious to list them all. Still, I would like to reserve a special thanks for Marva Seifert (a friend

267

since our childhoods in Amazonia) and our team at the University of California, San Diego, investigating how aerosols are produced during speech. That project, carried out alongside the writing of this book and some other work, has been a particularly invigorating one. I must also thank Elivar Karitiâna for his friendship and the many insights he has offered me over the years.

Thanks to the Carnegie Corporation of New York for a large and generous award that made the initial stages of this project possible. I wrote my proposal for a Carnegie Fellowship, which eventually morphed into a book proposal for Harvard University Press, over several days of very rough seas while traversing the Pacific, from Ensenada to Osaka, on the MV *Explorer*. The proposal for this book was accepted by Jeff Dean, my former editor, who also guided me during the writing and publication of my last book, *Numbers and the Making of Us*. This book's editor, Joseph Pomp, has been an invaluable source of helpful comments and suggestions. His meticulous feedback has been tremendous and he, along with Grigory Tovbis, came up with the book's title. Thanks are due as well to two experts who served as external reviewers for Harvard University Press: Nick Enfield, who offered extensive comments on an early version of the manuscript, and a second, anonymous reviewer who also offered very helpful feedback.

INDEX